William Byrd
and His Contemporaries

The publisher gratefully acknowledges the generous contribution to this book provided by the Sonia H. Evers Renaissance Studies Fund of the University of California Press Foundation.

William Byrd
and His Contemporaries

Essays and a Monograph

Philip Brett

Edited by Joseph Kerman
and Davitt Moroney

UNIVERSITY OF CALIFORNIA PRESS

Berkeley   Los Angeles   London

University of California Press
Berkeley and Los Angeles, California

University of California Press, Ltd.
London, England

Library of Congress Cataloging-in-Publication Data

Brett, Philip.
    William Byrd and his contemporaries : essays and a monograph / Philip Brett ; edited by Joseph
Kerman and Davitt Moroney.
        p.   cm.
    Includes bibliographical references and index.
    ISBN-13: 978-0-520-24758-1 (cloth : alk. paper)
    ISBN-10: 0-520-24758-2 (cloth : alk. paper)
    1. Byrd, William, 1542 or 3–1623.   2. Composers—England.   3. Music—England—16th
century—History and criticism.   I. Kerman, Joseph, 1924–.   II. Moroney, Davitt.   III. Title.

ML410.B996B74   2007
780.92—dc22   2006007433

Manufactured in the United States of America

16   15   14   13   12   11   10   09   08   07
10   9   8   7   6   5   4   3   2   1

This book is printed on New Leaf EcoBook 50, a 100% recycled fiber of which 50% is de-inked
post-consumer waste, processed chlorine-free. EcoBook 50 is acid-free and meets the minimum
requirements of ANSI/ASTM D5634–01 (*Permanence of Paper*).

CONTENTS

PREFACE

Philip Brett died in October 2002 on the eve of his sixty-fifth birthday. He is mourned by his many friends and admirers for his learning, lightly worn, his sensitivity, elegance, passionate activism, and exquisite musicality. His two signal contributions to musical studies extend over so wide a range that they might seem to come from different worlds. In the 1970s he was the first to break the taboo on the open discussion of composers' sexuality, and as he followed up on his powerful, subtle investigation of Benjamin Britten's *Peter Grimes* with further work on Britten operas, he became musicology's pioneer in gender studies and queer theory—known for polemics and forthright activism, not only scholarly writings.

A companion volume to this one, edited by George Haggerty, *Music and Sexuality in Britten: Selected Essays,* has been published by the University of California Press. After two years at King's College Cambridge, Philip spent his academic career at the University of California, first at the Berkeley campus and then at Riverside and Los Angeles.

Before that he had established himself in Renaissance studies, where he will be remembered principally as an editor, in particular as general editor of the works of the great Elizabethan composer William Byrd. He launched a new complete edition—*The Byrd Edition*—in the wake of an inadequate earlier one, which was floundering in revisions. Philip's intervention could be described as a rescue, for without him it is hard to believe the edition would have happened at all. He edited eight of the volumes himself—the Masses and the *Gradualia*, the consort songs and a volume of miscellaneous madrigals and songs—and brought the long undertaking (virtually) to completion. While his turn to Britten and gender studies made him a main precursor of the so-called new musicology of the 1980s, a musicology oriented toward hermeneutics, his work in the Renaissance preserved musicology's traditional emphasis on sources, historical analysis, and the establishment of texts. These zones of engagement were not altogether disparate, as he was well aware, and as we will see in a moment.

Musicology in Britain after World War II took its lead from Thurston Dart, and Philip Brett was Dart's star pupil. His affinity for the Elizabethan Golden Age, his nose for sources, his love of editing, his commitment to musical performance—all these and more resonated with Dart, who drew him into collaboration with several of his own editing jobs. (He took over two of Byrd's songbooks in Dart's revision of the earlier Byrd edition, by E. H. Fellowes: the *Psalmes, Sonets & Songs* of 1588 and *Songs of Sundrie Natures* of 1589). While still a student, he made two discoveries of moment in the field of Elizabethan music, establishing the provenance of a very large group of sources for vocal polyphony of the era, known as the Paston manuscripts, and identifying a group of consort songs preserved anonymously by Paston as late works by Byrd. (They remain, as of today, the last major addition to the canon.) Indeed, he named the genre "consort song"—earlier scholars had described it but never focused on it—and published the entire corpus in volume 15 of *The Byrd Edition* and volume 22 of *Musica Britannica*. When he addressed the Royal Musical Society on the subject of "The Consort Song, 1570–1615" in 1961, at a time when all papers were invited, he must have been the youngest speaker ever tapped.

Philip Brett became an exemplary editor, one who not only obsessed about minutiae in his text and, indeed, developed new ways of establishing it, but also assumed as full responsibility as he could for the music he edited. He sang it, researched it, and wrote about both the music and the research in commentaries of unusual extent and richness. It was in these commentaries and in his essays that he displayed his art as a historian and critic. This was especially true of his work on *Gradualia*, the large, two-volume collection of more than a hundred "sacred songs" (or motets) and motet segments for the Roman Catholic liturgy and private devotions, which Byrd published near the end of his career, in 1605 and 1607—his *magnum opus*. The edition, with its extraordinary book-length commentary, issued serially from 1989 to 1997, became Philip's *magnum opus* too.

Yet this was also the juncture for him where past and present, old musicology and new musicology, came together. The collection, he recognized, "had to be approached not simply as the fervent work of a remarkable composer but also as a peculiar manifestation of a set of unusual religious and cultural circumstances." In a postscript to his Cambridge Opera Handbook to *Peter Grimes*, he spoke about the impetus behind his work on Britten: "My ultimate concern is the social experience of oppression and its effects in the writing of *Peter Grimes*, not Britten's sexual preference. With appropriate changes to fit the conditions, I might write similarly about the social accommodation of another of England's greatest composers, William Byrd, who experienced another kind of oppression that affected his music."[1]

Gradualia was written and published for a persecuted minority, the recusant Roman Catholic community in England under Elizabeth I and James I. Philip made the connection with the cultural and political circumstances of present-day minorities on whose behalf he had taken up arms, as well as pen. Once he began examining the publication deeply—examining the printing process itself, which he was able to track in unusual detail; the confusing (sometimes confused) order of the contents in each of the two volumes; and especially the texts, with their arcane, explosive subtexts—he began to hear the music anew, and a radical interpretation emerged of Byrd's whole undertaking. A particular insight was that in setting the texts, Byrd considered not only their liturgical functions and biblical sources, but also the interpretation of those sources in a central polemical document of the time, the Douay-Rheims Bible, translated for the English Catholics and brought out serially during the composer's lifetime with profuse annotations. The Douay-Rheims annotations, Philip proposed, provide a key to the musical setting of many of *Gradualia*'s most striking numbers. In short, he saw *Gradualia* as a political act of defiance, one that in its own time placed new demands on Byrd's creative energies, and that now presents its own challenge to contemporary hermeneutics.

The outcome of all this was a series of five outsized prefaces, initiating the five volumes needed for *Gradualia* in the format of *The Byrd Edition*. As these volumes appeared one by one over a period of eight years, the study's true power was not immediately evident. Nor was the place where this research appeared conducive to the circulation it deserved. Philip intended to collate the prefaces and make them into a monograph (he even began drawing up an introduction for this monograph). To realize his intention is to pay him an apt tribute and to perform the important function, as we see it, of focusing some very bright light on the life and works of William Byrd.

Thus the final chapter (or, better, segment) of the present book brings together Philip's writings on *Gradualia* for the first time as an entity. And no document brings together his work as social historian, philologist, and critic more perfectly. The editors—Joseph Kerman, briefly his teacher and his longtime colleague at Berkeley, and Davitt Moroney, his student and collaborator—were both closely involved with the *Gradualia* project, and indeed we mapped out "Prefaces to *Gradualia*" even before a larger collection of Philip Brett's writings on Tudor and Jacobean music came under consideration.

Most of the other essays have been published before, sometimes in sources that are now hard to find; that they refer to so many of Byrd's contemporaries—the composers John Taverner, Thomas Tallis, Thomas Weelkes, and Orlando Gibbons, as well as the collector Edward Paston and the emblematist Geoffrey Whitney—provides, once again, a measure of the breadth of this scholar's purview. Some of the essays are addressed to his fellow musicologists, others to his fellow musicians. They range from the report of his findings on the Paston manuscripts—his first musicological coup, already accomplished in 1960—to an unpublished roundtable paper that he delivered a few months before his death (from two versions of this paper, filed on Philip's computer as " 'Blame not the Printer': William Byrd's Publishing Drive, 1588–91" and "Byrd's Soul Authority," we have abstracted a short chapter with the title "William Byrd: New Reflections"). Philip was a stylist, and apart from this case his own words have been left strictly alone, as free as possible from the depredations of editors and copyeditors.

A word on the opening chapter, which in its original form annotated a concert celebrating the 450th anniversary of Byrd's birth, given at Riverside and Claremont, California, in 1993. (Until recently Byrd was thought to have been born in 1543; the date has now been moved back to 1540.)[2] With only the slightest of editing, we think it makes a beautiful concise introduction to the composer, and while certainly the author would have revised it for inclusion in a book, also certainly he would have wanted such a book to acknowledge, up front, his commitment to musical performance. His work as a conductor, keyboard player, and violist meant at least as much to Philip as musicology. Those who lived around him will not forget his performances of *Gradualia* and a wealth of other music, from Ockeghem and Josquin Desprez via the Monteverdi Vespers, *The Fairy Queen, Susanna,* and the B-Minor Mass to Benjamin Britten and beyond.

Many of Philip's friends have helped with this book: most substantially George Haggerty and O. W. Neighbour, and Larry W. Allen, Kerry McCarthy, William Mahrt, Craig Monson, Louis A. Montrose, and William A. Peterson. In the area of production we are very grateful to Mary Francis and Lynne Withey of the University of California Press for their strong support and guidance and to Rebekah Ahrent, Michael Markham, and Camille Peters of the Berkeley Music Department for editorial assistance. Walter Frisch intervened most kindly at the last minute to help with permissions. The editors gratefully acknowledge the generous contribution to this book provided by the Edmund O'Neill Fund at the University of California.

We thank the following publishers and organizations for permission to reprint material that they first published or for which they now hold the rights: the Southern California Early Music Society (chapter 1), Oxford University Press (chapters 2, 3, 6, and 8), the Cambridge Bibliographical Society (chapter 4), The Lute Society (chapter 5), and Stainer & Bell Ltd. (chapters 7 and 10). Special thanks are due to Carol Wakefield of Stainer & Bell for granting permission to assemble and reprint the prefaces to *Gradualia* from *The Byrd Edition*. In his own acknowledgment pages Philip spoke warmly of his long and fruitful association with Allen Percival, former publisher and editor at Stainer & Bell. We wish also to acknowledge the firm's deep and even longer commitment to Elizabethan and Jacobean music.

Berkeley, October 2005
Joseph Kerman
Davitt Moroney

NOTES

1. Philip Brett, ed., *Benjamin Britten: Peter Grimes* Cambridge Opera Handbook Series (Cambridge, 1983), 192.

2. The earlier date rests on new archival studies and seems solid to us, as it seemed to Philip, even though it has not been accepted universally. See John Harley, *William Byrd: Gentleman of the Chapel Royal* (Brookfield, VT, 1997) and the *Oxford Dictionary of National Biography*.

ABBREVIATIONS

Byrd Edition   *The Byrd Edition* (London: Stainer & Bell, 1976–2004),
                  Philip Brett, general editor. Individual volumes edited by
                  Brett: vol. 4, *The Masses* (1981); vols. 5–6, *Gradualia I:* vol. 5,
                  The Marian Masses (1989), vol. 6a, *All Saints and Corpus Christi*
                  (1991), vol. 6b, *Other Feasts and Devotions* (1993); vol. 7, *Grad-*
                  ualia II: vol. 7a, *Christmas to Easter* (1997), vol. 7b, *Ascension,*
                  Pentecost, and the Feast of Saints Peter & Paul (1997)

Fellowes 48   Edmund H. Fellowes, *William Byrd*, 2nd ed. (London: Ox-
                  ford University Press, 1948)

Kerman 81   Joseph Kerman, *The Masses and Motets of William Byrd*
                  (London: Faber, 1981)

Neighbour 78   O. W. Neighbour, *The Consort and Keyboard Music of*
                  William Byrd (London: Faber, 1978)

NT   *The New Testament of Iesus Christ Translated Faithfully into*
                  English out of the Authenticall Latin (Rheims, 1582), repr. in
                  English Recusant Literature 1558–1640 , ed. D. M. Rogers
                  (Ilkley, Yorkshire: Scolar Press, 1975), vol. 267

OT   *The Second Tome of the Holie Bible Faithfully Translated into*
                  English out of the Authenticall Latin (Douai, 1610), repr. in
                  English Recusant Literature 1558–1640 , ed. D. M. Rogers
                  (Ilkley, Yorkshire: Scolar Press, 1975), vol. 266

CHAPTER ONE

William Byrd:
Traditionalist and Innovator

Sixteenth-century Europe produced a number of composers who possessed enormous technical facility and breath of vision. They are on the whole, however, a rather distant lot—especially those of the religious tradition represented by Gombert, Clemens, Palestrina and Lassus. This may explain why the early music movement has made a greater fuss over the more personal and intimate music of the subsequent century and a half, inaugurated most notably by Claudio Monteverdi, a character almost as colorful as his operatic music.

William Byrd (1540–1623) is clearly different from the European giants—even Victoria, who, though he also came from a country on the fringe of the Continent, was fully assimilated into the international scene in Rome. Bred up in a musical culture that had been isolated from that of the Continent during the late fifteenth century, Byrd completely assimilated Continental techniques, but he also strove to preserve various advantageous elements of insularity—particularly the rhapsodic sense of melody cultivated by his predecessors. Another notable difference of Byrd as a composer is that he

Notes for a concert of music by Byrd in November 1993, the 450th anniversary of his birth, given at the University of California at Riverside and Pomona College; published as "Traditionalist and Innovator: Aspects of William Byrd," *Southern California Early Music News* 18, no. 3 (November 1993): 1–15.

wrote fluently in several genres. He is arguably the most ambitious and accomplished composer of purely instrumental music of his age, as well as the creator of a highly individual style of vocal polyphony out of an imaginative amalgam of English and Continental traditions.

To an age like ours, fascinated with alienation and marginalization, Byrd also presents an intriguing dilemma. Revered by his contemporaries and honored by his chief employer, Queen Elizabeth, he appears in some lights as the perfect royal musician, writing on order for the newly established Church of England as well as clothing courtiers' ditties in substantial if often rather sober musical garb. The other, darker side of his life is represented by his stubbornly persistent Roman Catholicism. Clinging to his faith, he refused to conform and stayed away from his parish church in defiance of the law as long as he lived. His religious music, most of it in Latin, and some of it written expressly for the proscribed services of the Roman Catholic rite, has an intensity that appears to stem directly from his religious and political predicament as an outsider on the inside of Elizabethan society.

This anniversary concert program is divided into two sections, representing the earlier and later periods of Byrd's life. The separation occurs at the point around 1593 when Byrd appears to have retired from active life at court and to have moved from Harlington in Middlesex (near the present Heathrow Airport) to a house at Stondon Massey deep in the Essex countryside. There he lived a mere eleven miles from Ingatestone, the secluded home of the Petres, a Roman Catholic family of immense wealth (Lawrence Stone calls them "landed magnates") who protected his interests. Despite this umbrella, he continued to be cited as a recusant (one who would not attend Anglican services) at each quarter sessions of the local county court for the rest of his life, though it is likely he was excused the exorbitant fines and other penalties attached to such behavior.

Byrd had to face not only the persecution of his religion but also the Puritan suspicion of music, which affected even liberal thinkers like Roger Ascham, who in his *Toxiphilus* (1545) argued that instrumental music was effeminate and that while the young might learn singing, shooting was better. No wonder that Byrd in his first songbook, the much reprinted *Psalmes, Sonets & Songs of sadnes and pietie* of 1588, included a list of reasons "to persuade every one to learn to sing." These reasons carefully emphasize the spiritual and the physical; "it doth strengthen all parts of the breast, and doth open the pipes" is a fair example. The Oxford don John Case, in his *Praise of Musicke* (1586), was prepared to go much further in asserting that "the chief end of music is to delight." No doubt delighted by Case's defense, Byrd wrote a six-part song in his praise to words by Thomas Watson, a classically trained and musically involved poet who was a friend of Spenser (he is Amyntas in "Colin Clout's Come Home Again"). The piece was published as a broadside and only three of the six voice parts have survived; fortunately the survivors are the bass and the two sopranos, allowing the present writer to make a fairly convincing attempt at reconstruction.

Byrd's earlier secular vocal music gives a strong idea of his association with the more forward-looking literary people of his time. The 1588 songbook includes a beautiful setting of a rather plain-style poem by Sir Philip Sidney, "O Lord, how vain," along with "Constant Penelope," an awkward but lovable experiment in English hexameters, in which Byrd matches long and short syllables with long and short notes, in the manner of the contemporary French *vers mesuré*. The effect is to bring out the hexameter rhythm at the expense of the usual accentual emphasis, and this in turn reveals what Handel and Stravinsky knew but few native composers other than Byrd, Dowland, Purcell and Britten ever realized—that "speech rhythm" is not the only stable principle on which to base the intelligent setting of English poetry or prose.

It is ironic to find Byrd in the company of the literary avant-garde of the day, for he was a rather stubborn traditionalist in the matter of verse and voice. He preferred the English—and essentially medieval—tradition of setting the *form* of the verse rather than the new-fangled manner of reflecting its imagery and syntax, so conspicuous in the imported madrigal style that fascinated his younger contemporaries Thomas Morley, Thomas Weelkes and John Wilbye. Imbued with a strong sense of heritage and tradition, Byrd seems closer in spirit to the poet Edmund Spenser—whose verse, like that of Shakespeare, he never set.

Byrd's music for viols also reflects this traditionalism. He anxiously reworks the In Nomine tradition adopted by midcentury English composers from a mass setting of their preeminent forerunner John Taverner, and he plies himself at several other plainsong settings that tested his skill. The four-part work that we perform, *In nomine* no. 2, takes its point of reference from the work of the older composer Robert Parsons. But the climax of Byrd's earlier music occurs in the two sets of *Cantiones sacrae* published in 1589 and 1591. This serial publication, an unprecedented gesture in English music, was aided by Byrd's having secured a monopoly over the printing of music in his midthirties. The two collections contain a variety of Latin texts (very few of them drawn from the Catholic liturgy) which, though innocuous enough in themselves, taken together emphasize so heavily such symbolic matters as the Second Coming and the Babylonian Captivity that it seems clear they were intended to convey a political as well as a musical message.

Exurge, Domine is a typically vigorous appeal to God for action: "Arise, O Lord! Why sleepest thou?. . . Wherefore hidest thou thy face and forgettest our misery and trouble?" Byrd's repetitions of the opening words at the end, as a da capo, indicates the license he allows himself with his biblical texts as well as the urgent polemics of his settings. Like many of these motets, it is couched in music as demonstrative as any madrigal, exuberant in style and vivid in imagery. It is hard to escape the conclusion that it was written, like the rest of the contents of the *Cantiones,* to voice the outrage and despair of the English Roman Catholic community.

In this earlier period there is sometimes a roughness and vigor to Byrd's music that brings to mind Beethoven. Byrd, too, enjoyed a "late period" in which his music, increasingly cut off from its cultural surroundings (owing not to deafness, so far as we know, but to the religious enclave to which he belonged), took on a completely personal, visionary quality unmatched by any other composer of the age. To the new generation of court composers it would have sounded hopelessly old-fashioned. Few alive in Europe in 1611—the date of Byrd's last publication, the *Psalmes, Songs and Sonnets*—would have had any appreciation of its subtlety. Even Byrd seems a little self-conscious about it, issuing a solemn and unusual warning to the purchasers:

> Only this I desire; that you will be but carefull to heare them well expressed, as I have been in both the Composing and correcting of them. Otherwise the best Song that was ever made will seeme harsh and unpleasant, for that the well expressing of them, either by Voices, or Instruments, is the life of our labours, which is seldome or never well performed at the first singing or playing.

Byrd, we can imagine, would not have appreciated the modern myth that every educated Elizabethan could sit down and sing a madrigal at sight. He evidently liked to rehearse!

The music of this last publication is secular or domestic in function, even though almost half of its texts come from the Bible. Its style is more flexible and idiosyncratic than that of the early songbooks—particularly in its rhythmic vitality and sense of harmonic drive. It is matched by the subtlety of the later keyboard music: dance pairs such as the pavans and galliards named for the Earl of Salisbury and the mysterious "Ph. Tr.," and variations on popular tunes such as "O mistress mine"—the choice for our program—and "John come kiss me now" ("O mistress mine" is not Shakespeare's, but another text). A powerful number in the 1611 songbook, "Arise, Lord, into Thy Rest," is similar in message and intent to the earlier *Exurge, Domine*, but what a different musical world it inhabits! In place of the supremely energetic but slightly diffuse musical rhetoric of the Latin work, the English work has chiseled phrases, and a magnificent rising sequence near the end that sounds very much a part of seventeenth-century musical language.

If the 1611 collection is, as Byrd puts it, a swan song, the crowning achievement of his later period is the two-volume collection entitled *Gradualia*, first published in 1605 and 1607, which incorporates music for the chief festivals of the Roman Catholic rite. There are over a hundred items, most for the mass but also some for private devotions, as we have recently come to understand. Byrd is specific about its purpose in his prefaces, and it appears that copies of the first volume, published in the year of the Gunpowder Plot, may have been confiscated or withheld—both volumes were reissued in 1610 when the political climate had improved.

From the *Gradualia* we select music for one of the chief festivals of the church year, the Assumption of the Blessed Virgin Mary. Belief in the assumption of Mary was one of the dogmas that separated Roman Catholics from Anglicans, and Byrd pours the greatest intensity into his setting of these texts. At the same time he obeys a traditional law of decorum, which makes him refrain from making this music as flamboyant and demonstrative as the earlier motets. Its function after all is to be part of but not dominate the important actions of the liturgy.

In a famous personal statement in one of the *Gradualia* prefaces, Byrd speaks of the sacred words that he sets to music:

> In the very sentences (as I have learned from experience) there is such hidden and concealed power that to a man thinking about divine things and turning them over attentively and earnestly in his mind, the most appropriate measures come, I know not how, as if by their own free will, and freely offer themselves to his mind if it is neither idle nor inert.

He describes a process that we may mistake for inspiration but which he regards clearly as an *afflatus* from without. The Holy Spirit prompts one who ponders things divine with the right musical "measures," which appear as if unaided.

Byrd would have thought of Lassus in particular, perhaps, as having had access to such a source. But in the grand gestures of that great composer we can surely hear the lofty universality of a European Catholicism only slightly shaken in its conviction about its historical mission. In the more complicated, even tortured strains of the English master we can sense the kind of commitment that stops at nothing, even persecution and death, in pursuit of a faith that can never be taken for granted. This music retains its poignancy nearly four hundred years later.

CHAPTER TWO

Homage to Taverner
in Byrd's Masses

Byrd's settings of the Ordinary of the Mass are a special phenomenon in sixteenth-century music. For one thing, there are only three of them: set beside the dozens of mass settings by each of his Continental peers, these works take on extra significance as the single response of a great composer to the traditionally most important genre. For another thing, they are the only sixteenth-century English works of any consequence to have been published without any identification—no title page, colophon or date—other than the composer's name. Not until Peter Clulow made his definitive bibliographical study of the original editions did we know for sure that they belong to the years 1592 (or early 1593) to 1595, the Four-Part Mass being issued first, followed by the three-part and then finally the five-part works.[1]

Observers with stylistic sensibilities have always wanted to place the publication of the masses closer to *Gradualia* (1605 and 1607), whose musical characteristics they certainly prefigure. But Joseph Kerman has reconciled stylistic considerations with bibliographical facts in an eloquent and convincing way by linking the appearance of the masses with Byrd's removal to Stondon Massey, where at last he was able to enjoy the benefits offered by a comparatively secure Roman Catholic community headed by

Originally published in *Early Music* 9 (1981): 169–76.

8

his old friend and patron, Sir John Petre. This move marks a new phase in Byrd's Latin music, a phase which the masses inaugurated. In place of the exuberant conquering of difficult musical problems in the 1575 *Cantiones sacrae*, and the intense and often extravagantly poignant expression of a "political" and personal point of view as a Catholic in a Protestant country that characterizes the 1589 and 1591 collections, this last phase marks the realization of an ambitious plan to set major portions of the Roman liturgy to music—music that is as restrained in style as it is profoundly spiritual in content. In comparing the dissonance-laden and anxious "dona nobis pacem" of the Four-Part Mass with the serene setting of its five-part successor, Kerman has furthermore symbolically pinpointed Byrd's transition from, as it were, angry middle age to contemplative senior citizenship.

A third unusual feature of the masses, one that has been remarked on frequently, is their lack of borrowed or preexisting material. It was while contemplating a sentence of my own to that effect—in a draft for the preface to my edition of the masses in *The Byrd Edition*—that I paused to wonder afresh. There passed through my mind the discoveries of Kerman, Neighbour and Monson in tracing models for the motets, instrumental pieces and Anglican works in the music of such composers as Alfonso Ferrabosco the elder, John Bull, Thomas Morley and Thomas Tallis.[2] And in the almost trance-like state in which I suspect similar discoveries are made, I took my copy of the *Tudor Church Music* edition of Taverner's masses off the shelf and began leafing through. The book fell open at part of the "Meane" Mass, and the light dawned.

Taverner's "Meane" Mass is the one in which the older composer came closest to thoroughgoing imitation in the manner of the composers of the generation after Josquin.[3] And it was an influential work: according to Nigel Davison, three other Tudor masses were modeled on it—the Five-Part Mass by Tye, the "Frences" Mass of Sheppard, and the short Four-Part Mass of Tallis.[4] Taverner divided his setting into a large number of short sections many of which are separated from each other by a cadence and pause, and sometimes by a new time signature as well. Each section usually contains one or more imitative points—there are hardly ever more than three to a section—managed in a simple, straightforward manner. Variety is provided by changes in vocal scoring, meter and sometimes texture, alternating duets and chordal passages being the most common forms of relief. To encourage unity in the absence of the customary cantus firmus of his festal masses, Taverner employs not only the long-established head motive but also a "tail motive" common to all four movements (there is of course no Kyrie); and there are also internal thematic links between the movements. The result is a work of intense stylistic homogeneity limited on the one hand by the low level of contrapuntal development and on the other by the principally syllabic setting of the text (at least until the Sanctus). The soaring but shapely lyricism of Taverner's earlier masses has had its wings clipped with a vengeance.

The positive values of this new style can be observed in the Benedictus, possibly the most poetic moment of the whole piece. The breaking up into sections, most persistent in the Gloria, has given way by now to a more continuous texture in which the line flows expressively enough; and Taverner rather happily explores the warmth of the major triads centered on the third, fourth and seventh degrees of his transposed Dorian mode. Indeed, his insistence on F major until the piece is catapulted back to G by the final phrase of the Osanna (the "tail motive") is a harmonic strategy worthy of Byrd himself. So happy is the effect that one scarcely notices the slight stiffness of the contrapuntal technique betrayed by the regularity of the opening entries and the timidity of the attempted expansion of the second and third points.

In his Four-Part Mass, most probably composed as well as published first among the three, Byrd takes the ground plan of the "Meane" Mass much as it stands, duplicating the cadence points faithfully while managing to draw less attention, both in musical and notational terms, to the breaks between sections. Like Taverner, whose experience with the festal mass had some effect in this regard, Byrd tends to begin a movement (or major new section) with reduced voices, bringing in the tutti at some well-established point such as "Gratias agimus" in the Gloria, where in festal masses the cantus firmus traditionally made its first appearance. Comparing the reduced-voice sections in the two masses, it becomes clear that Byrd at times abandoned Taverner's example in the Gloria and Credo to assert an idiosyncratic division of the text on the basis of his own reading of its syntax and content. In the Credo, for example, Taverner includes "qui propter nos homines" in the section beginning at "Deum de Deo"; unlike him and almost every other composer, Byrd begins a new section here. And owing to the customary omission of text in Taverner's Credo, Byrd was without a guide for the latter part of the movement—one reason, perhaps, why the division at "et unam sanctam Catholicam" adopted in the Four-Part Mass was changed in the two subsequent works, which make the break at "Et in Spiritum sanctum," to achieve a better tripartite balance for the movement as a whole.

If Byrd adopts Taverner's basic plan, he nevertheless ignores his thematic links rather pointedly. In the Four-Part Mass the only movements to be linked by an obvious and straightforward use of a head motive are the Gloria and Agnus Dei; the openings of the Credo, Benedictus and Kyrie can each be heard as more or less distantly connected to this; but the Sanctus is totally unrelated—for reasons that will later become apparent. There is no tail motive. Clearly, thematic interrelationships applied in Taverner's schematic fashion could only have undermined the subtlety of Byrd's musical rhetoric, and would in any case have run counter to his belief, expressed so eloquently in the preface to *Gradualia*, in the generating musical power of the words themselves. The only striking internal correspondences occur between the unusual cadences of the two settings of "Jesu Christe" in the Gloria and that of "per quem omnia facta sunt" at the end of the first main section of the Credo (example 2.1); they make a rhetorical point that in the latter instance emphasizes the need for the change in Taverner's ground plan mentioned above.

It is not until the beginning of the Sanctus that Byrd openly acknowledges his debt. The four-part head motive of the "Meane" Mass begins in this movement as it had before with two sets of paired entries, the first of the pair ascending a fifth from G to D, the second a minor sixth from D to B-flat (example 2.2a). In a development not found in the Gloria or Credo, two further entries ascend a seventh from D to C. This kind of melodic expansion of the point was one of the few methods of contrapuntal development effectively used by the first English practitioners of

Example 2.1. Byrd, Four-part Mass

a. Gloria

b. Gloria

c. Credo

the art of imitation. Byrd reorganizes this expanding point into a new scheme that takes even greater advantage of its climactic potential: the three versions of the point (now in halved note values) are separated by three cadences, and each is introduced in stretto so that the line has time to exert itself before coming to a cadence (example 2.2b). The reworking also includes such tiny but significant details as the drop of a fifth at the beginning of bar 3 in the Altus, marked *x* in the example. This is a decoration of the dissonance, archaic by the 1590s, that not only mirrors the falling fifth succeeding the ascent in Taverner's first version of the point but also reproduces the triplex figure of Taverner's final cadence. See also bars 10 and 12. The literal but transposed borrowing of Taverner's bar 3 to form the cadential approach in Byrd's bar 7 may also be noted. The

Example 2.2

a. Taverner, "Meane" Mass: Sanctus

b. Byrd, Four-part Mass: Sanctus

whole passage is an inspired example of the kind of musical transformation Byrd practiced on all his models.

In what seems like a complementary but much abbreviated gesture toward Taverner's tail motive, and as if to hammer home his tribute to the older composer, Byrd also copies the final cadence of the Benedictus, transferring the passing notes from the Contratenor, where Taverner places them, into the Cantus. And in order to justify a figure that must have sounded a little antique in 1592, Byrd cleverly makes it seem to arise quite naturally and logically from the preceding line (example 2.3).

A number of other typical connections between the two works are set out in example 2.4. The first two, from the Gloria (example 2.4a, b, c and d), require little comment; but it should be made clear that if, as seems likely, Byrd's point for "Pleni sunt caeli" appears to derive from Taverner's by rearrangement of notes, then his second Agnus Dei might therefore conceivably begin with a reference to Taverner in retrograde (example 2.4g and h). On surer ground, it is clear that Byrd's setting of "filium Dei unigenitum" takes Taverner's point as its basis while showing to what ultimate expressive limits the older master's favorite 6–5 progression can be pushed (example 2.4i and j). Taverner's example in general might also explain other features of the Mass—most notably the curious figure in the bass at "miserere nobis" in the second Agnus (example 2.5), which is perhaps a reference to the kind of melodic and rhythmic patterning that is so notable a characteristic of the older composer's other masses.

Musical connections are slippery things, because in the case of a composer of Byrd's genius the development of the musical idea is likely so to transform the thing that prompted it that one is left with a handful of possibilities that reveal nothing. It might not be too wide of the mark, however, to imagine Byrd's having a copy of the "Meane" Mass open beside him as he composed, ready for him to check his bearings, to rework musical details or simply to borrow the rhythmic outline of a point here and there. Several of his patrons could have provided him with such a copy, for the work appears in one of the Petre manuscripts, and fragments of it are also found in the surviving Paston sources.[5] It would be misguided,

Example 2.3

a. Taverner: Benedictus

b. Byrd: Benedictus

though, to think of Byrd's choosing an unknown work by an unfamiliar composer at his own or his patron's whim. The modeling may have begun as a gesture to one of his most distinguished musical ancestors or as an attempt to place the masses firmly in the English tradition of Catholic liturgical music; but it evidently became an elaborate act of homage and criticism toward music that was very much alive for Byrd in spite of the fact that he could not at this stage of his career "learn" from it as he had earlier learned from his transformations of Tallis and Ferrabosco.

It is not too much to hope that the discovery of a model for the Four-Part Mass may lead to further discoveries of the kind. At the very least it validates what David Josephson cautiously labeled a "suspicion" when a few years ago he pointed out the similarity between the point in the "in nomine" section of the Benedictus in Byrd's Five-Part Mass and that of the famous passage to the same words in Taverner's *Missa Gloria tibi Trinitas.*[6] And this again makes more likely the possibility that the

Example 2.4

a. Taverner: Gloria

Gra - ti-as a - gi-mus ti - bi

b. Byrd: Gloria

Gra - ti-as a - gi-mus ti - bi

c. Taverner: Gloria

Cum san-cto Spi - ri - tu, cum san-cto Spi - ri - tu

d. Byrd: Gloria

Cum san - cto Spi - ri - tu

Cum san - cto Spi - ri - tu

Cum san - cto Spi - ri - tu

e. Taverner: Sanctus

Ple - ni sunt cae - li et ter - ra,

f. Byrd: Sanctus

Ple - ni sunt cae - li et ter - ra,

Example 2.4 *(continued)*

g. Taverner: Agnus Dei

h. Byrd: Agnus Dei

i. Taverner: Credo

j. Byrd: Credo

Example 2.5. Byrd, Four-part Mass: Agnus Dei

Sanctus movements of all three masses have connections with Taverner. The opening of the Sanctus of the Three-Part Mass (example 2.6) is a further reworking of the "Meane" Mass head motive, this time including an inversion, but still ending (at "Sabaoth") on a D cadence with the same archaic decoration of the cadential dissonance. About the opening of the five-part Sanctus it is less possible to be confident: but the combination of a three-note motive in breves, recalling a cantus firmus, and a graceful turning and rising countermelody is in general suggestive of Taverner's influence, and it may be more than mere coincidence that the initial notes of the cantus firmus are those of the first three notes of the triplex in the Sanctus of *Gloria tibi Trinitas*, and that the melodic shape of the countermelody can be found at "gloria tua" and its rhythmic outline both here and at several other points in Taverner's mass. The Sanctus and Benedictus constitute a special place in the early Tudor mass. It was here that the monorhythmic version of the cantus firmus was generally introduced, and where canons and other special devices tended to appear. Byrd's focusing on this movement of the mass to make both general and specific references to his musical grandfather, so to speak, is an act that shows knowledge of, as well as respect for, his native inheritance.

A further clue to Byrd's attitude to Taverner lies in the choice of the "Meane" Mass as a model for his four-part setting. One of the major points to arise from Oliver Neighbour's book *The Consort and Keyboard Music of William Byrd* is the debt Byrd owed to the melodic style of John Redford who, he says, "came near to sharing the acute feeling for linear balance, variation, extension and contrast that characterizes all Byrd's music."[7] Now Taverner, whom as a purely vocal composer Neighbour had less reason to explore so fully, was the other great master of line in Tudor music. But if what Byrd valued most about Taverner and Redford was their melodic sense, why then did he make the paradoxical choice of the "Meane" Mass? For in this work the challenge of the unfamiliar imitative technique diverts Taverner's creative energy away from line, as it continued to divert the energies of his successors of the intervening generation. Byrd must have recognized the importance of the work as the

Example 2.6. Byrd, Three-part Mass: Sanctus

first firm step along the road—the rather long road—toward his own style, while also appreciating the sacrifice it had entailed. And what the opening of the Sanctus of his Four-Part Mass shows so poetically is that the rift between early Tudor melody and middle Tudor texture—indeed, the crisis that occupied a whole generation of English composers—could be, and in fact had been, miraculously healed and resolved. Once the technique of imitation had been fully absorbed, it could be placed in perspective by a composer of Byrd's genius so that a truly lyrical style could again flourish—a lyrical style, moreover, that gained in expressiveness over the much more extravagant and rhapsodic early Tudor vein precisely because of its contrapuntal underpinnings. The Four-Part Mass, then, not only symbolizes the rebirth, phoenix-like, of Catholic ritual music in England, but also celebrates the reconciliation of a relatively new contrapuntal style with the melodic values of an earlier tradition; and the three- and five-part masses reaffirm the importance of this double achievement.

The discovery of Taverner's presence behind these works is important because it emphasizes, as nothing else has been able to do so powerfully, not only Byrd's positively Spenserian historical sense but also the intelligence and passion with which he approached the question of his artistic roots. While Elizabeth's court was playing at being medieval by holding tournaments, building castles, dressing gothic and reading and writing vast chivalric epics, this stubborn outsider at the center of the establishment was taking the literary and musical values of an earlier age seriously, and reinterpreting them in terms of contemporary technique. The result was an art which in the twilight of his composing career became, rather like that of Beethoven's late period, inaccessible to his contemporaries for the most part, but which is also, in the best sense of the word, timeless.

NOTES

1. Peter Clulow, "Publication Dates for Byrd's Latin Masses," *Music & Letters* 47 (1966): 1–9

2. Joseph Kerman, "Byrd, Tallis, and the Art of Imitation," in *Aspects of Medieval and Renaissance Music: A Birthday Offering to Gustave Reese*, ed. J. La Rue (1966); repr. in Joseph Kerman, *Write All These Down* (Berkeley and Los Angeles, 1994), 90–105; Neighbour 1978, 206–15; and Craig Monson, "The Preces, Psalms and Litanies of Byrd and Tallis: another 'Virtuous Contention in Love,' " *Music Review* 40 (1979): 257–71.

3. The work is printed under the title "Sine nomine" in *Tudor Church Music* (London, 1923), 1:50–69.

4. Nigel Davison, "Structure and Unity in Four Free-Composed Tudor Masses," *Music Review* 34 (1973): 328–38.

5. Essex Record Office, Petre MA D/DP Z6/1, fol. 12 (Bassus only). Of the Paston sources, Royal College of Music 2035 contains the "Crucifixus" at fol. 15, Tenbury 354–58 the "Et in terra pax" and "Laudamus te" at fol. 6v, and British Library Add. 29246 contains the "Et incarnatus" (as far as "sepultus est") in an arrangement for lute at fols. 10v and 19v. [Ed.: The Tenbury manuscripts now belong to the Bodleian Library, Oxford.]

6. See David Josephson's article in *Musical Times* 117 (1976): 739. Virginia Brookes's dismissive reply (ibid., 997) ignores the fact that Byrd had already shown his knowledge of, and involvement with, Taverner's In Nomine by quoting the opening point and adopting the same moment for his first cadence in his own consort In Nomine 4/1 (the first In Nomine in four parts).

7. Neighbour 1978, 112.

CHAPTER THREE

Facing the Music

Every so often in early music circles there occurs an event which sparks off discussion and prompts one to think about the nature of our endeavors to re-create the music of the past. Such an event for me was the attention suddenly thrown on Alessandro Striggio's 40-part motet, *Ecce beatam lucem*. It is almost too easy to accomplish my original assignment, a review of Hugh Keyte's 1980 edition of the work.[1] The only mistake here is the halving of note values; otherwise the edition is good, straightforward and accurate, full of discussion about the problems surrounding the work, and ingenious in its reconciliation of the two previously opposed systems of barring polyphonic music—it eliminates ties by providing ticks either side of the stave when a note traverses the barline and also provides the coherence only regular barlines can give by relying on them the rest of the time. This is a good compromise for a practical edition, giving the score reader the flavor of an original score (which would have had barlines and possibly even ties), and the individual singer something of the experience of the original parts (which would have had neither).

The background to the work can be extracted from literature surrounding it that has appeared in *Early Music* and in the correspondence

Originally published in *Early Music* 10 (1982): 347–50.

columns of the *Musical Times*. Striggio, a Mantuan of gentle birth with a widespread reputation as performer and madrigalist, appears to have written his motet for an occasion (or occasions) in Florence in 1561. The composer also wrote other mega-voiced pieces, now lost, around the same time. A performance of *Ecce beatam lucem* by Lassus in Munich in 1568, for the wedding of Wilhelm V of Bavaria to Renée of Lorraine, is described in the *Discorsi* of Massimo Troiano (2nd ed., 1569), which mentions a problematical instrumentation. The only surviving musical material, a set of parts dated 1587, relates to this Munich version. Through a charming and lucky discovery of Elizabeth Roche's and its interpretation by Ralph Leavis,[2] we are now tantalized by the very likely possibility that Tallis's 40-part *Spem in alium nunquam habui* was written in response to a challenge issued when Striggio's piece became known in England.

It is important in approaching these two works to watch one's critical assumptions. Why? Because since the day when Tudor music ceased to be regarded in a vacuum there has been an understandable, but no less fallible, tendency to assume almost automatically that music from the Italian "mainstream" must be superior to the insular product, whatever the actual evidence of individual pieces.

More important than nationality in this case, however, is the relative experience of the two composers. Striggio had barely reached majority when he wrote *Ecce beatam lucem*, whereas the aged Tallis had already weathered a major stylistic crisis in his own and his English contemporaries' music before composing *Spem in alium nunquam habui*. It comes as no surprise, therefore, to find that Striggio has less control of his medium than Tallis. Indeed, he has difficulty in doing much more than simply conducting his forty voices from one end of the rather expansive text to the other with appropriate, but scarcely well planned, gestures to the possibilities of contrasting groups. Real counterpoint he has no truck with (though he toys with an easy subject in bars 77–87); he prefers to build the work out of short-winded phrases occasionally enlivened with sprightly rhythms—the sort of thing that (in halved note values) was to become characteristic of the canzonet. Two rather automatic repetition schemes are what he seems to rely on for a sense of overall structure: one is set off by the two tutti appearances of the exclamation "O" in the text, the other is the conventional repetition of the final line, where Striggio badly mismanages the harmonic rhythm leading to the final cadence.

Tallis may have taken his cue from these repetitions when he planned his motet, especially in his treatment of the last line of text. (Owing to a quirk of the sources, which date from the Jacobean revival of the piece, the original word underlay is entirely lost; but the conjectural reconstruction, found in an eighteenth-century manuscript, cannot be too far wide of the mark in the broad essentials.) In Tallis the word "respice" mirrors Striggio's "O," but shows at the same time what an architectural sense can do for a piece of these dimensions. The A-major triad of the first instance, melting into the minor, initiates a set of ostinato entries in a remote harmonic arc that finally comes round to the dominant to prepare for the concluding G major "respice," in which the Mixolydian is powerfully reinforced by the typical pull toward C. This has no equal in Striggio, whose excursion to B-flat/G minor around bar 100, doubly welcome after so much penny-plain Mixolydian harmony, suddenly fizzes out and forfeits any structural importance it might have assumed had it been thought through as more than a diverting gesture.

Thrown onto the screen that Striggio unexpectedly provides, Tallis appears in his piece a superior composer. The sheer strategy of the 40-part motet is worthy of high admiration—its gradual unfolding by means of two imitative points passed around all the voices, the pseudo-harmonic entry of choirs 3 and 4 before the first tutti, the second tutti with its dramatic general pause heightening the tension and then the passage of quick *alternatim* exchanges among the four main choral groups (the eight choirs act in pairs) before the final passage already discussed. Most impressive of all, perhaps, is the way Tallis manages all forty voices without losing a sense of line, which is something that barely functions at all in Striggio's motet (so far as I can tell without having tried as yet to perform the work) and is in any case likely to be all but obliterated by the "Lassus" scoring. And all the while, except in those magnificent, regal homophonic exchanges, Tallis decorates his texture, not with Striggio's facile declamatory rhythms, but with the luxuriant detail of the earlier and more florid Tudor style, supported now (and enhanced) by the firm directional harmonic control he learned along with imitation. As a blend of old and new, *Spem in alium nunquam habui* is wonderfully successful. (Not all Tallis's "reconciliation" pieces are similarly inspired: it would not be hard to show how and why the *Puer natus* Mass, for instance, is a noble failure.) What it shows up in Striggio's attempt is the fatal disparity between the medium, which is monumental, and the technique, which is epigrammatic and miniaturist.

No amount of detective work about external matters, such as the size of Striggio's original forces, the acoustic of his performing space, the whim of his patron's taste and so on, could undermine to any serious extent these basic musical perceptions. But in asserting that, I realize I am swimming against the tide. For what is noticeable about all the words recently generated by *Ecce beatam lucem*, and by its relationship to Tallis and his motet, is that none of them attempts to address any of the fundamental musical issues involved. Can anyone imagine, say, the discovery of a likely model for a play by Shakespeare or Jonson resulting in a discussion devoted entirely to peripheral matters such as date of composition and first performance, method and venue of production, actors, patrons, audience and so on, without a single word being exchanged on the question of content?

Ah, but hasn't musicology usually focused on historical, cultural and textual matters? I fear it has, increasingly so: to the sad extent that, for all the vitality of the early music scene, what we do in a scholarly way seems intellectually suspect to many observers outside music, and the way we go about performing earns (and frequently deserves) the contempt of musicians. On the first score, I often wonder what accounts for the reluctance—if not outright refusal—of musicologists to deal with their main subject matter, music. Is it, for instance, a deep underlying insecurity, about most of the music's being able to withstand the sort of scrutiny that enhances one's admiration of a Mozart piano concerto or a Brahms

intermezzo? Or is it, perhaps, the more respectable fear that an anachronistic understanding will be the *only* result of applying to pre-Classical
works those techniques of analysis bred up on the Bach-to-Brahms
repertory?

Unfortunate, that word "analysis." With its metaphorical overtones of
dissection it suggests the very reverse of what it is needed for: to help the
average ear, capable of retaining only a few phrases at a time, to synthe-
size or build up an experience of the piece as a whole. The student of English literature generally learns as a basic skill something called, rather
happily, "close reading." I can understand the suspicion with which
some early music people regard analysis, either in the purely descriptive
form in which it was presented to me as an undergraduate at Cambridge
or in the more extreme "methodological" forms in which it is often now
encountered on both sides of the Atlantic; but I do think we need insights
into the intentions and the anatomy of early music derived from close
reading of the music itself and related not to some abstract method but
to the realities of the matter in hand. In fact I would go so far as to say
there is a desperate need for "close listening" everywhere apparent—in
articles and books and, perhaps most of all, in performances.

Take the presentation of the Striggio and Tallis motets during BBC
Radio 3's "Bavarian Wedding" program put on by the BBC's Radio 3 in
1981. The emphasis, not unexpectedly, was on capturing Lassus's performance of Striggio's motet as reported by Troiano. But that gentleman
doesn't tell us which parts Lassus gave to his twenty-four instruments, or
what reasons he had for his scoring. Furthermore, the music is not well
enough known yet for anyone to risk distorting it with a partially informed instrumentation and thereby sabotaging the composer's intentions. For example, the suspensions are a major element in the articulation of the phrasing and in the expressive language of the piece; the one
in the first part at bar 35 is certainly important, but it lost all effect in performance by being relegated to a footling recorder. A small problem, perhaps, but one that was indicative of larger-scale difficulties. And it was a
similar insensitivity to the way in which expressive details relate to the

overall design that undermined the performance of Tallis's motet, where a rather inappropriate bounciness substituted for the musically more essential qualities of line and shape.

The Tallis is of course very difficult, but even in recordings where the technical problems have been overcome, a concern for the peripheral tends to push the essential to one side. The Clerkes of Oxenford (Seraphim S-60256) strike a wonderful mood and take one's breath away by their virtuosity; but the young women are so busy reaching after those extraterrestrial notes occasioned by the transposition theories of their director, David Wulstan, that line and shape again suffer. The clarity of the Clerkes, however, shows up the other recording I know, by the Cambridge University Musical Society and King's College Choir under David Willcocks (ARGO ZK 30–31), for what it is: the work of an amateur choral society supplemented with professional "ringers." The grandiose musical gestures, like the insecurities of the singers, are almost but not quite concealed by yet another "peripheral" matter—a thick layer of that musically unsavory substance, the acoustic of King's College Chapel, Cambridge, which like the echo of Forster's Marabar caves tends to reduce everything to a dull boom.

This brings us back full circle. Of course it is important to know as much as possible about the external conditions of a piece of music like the 40-part motet by Tallis. It is important to know it was designed not for an over-resonant Gothic building but for an Elizabethan domestic long gallery, and that it was sung, presumably, by a professional choir of limited size, not a large band of amateurs. Everything we can find out about it and its presumed model, the Striggio piece, adds to our understanding. We *must* strive to get the best text and then respect it. Perhaps we even need to know which Elizabethan grandee commissioned it to get an added sense of ambience. On all these counts, musical scholars have done as well, if not better, than those in most other disciplines, and there is every reason to applaud them and to be thankful for the knowledge they have revealed.

I think the suspicion many scholars and performers have of going further is that the next step in so many musical discussions is to try to place a piece in terms of the externals of style rather than structure. Stylistic analysis, like every other method, has severe limitations when applied in an overmethodical way. Style is, after all, a rather superficial aspect of music when divorced from its basis in content; and all to often the stylistic critic is thrown off balance by a piece (like Tallis's) that lies outside any easily identifiable norm. Also, if style becomes the only yardstick, then the label that results from the measuring process tells us absolutely nothing about the inner logic of the piece or about the kind of compositional thought it embodies. What's more, the labels themselves (e.g., "conservative," "innovative") soon become critically loaded, and tend to do duty for a mature critical judgment where one is not otherwise earned. I suspect that the hard-line documentary musicologist and the proudly intuitive performer alike would be less averse to the notion of real musical thought if they realized that those who at present most frequently ask the question "But what about the *music?*" in a particularly patronizing way really mean "How quickly can you describe the style of this piece in such a way that I can file it securely away in my scheme without having to think too hard about it?" or words very much to that effect. (If you doubt me, take a really awkward problem work, like Monteverdi's *Missa In illo tempore* of 1610, and read everything that has been written about it.)

Another siren song, to which those with intellectual pretensions are particularly susceptible, is that sung by Criticism with a capital C. There are a lot of extremely fancy critical theories running around nowadays for anyone who wishes to pursue them. And it is all too characteristic of musicology to start running after them before it can properly walk. It is not that these theories, be they structuralism or semiotics, poststructuralism or deconstructionism, have nothing to offer, but that the grist they provide for the academic mill is likely to settle as a thickening dust in the scholarly journals before any real kernels of musical wisdom are extracted; and also that, as systems, they seem to one observer at least to have a tendency to direct attention onto the critic and onto the mechanics of the critical response, thus once again deflecting it from the work and from the composer's intentions and conception. The belated flirtation with Heinrich Schenker in Britain today seems by comparison almost endearingly sane and old-fashioned.

It would be sad if the cause of some real if minimal understanding of the conception of a mass by Josquin, or of what internal musical logic runs through a motet by Lassus, were sacrificed on the altar of the false god of methodology, whether of analysis, "style" or criticism. How then should we proceed? Why, by stealth, doing our best to meet the music on its own terms and produce our hard-earned findings before anyone has time to deflect attention from the real issues by asking what method has been used and suggesting a different one. True understanding will only be reached, as usual, when it outwits pedantry.

What distinguishes so many musicians involved in early music is their love and care for what they do. It is strange that this love and care should balk at the exercise of intelligent understanding. No human relationship thrives without some letting go of the self and of one's fears in an imaginative effort to reach out in understanding to another. Our relationship to music is not so very different, and it is perhaps a sign of the continuing immaturity of "early music" that such imaginative efforts at understanding, either in performance or scholarship, are so rare. For surely, inevitably, it is fear which makes us so anxious and determined to busy ourselves in doing anything and everything—to avoid making an honest attempt to face the music. It is high time we recognized our games for what they are and began to reach beyond them.

NOTES

1. London: Mapa Mundi, 1980.
2. *Musical Times* 122 (1981): 85 and 230. [Ed.: Roche drew attention to a doc-

ument from 1611 recalling that "there was a songe sent into England in 30 parts," and an unnamed duke asked if no Englishman could do better. "Facing the Music" seems to have been spurred by contributions on the matter in *Early Music* by Iain Fenlon and Hugh Keyte (8 [1980]: 329–34) and Denis Stevens (10 [1982]: 171–81). Earlier in his career Philip Brett edited *Spem in alium* (London, 1966) as a revision of the text first published in *Tudor Church Music*, vol. 6.]

CHAPTER FOUR

Edward Paston:
A Norfolk Gentleman
and His Musical Collection

The musician of the present day owes a great deal to the generations of
collectors through whose energy and enthusiasm so much music of the
past has been preserved. The heyday of the British musical collector was
the Victorian era,[1] when historical values began to assume a measure of
the importance attached to them today. Although the musical life of the
Elizabethans was in many ways more vital than that of the Victorians, the
collector appears to have been a much more unusual figure in their times,
and the lack of sufficient records makes him all the more difficult to trace.
Naturally, many Elizabethan gentlemen and musicians owned, or copied
out, quantities of music, but we are not justified in calling many of them
collectors on the evidence available, except by extending the sense of the
word beyond useful limits. The extant inventories of such musical households as those of the Kitsons at Hengrave and of the Petres at Ingatestone, for instance, show that their possessions were largely confined to
copies of contemporary English music acquired for the purpose of performance. But as Hyatt King points out, "For a man to be estimated a
true collector, we surely require evidence of something wider and deeper,

Originally published as "Edward Paston (1550–1630): A Norfolk Gentleman and His Musical Collection," *Transactions of the Cambridge Bibliographical Society* 4 (1964): 51–69.

something which denotes a breadth of outlook, a certain spirit of curiosity and a quest for knowledge of the musical past" (7).

Evidence of this nature occurs in the case of a Norfolk gentleman and amateur musician called Edward Paston, who therefore ranks with Henry Fitzalan, Earl of Arundel (d. 1580) and William Heather (1563–1627), founder of the chair of music at Oxford,[2] as one of the earliest British collectors. Judging from what remains of his collection, Paston's taste was definitely conservative, especially in English music. His manuscripts contain a lot of music by pre-Reformation and mid-sixteenth-century English composers, but very little by those flourishing after Tallis's death in 1585, and none by the leading madrigalists and lutenist composers of later Elizabethan, and Jacobean, times. This remarkable lacuna may have been remedied to some extent by his printed music books, which have not been traced; but since most of the music in his manuscripts, especially the Continental music, was already available in print, it is by no means a foregone conclusion. There was, however, one contemporary English composer whose music he collected with unusual thoroughness. Most of his manuscripts contain some pieces by William Byrd; some of them are devoted almost entirely to his works. Moreover, Paston possessed many pieces that were not published during Byrd's lifetime, and there is evidence to suggest that he knew the great composer personally. Appendix B lists the several dozen manuscripts and manuscript sets from Paston's collection that survive today.

Edward Paston belonged to a junior branch of the family known to posterity largely through its correspondence preserved from the fifteenth century, the so-called Paston letters. His life and details of his properties were sketched by the Rev. Francis Blomefield in his great *Essay towards a topographical history of the County of Norfolk,* and more recently Ruth Hughey and E. B. Burstall have printed biographical accounts of the man and documents dealing with his business transactions.[3] But none of them has commented in detail upon his musical and literary interests, and no one has so far connected him with the musical manuscripts that bear his name. The old *Grove's Dictionary of Music and Musicians* attributed the lute books stamped with Edward's name to the Mr. Paston who gave lessons upon the virginals to the Princess Mary in 1536–37;[4] none of the books, however, can have been written much before 1600, and Princess Mary's teacher was probably Edward's father.

Sir Thomas, the fifth son of the lawyer Sir William Paston, achieved some eminence at court. He became a gentleman of Henry VIII's Privy Chamber, and was sufficiently favored by the king to receive a knighthood in 1544 and the grant of many lands in East Anglia, including the manor of Thorpe-by-Norwich, which subsequently became the family home. His first son outlived him only to die in youth; King Edward himself was godfather to the second son, who was named after the king and christened in February 1550, eight months before Sir Thomas died.

On the death of his elder brother, Edward inherited all his father's property, but like most Elizabethan gentlemen he endeavored to enlarge his estate in order to provide for his family. His efforts in this direction were furthered by an uncle, Sir Clement Paston, the famous sea captain, who settled the manor of Appleton in North Norfolk and several other valuable properties upon Edward and certain of his sons.

Though Edward could not match the splendor of a Bess of Hardwick, a Burghley or a Hatton, he obviously shared the Elizabethan passion for building. He began in about 1590 by entirely remodeling Thorpe Hall. A few years later he evidently planned to build a new house at Binham, but abandoned the scheme as the result of an accident described by his contemporary Sir Henry Spelman:

> Mr Edward Paston many Years since was desirous to build a Mansion-house upon or near the Priory, and attempting for that purpose to clear some of that Ground, a Piece of Wall fell upon a Workman, and slew him; perplexed with this Accident in the beginning of this Business, he gave it wholly over, and would by no means all his Life after be perswaded to re-attempt it, but built his Mansion-house, a very fair one, at Appleton.[5]

The date 1596 appears on the lodge at Appleton, which is near Sandringham; the original house was burned down one night in 1707, the inhabitants narrowly escaping with their lives. In 1612 Paston began to build again, this time on his estate at Town Barningham some thirty miles east of Appleton. The distinguished house he erected there is standing to this day.

Edward's first wife, Elizabeth, daughter of Richard Lambert of London, died without issue. In about 1590 he married Margaret Berney, who bore him six sons and three daughters. After his death several of the children suffered under the recusancy laws, and three of them entered religious houses on the Continent, where a grandson named Edward achieved distinction as the president of Douay College from 1688 to 1714. Edward himself was never prosecuted for recusancy, but we learn of his Roman Catholic faith from Mary Berney, a niece by marriage, who lived at Appleton from about 1623 to 1632, when she entered the convent of the Canonesses of St. Augustine at Louvain.[6] Sister Mary reveals that Edward kept a mass-center in a house in the woods a mile from Appleton Hall. We can imagine the scene of its near discovery from her vivid account:

> It happened one day that the pursuivants came on a sudden and were kept in talk at the door sometime, whilst that the priest and church stuff were put up safe into the secret place, so that coming in they found nothing. But they brought with them a bloodhound which stood snuffing about the secret place where the priest was. Before the searchers espied him comes a great cat and fell a fighting with the dog, never leaving him till he departed from thence, which seemed an admirable thing that the poor cat was not afeared to set upon the dog. So would our Lord deliver them by this means.[7]

Undoubtedly this place would have been a rallying point for the papists of North Norfolk, and the Appleton household a refuge for many like Mary Berney.

Edward Paston died at the age of eighty, and was buried in Blofield church on 24 March 1629/30. The inscription on his monument there seems a sincere tribute to a quiet and dignified life:

To Edward Paston Esq Second Son of Sr Thomas Paston Knight one of the Gentlemen of Henry the eight his privy chamber truly noble noe lesse by stocke then all manner of vertue, most skillfull of liberall Sciences especially musicke and Poetry as also strange languages, Margaret his most loving wife and daughter of Henry Berney of Redham Esq alwaies mindfull of her most deare husband wth whom she lived most sweetly 40 yeares now alas in her funerall deprived of so great a solace of her life hath lamenting caused this howsoever a Monument of love to be set up.

It is not clear where Edward received his training in the "liberal sciences," for his early history is still obscure. The records of the universities, the Inns of Court and the larger schools fail to reveal his name, and I have been unable to trace him at any of the English colleges on the Continent. Yet he seems to have traveled extensively abroad, especially in Spain, where he may have received part of his education. A letter in Spanish addressed to the Count of Carcamo at the court of Madrid, and most probably written by Paston in his eighteenth year, indicates that he had many friends there and that he was about to return for a further visit.[8] Paston's Spanish travels were also mentioned by Bartholomew Young in the preface to his translation of the *Diana of George of Montemayor*, published in 1598:

> Well might I haue excused these paines, if onely *Edward Paston* Esquier (who heere and there for his own pleasure (as I vnderstand) hath aptly turned out of Spanish into English some leaues that liked him best) had also made an absolute and complete translation of all the Parts of Diana; the which, for his trauell in that Countrey, and great knowledge in that language, accompanied with other learned and good parts in him, had of all others, that euer yet I heard translate these Bookes, prooued the rarest and worthiest to be embraced.

Young's statement is an invaluable testimony to Paston's poetical leanings. What is more, Young writes as though Paston were known to Lady Penelope Rich, to whom this printed translation is dedicated. As we shall see, the association is further suggested in one of the topical songs contained in manuscripts from Paston's collection.

The interest that posterity has shown in Lady Rich owes more to the attentions paid to her by Sir Philip Sidney in his *Astrophel and Stella* than to any other event in her colorful life. Edward Paston was only a few years older than Sir Philip, and his social position and wide accomplishments would have recommended him to Sidney's literary circle, the so-called Areopagus. Sidney shared Paston's interest in the *Diana;* he himself translated two of the lyrics,[9] and his *Arcadia* was modeled to some extent on this famous pastoral romance. We learn that Paston was acquainted with at least one of Sidney's friends from Geoffrey Whitney's *A Choice of Emblemes*, a collection of symbolical pictures interpreted in verse, dedicated to the Earl of Leicester and published in 1585 at Leiden. Each of the two emblems dedicated to Paston in Whitney's book is placed next to an emblem dedicated to Edward Dyer, Sidney's closest friend (on 132–35, 196–99). The poem attached to one of Dyer's emblems is in praise of Sidney; similarly, one of those dedicated to Paston (beginning "The dyer, lo, in smoke and heat doth toil") is a eulogy for Dyer. It is possible that the association between Dyer and Paston implied by Whitney was one based primarily on common literary and musical interests, for Edward appears never to have been drawn into the court life of the Earl of Leicester's entourage. Indeed, he seems to have had no desire at any time of his life to advance himself in the public eye, either at court or in his own county.

Edward Paston's later life appears to have been spent mainly in the care of his family and property, and in the quiet pursuit of music and poetry. During this period he must also have built up his large library of books and music. We may suppose that the house at Thorpe was the scene of frequent musical gatherings, and the resort of the professional musicians and composers engaged in the comparatively rich musical life of nearby Norwich, one of the most important cities of the realm. Among them were Thomas Morley, organist and choirmaster at the cathedral from 1583 to 1587, and some lesser worthies such as Osbert Parsley, Richard Carlton and William Cobbold. A letter from Paston to his kinsman, the Earl of Rutland,[10] shows that these men could hope for advancement as a result of Paston's recommendation, but they must also have respected the master of Thorpe as a musician and performer in his own right. His instrument was the lute, and he was unusual among English lutenists in that he understood not only the French system of tablature used in this country but also the different system associated with Italy and Spain. Geoffrey Whitney, who may have visited Thorpe during the years he was employed at Great Yarmouth, left an account of Paston's playing in a poem attached to the only musical emblem of his collection. The emblem is dedicated to a certain "doctiss. virum D. St. Bullum" and the poem concludes with these lines, against which a marginal note refers to "E. P. Esquier":

> But, you are happie most, who in suche place doe staye;
> You neede not Thracia seeke, to heare some impe of Orphevs playe,
> Since, that so neare your home, Apollos darlinge dwelles;
> Who Linvs, & Amphion staynes, and Orphevs farre excelles.
> For, hartes like marble harde, his harmonic dothe pierce:
> And makes them yeelding passions feele, that are by nature fierce.
> But, if his musicke faile: his curtesie is suche,
> That none so rude, and base of minde, but hee reclaimes them muche.
> Nowe since you, by deserte, for both, commended are:
> I choose you, for a Iudge herein, if truthe I doe declare.
> And if you finde I doe, then ofte therefore reioyce:
> And thinke, I woulde suche neighbour haue, if I might make my choice.
> (186)

The dedicatee seems to have been the Stephen Bull, LL.B., who held posts in the Norwich archdeaconry in 1584 and 1585, and who would therefore have been for a time a neighbor to Edward Paston at Thorpe (Blomefield, 3:656, 659).

The nature and extent of the remarkable collection of music and books that Paston built up during his life are outlined in some detail in his will.[11] There he mentions "many lute bookes prickt in Ciphers after the Spanish and Italian fashion and some in letters of A.B.C. accordinge to the English fashion whereof divers . . . have singing parts sett to them," and many printed and manuscript "setts of lattin, ffrench and Italian songs some of three, foure, five, six, seaven, and eight parts." Most of the books seem to have been kept in a variety of places (a chest, a closet and "fower truncks" in the gallery) at Appleton, but there were also some at Thorpe and Town Barningham. How much of the collection perished in the conflagration at Appleton in 1707 we can only surmise; fortunately a good deal seems to have survived, though its identification presents certain problems. Only four items, three lute books and one set of part books, have Paston's name or initials stamped upon their covers; the others bear no trace of contemporary ownership—itself an unusual feature for musical manuscripts of the time—but I believe the evidence of handwriting, layout, content, binding and subsequent ownership is strong enough to connect them with Edward Paston.

The three lute books are now preserved at the British Library (Add. 31992), the Royal College of Music (2089) and St. Michael's College, Tenbury (340).[12] The covers of the first two are stamped in gold or silver with Paston's full name (figure 4.1).[13] The Tenbury lute book is less sumptuously bound, and has only the owner's initials and a conventional ornament blind-stamped upon the covers. These books are among those "prickt in Ciphers after the Spanish and Italian fashion"; they contain no lute music proper, but are entirely devoted to arrangements of vocal compositions. The contents of Add. 31992 suggest that this manuscript was the earliest of the three, and that it was completed about 1600.[14] It divides into two sections, one consisting almost wholly of songs by Byrd, the other containing a conservative selection of motets from popular Continental anthologies printed between about 1540 and 1590. RCM 2089, a more heterogeneous collection, includes motets from Byrd's printed sets of 1575, 1589 and 1591 scattered in small clusters among motets by Thomas Tallis and Alfonso Ferrabosco the elder (Italian-born but English-domiciled), and other motets, madrigals and chansons from Continental prints of the period 1560–85. Tenbury 340, a similar miscellaneous anthology, draws on later sources. On the basis of its contents it appears to have been written in the second decade of the seventeenth century.

Figure 4.1. Cover of British Library Add. 31992. (© The British Library Board. All Rights Reserved.)

With these three books we may safely associate a pair of lute books without an owner's name but in the same handwriting—the only other extant English sources of the period to employ Italian tablature (Add. 29246 and 29247). Together they form a comprehensive anthology of music for three to eight voices, and add to the repertory so far outlined works by older generations of English composers, reaching as far back as Taverner and Fayrfax; Add. 29246 also includes transcriptions of English music for viols. Much of Add. 29247 appears to have been copied directly from RCM 2089 (or from a source common to them both) in a virtually undisturbed order, but with shorter pieces interpolated here and there.

Many of the arrangements in these lute books were designed as accompaniments for a vocal performance. In Add. 31992 the Cantus part is omitted from the intabulation, and the singer takes his cue from a short direction in Spanish at the head of each piece. In this manuscript, and also in Add. 29247, folio numbers are given for companion sets of part books that have not survived.

The set of part books with Paston's name upon the covers is now at Tenbury (341–44). The contents, inscribed by the same hand as the lute books, consist chiefly of music by Byrd and the elder Ferrabosco. An index at the end of each book gives the folio number for each piece, and for some it gives in addition the "folio in the long Books," evidently referring to companion lute books (the surviving lute books are indeed "long," oblong quartos), which again have disappeared.

The person who inscribed all these books was an accomplished penman versed in several styles of handwriting. His most usual style was italic, but for the few English texts in the Tenbury part books he adopted secretary script. This same secretary hand appears in the letter from Paston to the Earl of Rutland in 1587 and in the following note on a flyleaf of RCM 2089, which identifies the scribe as one of Paston's servants:

> Wllm Corbett. I pray bynd this book in yellow letter duble fillytd w^t sylver, my m^r his Ovell and his name vppon it, the leaves be sprinkld w^t green & greene silke strings; look to fould it very even and cutt it as little as may be.

One other manuscript in the hand of this man has come to light: a single Bassus part book containing a selection of English and Continental motets (figure 4.2).[15] Its covers bear the name of Sir John Petre of Ingatestone in Essex, a neighbor and patron of William Byrd. It is conceivable that Paston's secretary was some time in Petre's employ, but more likely that the set of books to which this volume belonged originated from the Paston household—possibly as a present to one who shared not only Paston's musical interests but also his religious convictions.

The other manuscripts which I believe to have come from the Paston collection mostly answer to his description of "setts of lattin, ffrench and Italian songs some of three, foure, five, six, seaven and eight parts,"

Figure 4.2. Tenbury 342, fol. 73v. (The Bodleian Library, University of Oxford).

though they include sets of English songs as well. They were inscribed by a number of professional copyists whose handwritings fall into three main groups. Of the extant sets of part books, many of them now incomplete, seventeen are in the hands of group A (e.g., figure 4.3), six in the hands of group B (e.g., figure 4.4), and eight in the hands of group C.[16] Within these groups further subdivisions may be made. In group A, for instance, two copyists with very similar styles seem to have worked on different sections of the music; in group B the words are sometimes in two slightly different italic styles. It is also necessary to make a distinction between the music hands (A^m, B^m, C^m) and the hands which added the verbal text (A^w, B^w, C^w). In four further sets of part books some or all of the music is in one of the hands A^m, whereas the words are in one of the hands B^w. This establishes a definite link between these two groups of copyists; the connection between them and those of group C rests on very similar layout and binding, and on the large number and arrangement of concordant pieces they share.[17]

The copyists of these manuscripts employed slightly different methods of arrangement from those of Paston's secretary who wrote the lute books. His part books are small upright quartos, theirs are all oblong, mostly octavo, but occasionally quarto (RCM 2041) or duodecimo (Add. 29401–5). He adds the composer's name at the end of nearly every piece, but in their books composers' names rarely appear, and when present they are generally found in the Bassus book only, at the head of the compositions. As we have seen, he sometimes used secretary script, but they invariably used italic (with verbal incipits occasionally written in roman). Only two of his manuscripts are without an owner's name, whereas none of theirs has any indication of the original owner.

The considerations that suggest that the ownerless part books also came from the Paston collection outweigh these slight differences. Their contents represent merely a widening within the spheres of the repertory already described. Apart from the music of Byrd, a few instrumental pieces by John Bull and a handful of motets by Peter Philips, a Roman

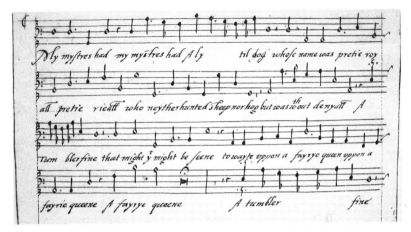

Figure 4.3. Harvard Mus. MS 30 (4), fol. 22v, showing the hands of Group A. (Courtesy of Houghton Library, Harvard College Library.)

Figure 4.4. British Library Add. 29401, fol. 28v, showing the hands of Group B. (© The British Library Board. All Rights Reserved.)

Catholic working for most of his life on the Continent, none of the identified music is by English composers flourishing after 1585. Morley,
Weelkes, Wilbye and Dowland, for instance, are completely unrepre-
sented. Some sets of part books resemble the lute book, Add. 31992, in
containing only one or two fairly well-defined categories of music
(motets by English composers, motets or songs by Byrd, Continental
motets, madrigals and chansons, and so on); others follow the other lute
books in presenting a cross section of all types of composition. Concordances with the lute book repertory are not difficult to find. Indeed, some
items occur again and again throughout the whole collection, often in association with certain other compositions. The scribes seem to have
copied small clusters of pieces at a time, possibly from some central
source, constantly rearranging the order of the clusters themselves and
the order of items within them, and sometimes interpolating extra items:
see table 4.1.

The original bindings, when they still exist, offer another means of
connecting the groups of manuscripts. Some books (including those written by Paston's secretary) are bound in boards covered in calf and stamped
with various devices in blind, silver or gilt. The same device recurs on
more than one set of books: one on the covers of one of the lute books
(Add. 31992) appears on the Petre Bassus book and on a set of part books
of group A (Tenbury 369–73); a fleur-de-lis device on the covers of the
Tenbury lute book turns up again on seven sets from groups A and B;[18]
and another which appears on two sets of group A is also found on one of
group C.[19] The other books of the collection preserved in their original
state are bound in limp vellum covers with a description of their contents,
or the title of the first item written on the outside in ink. One of these, a
miscellaneous anthology of three-part compositions (RCM 2036), is entitled "Preciosas Margaritas," and is therefore likely to have been a present
from Edward to his wife, Margaret. We know the name of one of the
binders, William Corbett, from the note in the lute book mentioned
above. I have not been able to trace this man, but Corbett was a common
name in Norfolk at the time, and he may well have worked in the county.

Table 4.1 *Typical Concordances between Paston Manuscripts*

Title	Composer	Year	Add. 31992	RCM 2089	Add. 29247	Tenbury 340	Tenbury 341–44	RCM 2041	Add. 29388–92	Mad. Soc. G21–26	Add. 30361–66	Add. 30810–15	Tenbury 379–84
Memento homo	Byrd	1575			75	36	68	83		13		24	44
Aspice Domine, quia facta	Byrd	1575		69	76 96	51		86				26	26
Attolite portas	Byrd	1575		70	77 97	52	69	87				23	
O lux beata Trinitas	Byrd	1575		71	78 95	49	79	84				25	
Infelix ego	Byrd	1591			79	10	71					22	
Peccata mea	Gombert	1549	119		86	38		33					
Domine da nobis	Crecquillon	1554			80	37		34					1
Jesu nostra redemptio	Lassus	1568	120	67	81	34		35					2
Cum natus esset Jesus	Lassus	1568		68	84	35		37			31		3
Caesaris auspitiis	Crecquillon	1554	121						26				
O vos omnes	Ferrabosco	1585	123	22				55	25	12	35		
Salve Regina	Vaet	1568	124			13	67	26	37	3	7	1	
Veni Creator	Lassus	1568	125	33				62	35		30		
Timor et tremor	Lassus	1568	126					65	14				
In monte oliveto	Lassus	1568	127					29	15	10	33	15	18
In monte oliveto	Ferrabosco	1568	128					30	16	11	34	16	19
Timor et tremor	Ferrabosco	1585	131					64	10				

NOTE: The numbers refer to the position of the items within the manuscripts. Nos. 2–4 occur twice in Add. 29247 in slightly different arrangements for the lute. The manuscripts in the first five columns are in the hand of Paston's secretary; those in the next three in the hands of group A, and those in the last three in the hands of group C.

One set of part books (Egerton 2009, 2011–12), a collection of songs and madrigals written in the hands of group A, can be ascribed to Paston's collection on the evidence of a later owner; in 1669 it belonged to Stephen Aldhouse of Matlask, near Town Barningham. Since Aldhouse was one of the witnesses to Paston's will, there can be little doubt that this set originated from Paston's library. Another set of part books owned by Aldhouse in 1670 (Add. 18936–39) was not written by any of the copyists mentioned above, and it differs from their fair copies in its haphazard arrangement and rough appearance; the compiler evidently copied from Paston sources, probably from part books without composers' names, since his attributions are frequently inaccurate. But as the later folios indicate a slightly more advanced taste in contemporary English music than that of the Paston manuscripts, the set may have been compiled by a younger member of the family, or by a musician in attendance, for his own private use. The earliest owners that can definitely be associated with the rest of the manuscripts under discussion are nineteenth-century collectors, principally George Ebenezer Williams, Joseph Warren, Stephen Groombridge, Frederick Lygon, sixth Earl Beauchamp, John Reekes, R. P. Carr and the Rev. Sir Frederick Ouseley.[20] It seems probable that the collection, having been split up in Paston's will, began to come onto the market in the middle of the eighteenth century when the family fortunes were low.

The evidence that has so far come to light suggests that during later life (after about 1590) Paston employed several copyists to produce manuscripts for his private collection. At least one of them was a personal servant of his, and the others may well have worked in the household. The frequent reappearance of certain pieces of music throughout the collection might mean that some manuscripts, like the book belonging to Sir John Petre, were inscribed for other persons; but in that case we should expect to find in them some clue to their owners' identities. The duplication of music within the collection was not without reason: many pieces were provided with transposed versions which enabled them to be played or sung by different combinations of instruments and voices; and we may conjecture that Paston wished to have a similar selection of music available at each of his three houses. A look at the manuscripts themselves suggests a slightly different reason. They are clearly and often beautifully written, but they are by no means always accurate or even complete, and few of them show signs of having been used by performers. It almost seems as though the scribes copied out the same pieces over and over again to fill out part books that might never be examined. One wonders whether Paston eventually became more concerned with the size of the collection than with the growth of the musical repertory it contained.

Three songs whose words refer to events in the life of the Pastons and their circle form the last link in the chain of evidence connecting the ownerless part books with Edward's collection. They occur in Add. 29401–5 (group B), and one is also found in Harvard Mus. 30 (group A).

"My mistress had a little dog" portrays a curious incident at Appleton. The pun in the couplet at the end of the third stanza surely identifies the lady in question as Penelope Rich. It is possible that, as I have said, she knew Edward, and that she was visiting his home at the time, which must have been between 1596, when Appleton was built, and 1605, the year of her divorce and second marriage.

> My Mistres had a litle Dogg
> Whose name was pretty Royall,
> Who neyther hunted sheepe nor hogg,
> But was without Denyall
> A tumbler fine, that might be seene
> To wayt vpon a fayrie Queene.
>
> Vpon his Mistres he would wayte
> In Curteous wise and humble;
> And with his Crafte & false deceyte,
> When she would haue hym tumble,
> Of Conyes in the pleasant pryme,
> He would kill twentye at a tyme.
>
> The Goddesse wch Dyana hight,
> Among hir Beagles dayntye

Had not a hound soe faire & white,
  Nor graced with such beautye;
And yet his beautye was not such,
But his Conditions were as Rich.

But out Alas! Ile speak no more,
  My hart with griefe doth shake,
This prettye dogg was wounded sore,
  Euen for his Mistres sake,
A beastly man, or manly beast
Knockt out his braynes—and so I rest.

A tryall royall, Royall a tryall!
  Oh yes!
Ye hounds & beagles all,
If ye satt in Appleton hall
Would you not iudge y^t out of doubt
Tyburne were fitt for such a loute?[21]

In 1608 Edward's eldest son, Thomas, married Mary Browne, a member of the famous Sussex family which had enjoyed Queen Elizabeth's favor in spite of its adherence to the old faith. The match must have delighted Paston, and it is natural that he should wish to hear the bride's praises sung.

Though I bee browne yet am I fayre
  As ys the sable mixt wyth gold,
I am not parched wyth the Ayre,
  Nor change my hew for heat or Cold.
This prayse my brownnes doth retayne,
Noe Coulour can my beauty stayne.

I am not lyke y^ee fading whyte,
  A coulor proper to the snowe,
Wherin, though louers vayne delight,
  Yet hath y^t this (as all men know):
That euen as doth the silver Moone,
Nothing on earth doth change soe soone.

> But Brownes sweet favour ys not soe;
>   Yt ys a gift of Nature's grace
> Passing ye Rose, Lyllye & Snowe
>   Which shyne for fayre in womens face;
> And y^t which most adornes ye same
> Is that Browne beares a vertuous Name.[22]

The last of these songs records a sadder occasion of 1608—the death of Mary Browne's grandmother, Lady Magdalen Montague. This lady outlived her husband, Sir Anthony Browne, first Viscount Montague, to become a dowager of great holiness and considerable celebrity. Her confessor wrote her biography, stressing among other things her endeavor to attain "the second degree of chastity," and telling how she had repulsed even the playful attentions of the king of Spain during his stay at the court of Queen Mary.[23] It is upon this aspect of her virtuous life that the poem dwells:

> With Lillies white those Virgins fayre are Crowned
>   Y^t wedd themselues to our great Lord & Sauior,
> & neuer weare in worldly pleasure drowned,
>   But solely liu'de in chast & sweet behavyour,
> Expecting still, wth Lamps of Christall shyning,
> The brydegroomes call to bidd them to his Dyning.
>
> Among these Maydes fayre Mawdlyn lat deceased
>   May well be plac'te in virgin's weede attyred;
> Who, as in yeares, in vertue still encreased,
>   And was a flower of beutye most admired;
> Whose corps in earth in marble tombe reposes,
> And soule in heaven Crowned with sacred Roses.[24]

These verses and the music to which they are set are anonymous. It seems probable, however, that Paston himself was the poet, and William Byrd the composer. Paston's memorial mentions his skill in poetry as well as in music, and Bartholomew Young refers to his activities as a translator. We know from his will that he possessed "collections of Italian Poetts," and it would be disappointing if the musical side of his library gave no indication of his literary interests. In one of the sets subsequently owned by Stephen Aldhouse (Egerton 2009–12) there are a number of Italian madrigals and French chansons adapted to English words.[25] Admittedly, there are few translations or imitations; the poet seems to prefer setting his own frequently sententious verse to the music in a manner that is often far from graceful. He is fond of elegy, and moralizes quaintly upon the calamities that befell such famous historical figures as Henry VI, the princes in the tower, Mistress Jane Shore, Thomas Cromwell and Lady Jane Grey. The adaptations are not restricted to foreign songs that the Paston family might wish to perform in English; the two manuscripts containing the verses printed above also include a few of Byrd's songs (all known from earlier printed or manuscript sources) to which new verses have been set. They are mostly elegies—one in rather acid terms for Queen Elizabeth, and two for Mary, Queen of Scots that leave us in no doubt about the poet's religious and political sympathies.[26] The person who wrote all these verses must also have been responsible for the topical songs printed above. The amateurish technique, conservative style and generally sententious mood of this series of poems suggest an author of Paston's age and background. What fitter exercise for a person of his talents than the setting of new words to old favorites and the celebrating of events important to the family in verse?

Judging from the contents of his collection, Paston's musical tastes, like his literary style, were formed in the late 1560s and 1570s, when he seems to have come into contact with the leading English composers working in London. In 1574 he appears in the will of Ellen White as a debtor to her and her husband, Robert White, choirmaster of Westminster Abbey and one of the most important English composers of the time.[27] The large amount of unpublished music by Alfonso Ferrabosco the elder in Paston's manuscripts suggests that he was an admirer, and possibly a patron, of this Italian composer, who lived in England for long periods between 1562 and 1578.

Byrd arrived in London in 1572, and it is probable that Paston took an early interest in this promising newcomer to the musical scene. Byrd, like Paston, seems to have had some connection with the Sidney circle. His setting of two verses in quantitative meters in a manner reminiscent of the French *musique mesurée* argues an interest in their metrical experiments; he certainly set three poems by Sidney and two by Dyer, and at least two of his printed songs refer to the unhappy plight of Lady Rich, who was Byrd's near neighbor when he took up residence in Essex. Whitney's emblem book was also well known to him, for he took as many as six poems from this collection, including "In crystal towers," one of the two dedicated to Paston.[28]

Byrd's relationship with these people is no less conjectural than Paston's; but conjecture diminishes a little when one discovers hints that both of them were connected with the same group of people. The association between Byrd and Paston themselves rests on firmer evidence. How early it began we cannot say. "Ah, golden hairs," one of Byrd's earlier songs dating from before 1588, is a setting of an imitation of the first lyric in Montemayor's *Diana*. The coincidence is almost too good to be true, but the style of the poetry is not noticeably similar to that of the verse I attribute to Paston. However, "Crowned with flowers," a poem based on this same lyric of Montemayor's, appears first in one of Paston's manuscripts adapted to Italian music,[29] and was later set by Byrd and published in his *Psalmes, Songs and Sonnets* of 1611. It is Paston's musical collection as a whole that argues his connection with Byrd most eloquently. Byrd's music takes pride of place, and a few volumes are devoted almost exclusively to his work. One of the lute books (Add. 31992) includes an almost complete collection of the songs written up to the date of its compilation; no fewer than twenty-five songs—many of them sadly incomplete—are known only from this book and other sources of the collection.

The three topical songs in question appear in two sets of part books (Harvard Mus. 30 and Add. 29401–5) almost entirely filled with songs which we may ascribe to Byrd from concordances with reliable manuscripts and printed sources. The composition of these part books strongly suggests the attribution to Byrd of the three anonymous songs, but their musical style presents even greater evidence of his authorship—evidence which cannot be considered here in detail. They are designed to be performed by a solo voice to the accompaniment of a quartet of viols. This somewhat conservative English form was one which Byrd cultivated and developed throughout his working life, but one which was driven out of fashion during the last decade of the sixteenth century by the enormous vogue of the new Italianate madrigal and the equally novel lute air from France. The music of the three songs is characteristic of Byrd's later, more complicated style, and there is no possibility that the words were adapted to already existing music. By the time these songs were composed (between about 1596 and 1608) no other composer writing in this old-fashioned style had at his command the fluency of technique and intensity of expression which they display.

Among the other anonymous songs that appear in these manuscripts are eight more that would seem to belong to Byrd on the grounds of their musical style. The manuscripts of the collection also contain a motet of Byrd's unknown from other sources, and the original versions of several songs published in revised form. Indeed, they are a rich source of the unpublished English music of the sixteenth century—one upon which the editors of *Tudor Church Music* had often to rely in the absence of earlier, more authentic manuscripts. There may still be more undiscovered English music of the period lying in the part books which do not give attributions. As Joseph Kerman has remarked: "After all the Continental music has been filtered out of these sources, unsuspected works by Byrd and other English composers may perhaps be identified in the residue."[30] The Paston collection is indeed of great value as a record of the tastes and enthusiasms of an Elizabethan amateur musician, but it is even more remarkable to the musical historian as an important source of compositions by William Byrd and his English predecessors.

APPENDIX A: EXTRACTS FROM THE WILL OF EDWARD
PASTON DEALING WITH HIS COLLECTION

Item wheras I have many lute bookes prickt in Ciphers after the Spanish and Italian fashion and some in letters of A.B.C. accordinge to the English fashion whereof divers are to bee plaid vpon the lute alone and have noe singinge partes and divers other lute bookes which have singing *pts* sett to them wch must be sunge to the lute and are bound in very good bookes and tied vp with the lute parts whereof some have two singinge bookes some three and some fower I will that my sonne William Paston after my decease shall have the keepinge of the said bookes vntill my Grandchild Thomas Paston shall come to his age of eighteene yeares And then I doe give and bequeath the same to my said Grandchild Thomas Paston: Item whereas I have standinge in my Study next the Parlor at Appleton a Chest wherein there are many setts of lattin, ffrench and Italian songs some of three, foure, five, six, seaven, and eight parts whereof all are pricked and as yet not printed I doe will and my minde is that my said sonne William Paston shall have the keepinge of the said Chest and the bookes therein conteyned vntill my said Grandsonne Thomas Paston shall attaine vnto his said age of eighteene yeares And then I will and bequeath vnto him the said chest and the bookes therein contayned: Item whereas I have divers other singinge bookes at my house at Townebarningham and some at my house at Thorpe by Norwich whereof many are prickt songs and not printed and many songes printed and not prickt, the prickt songes I doe give and bequeath vnto my sonnes William and John Paston to bee equallie devided betweene them And whereas I have alsoe many setts of printed songs in the foresaid Study by the parlor at Appleton whereof some are of lattin and some of ffrench and Italian I doe alsoe will and bequeath the same vnto my foresaid sonnes William and John Paston to bee equallie devided betweene them: Item whereas I have in my Study at Appleton and in my Study at Thorpe aforesaid many lattin, spanish and ffrench bookes all the lattin bookes I doe will and bequeath vnto my sonne Wolstan Paston, and the Italian, ffrench and Spanish the one halfe I doe give to my said sonne William Paston, and the other halfe to my said sonne John Paston and I doe the like devision make of a whole Chest of bookes wch stand in my great Chamber at Thorpe: Item whereas I have many bookes in Spanish and some in Italian all of singuler workes and collections of Italian Poetts written by one Richard ffox and others I doe will and bequeath the same to my sonne William Paston to have the keeping thereof vntill my Grandchild Thomas Paston shall come to his age of eighteene yeares And then I give and bequeath the said bookes vnto him which I could wish him to

make a very good account of: Item whereas Clement Paston my vncle Esq[r] de-
ceased did give and bequeath vnto mee two Snakes of gold linked together and a
faire bowle silver and gilt w[ch] he had of a noble french Captaine called Baron S[t]
Bancart whom my said vncle tooke prisoner in a fight at Sea I doe give and bequeath the said Snake & bowle to Clement Paston my grandchild who I hope will
keepe the same as a remembrance of my foresaid good vncle who was very boun-
tifull besids the said gift to divers of my sonnes: Item whereas I have lyinge in my
Study at Thorpe by Norw[ch] a goodly auncient faire booke of davids Psalmes all
full of faire letters richly gilded wth gold w[ch] my foresaid vncle gave me I do will
and bequeath the same to my Grandchild Clement Paston willinge him to save
and keep it . . .

Item whereas I have standinge in the Gallery at Appleton where I now dwell
fower truncks wherein are conteyned divers setts of lute bookes prickt in Cyphers
and divers singinge bookes tyed vpp wth the same, And whereas I have alsoe in
the Closett next vnto the said Gallery divers lute bookes pricked all in Ciphers
according to the Italian fashion, my will and minde is that my sonne William Paston Gent or his assignes shall have the keepinge of the said truncks and bookes
vntill my Grandchild Thomas Paston shall come to his age of Eighteene yeares
And then I will have all the foresaid lute bookes and singinge bookes delivered
vnto the said. Thomas Paston or his assignes to vse the same at his will & pleasure And if he die before he come to the foresaid age, Then I will and bequeath
All the said bookes to my said sonne William or his assignes.[31]

APPENDIX B: LIST OF MANUSCRIPTS

The manuscripts are arranged according to the predominant features of their contents;[32] those comprising two coherently planned collections of different kinds of
composition are placed under the heading of the larger one. Manuscripts containing a loosely arranged selection of three or more kinds of music are classified
under the heading "miscellaneous." A specimen entry shows the system of abbre-
viations:

Madrigal Society G. 16–20 * (incomplete) † (gives none or very few of the
composers' names): group A (L = manuscripts in the same hand as the lute
books), a 6–7 (contains mainly six- and seven-part compositions), 1597
(first date of publication of the latest identified pieces); Tallis (includes
works by this composer in spite of the classification under "Continental
motets").

Continental Motets and Masses

*British Library Add. 34001–2 †	A	a 8	1597
Madrigal Society G. 9–15 and British Library Add. 34000†	B	a 7–8	1597; Tallis, Byrd
*Madrigal Society G. 16–20†	A	a 6–7	1597; Tallis
*Madrigal Society G. 21–26†	A	a 6–7	1595; Tallis, Byrd
*Add. 29388–92†	A	a 6	1585
Tenbury 379–84†	C	a 6	1591; Byrd
Add. 30361–66†	C	a 5–6	1591; Byrd
Add. 30810–15†	C	a 5–6	1591; Byrd
Tenbury 349–53†	A	a 5	1607; Byrd
Tenbury 374–78†	B	a 5	1605; Byrd
*Madrigal Society G. 27†	C	a 5	1591; Byrd
*Tenbury 385–88	C	a 5	1612
Tenbury 359–63	A	a 4–5	1607; Byrd
*Folger Shakespeare Library 460328†	A, B	a 4	1605; Byrd

Madrigals and Chansons

*Add. 30816–19	C	a 6	1601
Madrigal Society G. 28–32†	B	a 5 ?	
Fitzwilliam Museum: Mu 278–79	A, C	a 5	1587–95
Tenbury 364–68	A	a 5	1596
*Add. 30450†	A	a 5	1604; some English versions; Byrd
*Add. 30820–22	B	a 5	1593
Manchester, Henry Watson Library BRm 470.I. CR 71†	A	a 4	1585
*British Library Egerton 2009, 2011–12†	A	a 4–5	1611; mostly English versions; songs by Byrd
*British Library Egerton 2010†	A	a 5	1597; mostly English versions
Add. 30823–25†	B	a 3	1604

English Motets and Masses

*Tenbury 1469–71†	A	a 5–6	1589; Lassus; songs and psalms by Byrd and Tallis
*Add. 34049†	C	a 5	1575
Tenbury 354–58	A	a 4–5	all apparently unpublished
RCM 2035	A, B	a 2–3	fragments from larger works, 1605

Music of William Byrd

*Add. 31992	L	a 4–6	1611; Continental motets; a lute book
Tenbury 369–73†	A	a 5	1605; Tallis, Ferrabosco, Desbuissons
*Harvard College Library Mus. 30†	A	a 5	1611
Add. 29401–5†	B	a 5	1611; completed after 1612; Tallis, Ferrabosco, White, Parsons, Bull

Miscellaneous

Tenbury 340	L	a 6–8	1613; a lute book
Add. 29246–47	L	a 2–8	1611; lute books
*Essex Record Office D/DP Z6/I	L	a 5–6	1591; belonged to Sir John Petre
*Tenbury 341–44	L	a 5–7	1591
RCM 2089	L	a 5–6	1591; a lute book
*RCM 2041†	A	a 4–8	1611
RCM 2036†	A, B	a 3	1605
*Add. 41156–58†	A, B	a 3–4	1605

NOTES

1. See Alec Hyatt King, *Some British Collectors of Music*, Sandars Lectures, 1961 (Cambridge, 1963).

2. See Joseph Kerman, *The Elizabethan Madrigal: A Comparative Study*, American Musicological Society Studies and Documents 4 (New York, 1962), 45; Hyatt King, 7–8.

3. See Blomefield's work (London, 1805–10); Ruth Hughey, *The Correspondance of Lady Katherine Paston, 1603–1627*, Norfolk Record Society Publications 14 (Norwich, 1941); E. B. Burstall, "The Pastons and Their Manor of Binham," *Norfolk Archaeology* 30 (1950): 101–29.

4. *Grove's Dictionary of Music and Musicians*, 5th ed. (London, 1954), 6:589; see also F. Madden, *Privy Purse Expenses of the Princess Mary* (London, 1831), 5, 22 and 26.

5. *The History and Fate of Sacrilege . . . Wrote in the Year 1632* (London, 1698), 253.

6. See T. B. Trappes-Lomax, "Roman Catholicism in Norfolk, 1559–1780," *Norfolk Archaeology* 32 (1961): 31. Paston also harbored Helen Draycott, a "cousin-german," before she entered a convent in Brussels sometime before 1625.

7. *Chronicle of the Augustinian Canonesses of Louvain*, ed. A. Hamilton (Edinburgh, 1904–6), 2:101–2.

8. British Library Harleian 1583, fol. 378. The letter is addressed from London and undated, but since it refers to the detention in an English harbor of a ship carrying money for the Duke of Alba's campaign in the Netherlands, it must have been written during the winter of 1568.

9. "What changes here, ô haire" and "Of this high grace"; see *The Poems of Sir Philip Sidney*, ed. William A. Ringler (Oxford, 1962), 157–59.

10. Royal Historical Manuscripts Commission, *Rutland MSS*, Reports and Calendars Series 24, 1:223. The bearer of the letter was engaged to give lessons upon the virginals to the Earl of Rutland's daughters. According to Paston, "he was placed at Norw[ch] Organest, And by my perswacion he hath left his rome to come vnto you[r] L." The letter is dated 3 August 1587. Could the musician in question have been Thomas Morley, who was paid his last salary as choirmaster by the cathedral authorities on 24 June of that year? The functions of organist and choirmaster were apparently fulfilled by the same man at Norwich until as late as 1591. For the record of Morley's tenure of the post see the remarks by F. L. Harrison in *Music & Letters* 42 (1961): 97–98.

11. Prerogative Court of Canterbury [P.C.C.], Scroope 43. The relevant extracts are printed in appendix A at the end of this chapter.

12. [Ed.: The Tenbury manuscripts now belong to the Bodleian Library, Oxford.]

13. The covers of RCM 2089, now in poor condition, have Paston's coat of arms—his "Ovell"—stamped on them.

14. The manuscript contains one song published by Byrd in 1611, but this item may well have been written and circulated well before the date of publication. I am indebted to Mr. Eugene Porter, of the University of California, for the dating of the Continental motets in the lute books.

15. Essex Record Office, D/DP Z6/I. The scribe uses secretary script for the verbal texts, and a heavy gothic lettering for the titles and composers' names.

16. These books have already been described in some detail; see Philip Brett and Thurston Dart, "Songs by William Byrd in Manuscripts at Harvard," *Harvard Library Bulletin* 14 (1960): 343–65.

17. Cf. Madrigal Society G. 27 (group C) with Tenbury 349–53 and 359–63 (group A), and Tenbury 379–84, Add. 30361–66 and 30810–15 (group C) with Madrigal Society G. 16–20, G. 21–26 and Add. 29388–92 (group A).

18. Add. 29388–92, 30450, 41156–58, Tenbury 364–68, 1469–71 and Madrigal Society G. 16–20 and 21–26.

19. Tenbury 349–53 and 354–58 (group A), and Add. 30361–66 (group C). These blind-stamps are not exclusive to the Paston books. I have traced two of them elsewhere: the one on Tenbury 349–53 and 354–58 (group A) appears also on the covers of Robert Dow's part books, compiled from 1581 to 1588, and bound by a later owner—his initials G.T. also appear on the covers (Christ Church, Oxford MSS 984–88); see the covers of a copy of Nicholas Yonge's *Musica Transalpina*, 1588 (stamped with the initials W.S.) at the Folger Shakespeare Library, Washington DC, and a set of manuscript part books in the Filmer collection at Yale University.

20. Joseph Warren owned Add. 29246–47, Tenbury 359–63 and 369–73; it appears that all the Paston manuscripts in the Madrigal Society Library were presented by Stephen Groombridge; Lygon owned Tenbury 340 and 341–44; Williams owned another of the lute books (see Hyatt King, 27); Reekes possessed Add. 34049 and 34050; and Carr owned Add. 30810–25 (4 sets) and Add. 34001–2.

21. Add. 29401, fol. 33v. Punctuation has been supplied, and capitalization standardized for the first word of each line.

22. Add. 29401, fol. 21v.

23. *An Elizabethan Recusant House, Comprising the Life of the Lady Magdalen, Viscountess Montague (1538–1608)*, trans. from the Latin of Dr Richard Smith by Cuthbert Fursdon, ed. A. C. Southern (1627; London, 1954).

24. Add. 29402, fol. 39v.

25. A few more madrigals and chansons occur in the later folios of Add. 34050.

26. "I that sometime," the elegy for Queen Elizabeth, is set to the music of Byrd's "When first by force," published in 1589; "The noble famous queen," for Mary, Queen of Scots, appears first as "While Phoebus used to dwell," and the other elegy for Queen Mary, "In Angels' weed," appears to have been adapted to a song, "Is Sidney dead?" appearing in the lute book Add. 31992.

27. P.C.C. 11 Carew, printed in *Tudor Church Music* (London, 1926), 5:xix. "Item Edward Paston esquire Xs. viijd. and she hath in pawne a Jewell of golde." The payment may have been for copying or composing music; but none of the Paston manuscripts discussed here can date from as early as 1574.

28. For details of these settings see Philip Brett, "The English Consort Song, 1570–1625," *Proceedings of the Royal Musical Association* 88 (1961–62): 82–84.

29. Egerton 2010, fol. 24v. The words are adapted to Philippe de Monte's madrigal "Dolce mio duol," first published in 1572. See also Egerton 2009, 2011–12 and Add. 29247, fol. 76, where the scribe—evidently with some pride—has placed the Monte version next to Byrd's setting of the words.

30. Joseph Kerman, "Byrd's Motets: Chronology and Canon," *Journal of the American Musicological Society* 14 (1961): 372.

31. P.C.C. Scroope 43. Clement and Thomas Paston, the grandchildren, were the sons of Edward's eldest son, Thomas, who died in 1622. William was Paston's second son and heir. Richard Fox may have been one of the musical copyists.

32. Further descriptions of many of the manuscripts may be found in the following library catalogs: A. Hughes-Hughes, *Catalogue of Manuscript Music in the British Museum* (London, 1906–9), 3 vols; W. B. Squire and R. Erlebach, "Catalogue of the Manuscripts in the Library of the Royal College of Music" (typescript, 1926–31); E. H. Fellowes, *The Catalogue of Manuscripts in the Library of St Michael's College, Tenbury* (Paris, 1934). See also *Tudor Church Music*, ed. E. H. Fellowes (London, 1948), app. (Tenbury 1469–71 and the Petre Bassus book); Brett and Dart, 359–64 (Harvard MS Mus. 30). The manuscripts in the library of the Madrigal Society are now on loan to the British Library; I am grateful to Mr. J. G. Craufurd, secretary of the society, for permission to examine them and for information about them.

CHAPTER FIVE

Musicae Modernae Laus: Geoffrey Whitney's Tributes to the Lute and Its Players

In May 1586 the house of Christopher Plantin in Leiden published the first English emblem book, Geoffrey Whitney's *A Choice of Emblemes and other devices.* The author had followed or accompanied his patron, Robert Dudley, Earl of Leicester, to the Netherlands on that famous and ill-fated expedition, and had eventually taken up residence at the university in Leiden.[1] In the preface Whitney explains that he was persuaded by friends to publish the book which he had presented to Leicester in manuscript shortly before the earl embarked for the Netherlands in December 1585. For the printed version, Whitney secured commendatory verses from distinguished Leiden scholars, and dedicated many of the individual emblems, not only to personal friends and relatives, but also to Dutch scholars and to those Englishmen chiefly associated with Leicester and his cause. The publication, therefore, belongs partly among the propaganda aimed at cementing Anglo-Dutch relations and enhancing the prestige of the lord lieutenant and his English followers.

Consisting of a large number of allegorical pictures interpreted in verse, the book followed a Continental fashion that had quickly grown in popularity since the appearance of the first emblem book, Andrea Al-

Originally published in *Lute Society Journal* 7 (1965): 40–44.

ciati's *Emblematum Liber*, published in 1531. Indeed, *A Choice of Emblemes* leans heavily upon the well-known Continental anthologies (Whitney himself refers to it as "my gatherings and gleaninges out of other men's haruestes"), and most of the plates are taken from the Italian and French books already printed by Plantin.[2] Yet Whitney's moralizing verses are rarely literal translations, and he was capable, as we shall see, of placing an entirely new meaning upon an old device.

Unlike some Continental collections, and those of later English emblematists such as Henry Peacham and George Wither, *A Choice of Emblemes* does not at first glance promise much of musical interest. Instruments occasionally appear as conventional subsidiary symbols in some of the devices, but only 2 out of the 248 emblems give a prominent place to music. The first of these, showing Mercury stringing the lute, comes from John Sambucus's *Emblemata*, published by Plantin at Antwerp in 1564. The motto *industria naturam corrigit* is also from Sambucus, but the accompanying verse misses the finer symbolical points of the original, which dwells upon the skill and effort required to produce harmony from intractable materials. Whitney seems content with a loose reference to the magical powers attributed to the classical lyre or *kithara*, which by common Renaissance usage becomes the lute. The totally new idea introduced rather awkwardly in the final couplet was probably intended as a compliment to Leicester (or to the Dudley family in general), whose device was a bear chained to a post. The poem is a fair example of Whitney's homely and unpretentious style:

> The Lute, whose sounde doth most delighte the eare,
>   Was caste aside, and lack'de bothe stringes, and frettes:
> Whereby, no worthe within it did appear,
>   MERCVRIVS came, and it in order settes:
> Which being tun'de, suche Harmonic did lende,
> That Poëttes write, the trees their toppes did bende.
>
> Euen so, the man on whome dothe Nature froune,
>   Whereby, he liues dispis'd of euerie wighte,

Industrie yet, maie bringe him to renoume,
    And diligence, maie make the crooked righte:
Then haue no doubt, for arte maie nature helpe.
Thinke howe the beare doth forme her vglye whelpe. (92)

The source of the other musical emblem has not been traced, but it seems likely that the device, a conventional picture of Orpheus with his lyre surrounded by birds and beasts, and the first half of the poem, dealing in general terms with the classical legend (and referring to the lyre this time as a harp), are derived from elsewhere. In the second half Whitney strikes a personal note, praising one "who Linvs, and Amphion staynes, and Orphevs farre excelles" (186).

A marginal note, referring to "E. P. Esquier," gives the clue to the identity of this prodigy: the amateur lutenist and musical collector Edward Paston, to whom Whitney dedicated two further emblems (see chapter 4). Paston owned a house at Thorpe, near Norwich, where Whitney may have met him frequently during the years 1580–85 when the emblematist held the post of underbailiff at nearby Great Yarmouth. As I have pointed out elsewhere, Whitney's book suggests that Paston was in some way connected with Edward Dyer, close friend of Sir Philip Sidney and noted member of Leicester's circle, and helps to confirm Paston's association with William Byrd, who set six of Whitney's poems to music, including "In crystal towers," one of those dedicated to Paston.[3]

Yet my chief concern here is with another lutenist, not a distinguished amateur like Paston, but a noted professional player and composer. In the Houghton Library at Harvard there is a small folio manuscript of Whitney's book that has all the appearances of the original presentation copy.[4] It contains fewer emblems than the printed book (199 compared with 248), none of them have individual dedications, and far fewer of the poems refer to contemporary figures. The Orpheus emblem is not included, and there is no mention of Edward Paston or of Dyer. The manuscript does, however, contain a musical emblem excluded from the print. The device, copied from one of Plantin's editions of Alciati, shows a lute and open music book lying on a cushion beneath a canopy. Alciati's emblem, dedicated to Maximilian, Duke of Milan, on his entering into a new treaty, proclaims the lute as a symbol of alliance (the motto is *Foedera*), and the poem, a political allegory, deals with the difficulty of keeping the strings in tune and preserving *ilia omnis harmonia.*[5] Whitney, who has a different aim in view, changes the motto to *musicae modernae laus*, and in a poem that for him is unusually terse and crisp pays tribute to contemporary English music by summarily dismissing a current humanistic belief in the superiority of "ancient music":

> When that Apollo h[e]arde the musicque of theise daies,
> And knewe howe manie, for theire skill, deserved iustlie praise,
> He left his chaire of state, & laide his lute away,
> As one abash'd in English courte, his auncient stuffe to plaie.
> And hyed vnto the skyes somme fyner pointes to frame:
> And in the meane, for cunninge stoppes, gaue Johnsonne all the fame.
>   (fol. 87v)

Johnson, alas, is a common enough surname. Who, then, was this custodian of the lute-lyre, this champion *kitharista?* His appearance in Whitney's book suggests that he was one of Leicester's most noted musicians, past or present. In the patent issued to the earl's players and musicians in 1574 a William Johnson is named, but he was probably only an actor, and by 1585 he had joined the Queen's Men.[6] Edward Johnson the musician has a stronger claim. He went from Hengrave, where he served the Kitsons, to assist at the magnificent entertainment given by Leicester to the queen when she visited Kenilworth in 1575:[7] yet it seems that this was a temporary arrangement, and Edward is known neither as a lutenist nor as a court musician. His achievements, such as they were, belong to later Elizabethan times when he contributed to East's *Psalmes* (1592) and Morley's *Triumphs of Oriana* (1601), gained his Mus.B (1594), and was mentioned by Francis Meres as one of the sixteen best composers in the land (1598).

The most likely candidate is John Johnson, a virtuoso lutenist who entered the queen's service in 1579, and remained in her employ until mid-summer 1594, the probable date of his death.[8] All the extant compositions that can be ascribed to him are written for the lute, and the number of them suggests that he was one of the more important lute composers of his time.[9] It is perhaps worth noting that a John Johnson appears in a list of those who were with Leicester in the Netherlands, yet he is entered separately from the "musicioners" who also appear in the list,[10] and I have been unable to establish any definite connection between the lutenist and the earl. Nevertheless, in view of John's reputation as composer and lutenist, and his position at court, it is almost certainly to him that Whitney's verse refers.

Why was the emblem omitted from the later printed version of *A Choice of Emblemes?* The circumstances of publication offer a possible explanation. Dutch readers might not take kindly to such lavish praise of music "in English courte," and Whitney may have feared censure from the Leiden scholars for changing the meaning of Alciati's famous device so radically. Perhaps, on the other hand, it was a matter of decorum—an important consideration in Elizabethan times. Having dedicated two emblems to Edward Paston, and having devoted yet another to the musical abilities of this gentleman amateur, Whitney may have considered it unwise and unfitting to invite comparison by including a further emblem in praise of another lutenist of superior musical ability, no doubt, but of inferior social standing.

NOTES

1. See J. A. van Dorsten, *Poets, Patrons, and Professors* (London, 1962), 124.

2. See Henry Green's facsimile reprint with copious annotation (London, 1866), 252 for this and further details. Rosemary Freeman's standard work, *English Emblem Books* (London, 1948) further assesses Whitney's book in relation to the tradition.

3. Not Edward Pearce, as M. C. Boyd ingeniously suggests in *Elizabethan Music and Musical Criticism* (Philadelphia, 1940), 203. Apart from other considerations, Pearce does not appear to have been of sufficient social standing to warrant the title "Esquier."

4. MS Typ 14 (English). So far as I can discover, the manuscript has eluded those who have written about Whitney's emblem book. An examination of its contents confirms Ms Freeman's view (238) that the other manuscript (Bodleian MS Rawl. poet. 56) cannot represent the original version, and may well have been copied from the print. The Harvard MS occasionally varies from the print, as in the final couplet of the poem quoted above, which reads, "Then, thoughe thou be like beares misshapen whelpe, / Yit haue no doute, for arte maie nature helpe"; here the Bodleian MS follows the print.

5. The complete emblem is reproduced as an illustration in John Hollander's *The Untuning of the Sky* (Princeton, 1961), which also discusses its significance and the whole question of the lute-harp-lyre constellation at 43 ff.

6. E. K. Chambers, *The Elizabethan Stage* (London, 1923), 2:86–89.

7. For the identity of the Hengrave Johnson see Ian Harwood's remarks in *Lute Society Journal* 5 (1963): 36.

8. See the entries from the Audit Office accounts printed in the *Musical Antiquary* 2 and 3 (1910–11).

9. See D. Lumsden, "English Lute Music, 1540–1620—an Introduction," *Proceedings of the Royal Musical Association* 83 (1956–57): 8; with 23 extant pieces, Johnson is outmatched by only four other lute composers—Dowland (74 pieces), Daniel Bacheler (52), Francis Cutting (51) and Anthony Holborne (42).

10. British Library MS Galba CVIII, fols. 96–101; see app. 1 and 3 of *Leicester's Triumph*, by R. C. Strong and J. A. van Dorsten (London, 1964).

CHAPTER SIX

The Two Musical Personalities
of Thomas Weelkes

In preparing a study of Byrd's sacred and secular settings of English
words I have approached the works of his contemporaries from a special
point of view which at times, I believe, reveals their achievements in a different light. Among them there is no more intriguing figure than
Thomas Weelkes, who by and large practiced one style in his madrigal
publications and another, much closer to that of the older master, in his
Anglican services and anthems. Until recently commentators have
tended to view these two major parts of Weelkes's output in isolation
from each other; but the challenge of accounting for their differences,
understanding them as complementary parts of the composer's musical
personality and building up a new profile of him as a result has now been
undertaken by David Brown in the most serious and detailed monograph
on any English composer of the period to have been published.[1] The
book is invaluable—and a good deal more impressive than most of its re-
viewers would allow; yet in using his analytical expertise virtually to reverse the previously held (though largely unwritten) view on the relative
merits of the madrigals and church music, Brown has created a new
image of the composer that is not entirely convincing. The purpose of

Originally published in *Music & Letters* 53 (1972): 369–76.

this article is to question some aspects of his critical assessment, to re-affirm as strongly as possible the preeminence of Weelkes the madrigal-ist and finally to suggest a partial explanation for some of the composer's structural tendencies that links him more firmly to the native tradition of Byrd—even in the implied revolt of his most extravagantly Italianate manner.

Before turning to my main purpose, it is a pleasure first to commend David Brown's thoughtful and penetrating approach to the musical material. Rarely is such concern to pierce to the heart of the matter encountered in writing about music of this vintage. It is not merely that coverage of all parts of the composer's output is generous, but also that the greatest care has been exercised over the analysis and its presentation. Even more impressive is the overall account of Weelkes's style, procedures favored by him—especially in the matter of formal articulation and design—being effectively isolated by comparison with the methods of the most important English composers of the time. The author has been taken to task for not extending the comparisons further afield,[2] yet to cry parochialism in this case is to chase a hare more apparent than real. Although a transalpine overview is important to maintain perspective, an intent gaze at the English scene, which after all formed the composer's basic working methods, is likely to bring the picture into clearer focus. Limiting the comparative discussion, furthermore, makes the analysis all the more cogent and profound; no one can fail to be impressed by such things as Brown's new interpretation of the three-part pieces in Byrd's *Songs of Sundrie Natures* (52), his comparison of Byrd and Morley (50–51) and his discussion in chapter 7 of repetition and sequence in the works of Morley, Wilbye and Weelkes.

After such a display of analytical acumen Brown's critical judgments come as something of a disappointment. Indeed, it could be argued that analysis in this instance leads criticism astray, for the technical devices that can most readily be demonstrated and discussed insinuate themselves as qualities in their own right, and the technical means begin to dominate the artistic ends in the writer's judgments. Brown is too intelligent to be unaware of the danger, and specifically warns (205) against overestimating the significance of repetitive devices, for example; yet he cannot avoid a tone of warm approbation whenever these and other of Weelkes's structural preoccupations are mentioned. Perhaps he is also sufficiently conditioned by the popular belief that good composers get better and better to propose a rising graph for Weelkes's musical development, even though the available evidence suggests a distinctly downward spiral in all spheres of his life from about 1609 to the end in 1623. Whatever the reasons, Brown creates a vision of Weelkes the talented young madrigalist giving way shortly after 1600 to Weelkes the serious church composer:

> At heart Weelkes was a contrapuntist who turned away from the madrigal partly because his more brilliant and imaginative works were almost certainly too advanced for all but very limited circles, partly because of the circumstances connected with his move to Chichester and his Chapel Royal aspirations, but also because the trends which had been developing in his work were hardly suited to a further pursuit of the madrigal. The sphere in which they could find a full and fitting expression was church music, and when Weelkes moved to Chichester [sometime between October 1601 and October 1602], he plainly took the decision to pour everything into this type of composition. (201)

As we ponder this transformation, we are assured that "Weelkes' music really lost nothing essential through foregoing its more purple moments" (204).

The first and foremost casualty of this new interpretation is the *Ayeres and Phantasticke Spirites for Three Voices* of 1608, which Brown considers too light and frivolous for serious attention. I think on the contrary one could maintain it is the most polished of Weelkes's sets, where conception and design rarely fall out of step and where technique is always equal to imagination: art conceals art to bring sheer delight. Campion's likening of the air to the epigram may have influenced the choice of the title, but any connection with the lutenist air ends there. Involved as deeply as ever in the madrigalian ethos, Weelkes evidently aimed in this set at appealing to the more sophisticated (and less elevated) tastes of the new reign by creating an English counterpart to the humorous and parodistic forms of Italian music, such as the *villanella* and *villota*.[3] There is no sign here of his succumbing to provincialism or surrendering himself entirely to lofty contrapuntal ideals.

It was nevertheless a highly ingenious idea to portray Weelkes running through the madrigal, and then fulfilling his essentially contrapuntal nature in a more serious and responsible fashion by making out of the necessity of Chichester the virtue of good church music; but quite apart from the awkward testimony of the 1608 set, the remaining music simply does not bear it out. First of all, Brown is obliged to sow seeds of confusion about what is, and what is not, church music in order to gather in as supporting evidence pieces like "Hosanna to the Son of David," which probably never graced a church service before the present century. True, he notices that some pieces with sacred texts were not intended for the Anglican rites, but characterizes them by the thumping contradiction "domestic 'church' music" while subsuming several thoroughly unecclesiastical works under the heading "true anthems." Yet if a piece does not appear in the liturgical sources, and if it does not observe the decorum that in spite of increasing High Church license remained a predominant feature of the Jacobean Anglican idiom, it is surely misleading to classify it as church music.[4] "Hosanna to the Son of David" is no more or less a "true anthem" than the three sacred pieces Brown excludes from that category. It occurs only in secular sources; it sounds madrigalian; and its words are as likely to apostrophize James I (or one of his sons) as to commemorate Jesus Christ. It is probably a welcome song intended to adorn one of the king's progresses, if not his initial entry into the kingdom in 1603. *Gloria in excelsis* and *Laboravi in gemitu meo* are two more works noticeably un-Anglican in manner, and the sources also point to their secular origin.[5] Some pieces, like "Alleluia! I heard a voice," eventually led a double life, and their initial purpose cannot be determined. But even when doubtful cases like "O Lord, arise into thy resting place" are put on one side,[6] the conclusion remains that several of the works most essential to Weelkes's reputation as a church composer are not church music at all; and we are therefore entitled to assess that reputation afresh in order to understand more fully where his artistic strength lay.

Second, the almost complete lack of evidence for dating the genuine church music, while not seriously undermining Brown's theory, scarcely invites confidence in it. The extant choir books are too late to have any bearing on the problem, which—to put it in extreme terms—leaves only a couple of post–Gunpowder Plot verse anthems (one of them incomplete) and three "royal" anthems safely assigned to the Jacobean period.[7] Yet the last major piece to be dated at all convincingly (two contributions to Leighton's *Tears or Lamentations,* 1614, are of no great consequence) is a secular work—the elegiac madrigal "When David heard that Absalom was slain"—occasioned in all probability by the death of Henry, Prince of Wales, in 1612.[8] Did Weelkes write anything of comparable stature in the remaining years? We do not know, but a positive answer might carry more weight if the church music bore signs of stylistic development and artistic growth. These are notably lacking, however, and it is difficult to avoid the feeling that Weelkes could sink back into the well-worn Anglican mold, as into a comfortable old armchair, with equal ease throughout his working life, and that his faculties generally dozed a little as a result.

Third, to invest heavily in Weelkes the contrapuntist is to put too great a risk upon the safety of one's critical capital. Granted, there is plenty of contrapuntal and pseudo-contrapuntal activity in the music, none of it to my mind shows any really outstanding expertise; at best it is used for dramatic ends or to create lively textures, at worst it merely prolongs the piece. The only example I have noticed of his working anything so complicated as a genuine double point (in which two independent melodies are combined in the construction of a contrapuntal period) occurs in *Laboravi in gemitu meo,* again not a church work but apparently an academic exercise modeled on Morley's setting of the same words. As for the quality of Weelkes's counterpoint as counterpoint, one needs only to glance at Brown's example 114, intended to show "how close Weelkes

Example 6.1

a. Byrd, Great Service: Magnificat

[He remembering his mercy]

b. Weelkes, Service for Seven Voices: Magnificat

[He remembering his mercy]

has drawn to Byrd" in the seven-part Magnificat, to realize how far he still had to go (example 6.1): his regular entries, predictable rhythm and insistent suspensions seem primitive beside the older master's effortless control—the rhythmic resemblance of the subject itself is about the only thing the two have in common. Brown also writes approvingly of Weelkes's close and repetitive entries because they produce what he calls "thematic concentration." I see no reason for approbation: better contrapuntists are less dense. But close entries, terse points of imitation and dense textures were all part and parcel of the Jacobean Anglican style—that dim religious manner barely altered in its essentials from the prototype established by the generation of Tallis and Tye. Good contrapuntists like Byrd and Gibbons could generally make something out of it, but one can only regret that Weelkes practiced it in so orthodox a manner since it caught him on his weakest points.

It would of course be wrong to imply that the church music is completely derivative and empty. Many of its best moments arise from the application of techniques used with success in the madrigals, like the "organic repetition" or sequence which Brown describes so well. This appears at its crudest and most unattractive in "Alleluia! I heard a voice," where two well-worn clichés (one incorporating a false relation, the other an unprepared seventh) are ground out ad nauseam at different pitch levels. In a different class are the unison repetitions of the treble dialogues in the Fourth Service or the similarly constructed four-part section for trebles and altos at "to be a light" in the Nunc Dimittis of the Eighth Service for five voices, where the *rota*-like technique combined with a welcome change of texture saves an otherwise routine piece. Is there anything like these passages in the Anglican repertory of the period? Furthermore the *ostinato* effect of regular entries, well worn though the device is by Weelkes's time, can take on a new dramatic urgency at his hands in a work like the Nunc Dimittis for seven voices, where the resulting tension finds release in a startlingly—and surely consciously—archaic cadence incorporating both the simultaneous false relation and the 6/5 progression (now resplendent in the major) that have been relentlessly repeated during the course of the piece. Such an extravagant evocation of the musical language of the earlier part of the century, however, argues the work of a composer more youthfully exuberant than stylistically secure (example 6.2).[9]

Fine though such passages may be, Weelkes's bona fide church music hardly qualifies him for prolonged attention; one gains the impression of a strong musical imagination leashed in by counterpoint and reduced to routine by the exigencies of a style too familiar and too restricting. Neither a lutenist nor (as Brown rightly points out) a good melodist, there was no recourse for him in the air. Yet the Italianate idiom promulgated so energetically by his friend Morley answered all the needs of his wayward talent, and his quick ear instinctively grasped its essential musical ingredients if not its literary aesthetic. Here his counterpoint could be put to a number of expressive purposes, though he let it ramble on in the English manner on occasions; here the imitative material gained character from that virile rhythmic sense stifled in church; and

Example 6.2. Weelkes, Service for Seven Voices: Nunc Dimittis

even more important, here the counterpoint was thrown into dramatic relief by *alla breve* passages in which new harmonies were explored and rich suspensions and passing notes introduced, passages in which the old clichés (particularly those involving the false relation) suddenly took on fresh and truly expressive connotations. If Weelkes sometimes overextended himself in either kind of texture, he seems to have done so out of sheer musical high spirits, and when he struck the right balance (as in "Hosanna," "When David heard" and a dozen or so of the printed works) he rose as high as any of his contemporaries, English or Continental.

It appears from Weelkes's work (and from the anti-intellectual tone he adopts in the dedication to the *Madrigals of 5. Parts* of 1600) that he possessed that almost subcutaneous kind of musicality residing as much in the fingertips as in the head. His imagination was headstrong, yet needed a good stimulus to set it afire. This happened, I believe, in his release from the musical tradition of his youth by means of the imported madrigal style and in his response to the vivid images of the Petrarchan and "fantastical" poetry that came with it. Yet his preoccupation with form and structure shows that he had a lively mind and perhaps some realization that he lacked the ability to construct developing and self-generating contrapuntal forms after the manner of Byrd and Gibbons. He appears to have settled upon a simple but strong block-like method of construction with clearly articulated sections bound together by repetition, thematic relationships and so on.

Yet another reason for the schematic nature of Weelkes's formal planning may have to do paradoxically with his obvious lack of sensitivity to the madrigal's literary background. The English secular tradition, exemplified at its best in the music of William Byrd, still clung to a method in which the setting was usually strophic and the musical shape determined largely by the poetic form and not by the content of the verse. It was easy enough for Weelkes to grasp Morley's rules for "dittying" in the Italian manner; indeed, attention to verbal imagery brought about some of his most imaginative strokes. But could he forget the basic formal principles in which, as the old-fashioned verse anthems so clearly demonstrate, he must have been trained? I think not. To begin with, the poetry Weelkes set almost always seems native in appearance; alone among the important English madrigalists he chose no text from the Italian anthologies of Yonge, Watson and Morley.[10] Apart from the Oriana madrigal "As Vesta was from Latmos hill descending," its irregular ten-line text probably provided by Morley, Weelkes's most ambitious works generally employ two (in one case three) stanzas of identical and regular form, and he comes as close as possible to strophic setting in these works without losing his madrigalian integrity. "Come clap thy hands," "What have the gods their comfort sent?" and "Thule, the period of cosmography" all incorporate verbal and musical refrains; "O care, thou wilt despatch me" is interspersed with fa-las possibly (like those in Henry Youll's setting of Sir John Davies's "Early before the day") introduced by the composer himself, who must at any rate have engineered many of those refrain-like repeats in the anthem texts. When there is no refrain, as in the three-stanza "My flocks feed not," Weelkes nevertheless pursues a similar plan in setting each stanza; indeed, the telescoping of lines 1–3 and 5–7 in this piece—a practice Brown interprets wrongly as careless word setting—reflects this formal concern over the verse particularly well. Furthermore, the rigorous division of the single stanza itself into fast and slow sections, a feature that Kerman relates to instrumental music (229–30), appears to be generated as often as not by the sets of rhyming couplets out of which Weelkes's madrigal poems are usually built; and the other formal devices encountered in the single-stanza settings can perhaps be seen as compensating musically for the disintegration of the poetic form in the madrigalian idiom, essentially discursive as it is. In other words, what critics have so far considered a "purely musical" concern may well spring from a conscious awareness of that formal approach to poetry observed by Byrd and others in the native tradition, and from a determination not to lose its advantages in writing madrigals (Byrd's methods are discussed in chapter 8).

Whatever way one looks at it, Weelkes's solution to the stylistic and formal problem in the English madrigal constitutes his own personal triumph and one of the greatest artistic achievements of the Elizabethan age. Yet in view of its special nature it seems meaningless to try to relate it to a broader historical process and to conclude, as David Brown does, that "Weelkes was in every way a transitional figure, standing with one foot in the Renaissance and the other in the Baroque, applying the contrapuntal legacy of the former to the incipient demands of the latter." So it may seem from a vantage point in this century. But if we "put off our Anno Domini," as Roger North prescribes, and fall less readily into conventional notions of periodization, I believe we reach something less grand but more real: a brilliant talent, musically ambitious but professionally unlucky, working in conditions that eventually appear to have stifled his creative spark, yet arriving very early in his career at a fruitful synthesis of foreign style with native tradition that allowed him to fulfill his own highly individual artistic nature.

NOTES

1. David Brown, *Thomas Weelkes: A Biographical and Critical Study* (London, 1969).

2. See Denis Arnold's review in *Musical Times* 110 (1969): 1142–43. Arnold gave an exemplary lead in this direction himself in "Thomas Weelkes and the Madrigal," *Music & Letters* 31 (1950): 1–12.

3. As one might expect, the fa-la refrain of the ballet is much in evidence, and there are more instances of the *aabcc* form of the canzonet than appear in Fellowes's edition, which misplaces repeat marks (see Thurston Dart's revised issue for the correct readings). An interesting combination of the two forms is found in a three-part piece of the same genre by Weelkes, "Thus sings my dearest jewel," published in the *Musical Times* 112 (1972), together with an article by Craig Monson, who discovered it. See also the April 1972 issue (on 361) for a further addition to the composer's output.

4. Terminology was haphazard in Weelkes's time, and causes problems now. The *OED* gives "anthem" a wide meaning, and there *is* no reason to restrict it to church music. But in view of the generally understood ecclesiastical connotation and the important musical issues involved, it would seem wise to follow the lead given by Peter le Huray, *Music and the Reformation in England, 1549–1660* (London, 1967), who describes verse anthems appearing in the secular sources with viol accompaniment as "consort anthems," and likewise to distinguish non-Anglican full anthems, such as those mentioned in this paragraph, as "sacred (or spiritual) songs" or even "secular anthems."

5. *Gloria in excelsis* appears with its Latin refrain translated in Tenbury 1382 [now in the Bodleian Library, Oxford]; this has generally been considered a liturgical source, but John Morehen comes to a different conclusion in his article on the manuscript in *Music & Letters* 50 (1969): 363. *Laboravi in gemitu meo*, a sturdy exercise in the high art of the Latin motet, may perhaps be identified, as Brown suggests, with the "hymnum coralem sex partium" that Weelkes submitted for his Oxford B.Mus. in 1602.

6. This piece may also have celebrated some academic occasion, since its earliest appearance—side by side with a companion piece, "O sing unto the Lord," by Thomas Tomkins—occurs in a set of decidedly unliturgical manuscripts originating from Oxford (BL Add. 17786–91).

7. Even here caution must be exercised, since one of them may easily have referred to "the Queen" in its original state.

8. That the many English settings of this text were occasioned by this tragedy has been suggested by Thurston Dart in "Two English Musicians in Heidelberg

in 1613," *Musical Times* 111 (1970): 29; confirmation is forthcoming from Charles Butler, who while dealing with "Lydian music" in his *Principles of Music* (1636) refers to another famous setting as follows: "Of this Moode is that passionate Lamentation of the good musical King, for the death of his *Absalom:* Composed in 5. Parts by Mr. Th. Tomkins, now Organist of his Majesties Chappel."

9. I am indebted to Jeremy Noble for the use of his transcription of this still unpublished work.

10. Joseph Kerman, *The Elizabethan Madrigal: A Comparative Study*, American Musicological Society Studies and Documents 4 (New York, 1962), 224.

CHAPTER SEVEN

English Music for the Scottish Progress of 1617

To contemplate the musical institutions of any society is to reach some understanding of its attitude to the art.[1] More imaginatively, it is to gain some sense of the composers' environment, and particularly of such elusive matters as musical traditions and shared artistic assumptions—a sense that leads inevitably to a finer perception of the music itself. The preeminence of the Chapel Royal and of the King's Musick in Tudor and Stuart England has long been recognized. The archival researches of this century have demonstrated how sporadic and uneven, by comparison, were the maintenance and achievements of other establishments both sacred and secular. Yet the musical implications of this state of affairs have never been fully explored. Continuity of both composers and repertory creates a special situation, particularly within the Chapel Royal: Byrd absorbed the work of Tallis, Purcell the music of Gibbons. Indeed, it is arguable that it was the chapel in particular, giving a lead to the English church in general, that helped most to preserve and foster an indigenous musical idiom that endured in spite of the influx of French airs and

Originally published in *Source Materials and the Interpretation of Music: A Memorial Volume to Thurston Dart*, ed. I. Bent (London: Stainer & Bell, 1981), 209–26.

dances, Italian madrigals and motets and so on, and shaped the musical thinking of each successive generation.

In roughly the same way that an ecclesiastical style had remained little altered from the death of Dunstable to the advent of the Reformation, so the Anglican style initiated by Tallis and Tye was hallowed by Byrd, and lived on to be revitalized by Orlando Gibbons and transformed by Henry Purcell. Its characteristics—thick texture, close imitation, short-winded points and a liberal and gratuitous display of false relations—can be heard in the church works of a host of composers, minor and major, Elizabethan and Jacobean, many of whom donned quite different musical garb when they hung up their cassocks and surplices. It is as difficult to recognize the hand of "April is in my Mistress' Face" behind *Nolo mortem peccatoris* (difficult enough, indeed, to cast doubt on Thomas Myriell's ascription of the latter to Morley)[2] as it is sad to contemplate the adventurous spirit of Weelkes's "O Care, thou wilt despatch me" reduced to the tired clichés of his "Alleluia! I heard a voice." Yet these are only extreme instances of a general and readily perceptible phenomenon.

To all but the most partial critic, achievements in the secular sphere appear to shine rather bright against this dim religious light. Yet instrumental music aside, no vocal idiom other than that patronized by the chapel composers survived or flourished so long. The English madrigal enjoyed and lost its vitality in less than twenty years. Its initiator, Thomas Morley, did hold a chapel post, but its two brightest stars, Wilbye and Weelkes, were respectively a successful estate agent and the bibulous organist of a low-grade provincial cathedral. The high ideals of the Dowland lute song had scarcely been displayed in print before they were first undermined by an intelligent dilettante, Thomas Campion, and later sacrificed for charm and a new set of Italianate notions by a number of lesser lights. Yet Thomas Tudway could report with some accuracy at the end of the seventeenth century: "the Standard of Church Music begun by Mr. Tallis & Mr. Bird, &c. was continued for some years after the Restauration, & all Composers conform'd themselves to the Pattern which was set by them."[3]

Owing, moreover, to the inclusive use of the terms "madrigal" and "air," and the desire of E. H. Fellowes (most notably) to create a national school out of an odd assortment of classmates, it was not until recently appreciated that certain composers, and leading chapel composers at that, pursued in secular music a vein as indigenous as that of their church composition and in many respects related to it. To fall back on critical terms like "old-fashioned," "conservative" and "unliterary" to describe this phenomenon, as more recent scholars have done, is eventually to invite misunderstanding. If a style can regenerate itself from time to time in music of such quality as that of Byrd and Gibbons, if it can take from outside what it needs and still remain true to its own character and ideals, then it is "adventurous" and "progressive" enough to be judged without the prejudice such labels are bound to suggest. But I have argued this at length elsewhere, attempting to show, in the case of Byrd, how his means of setting poetry, so very appropriate and intelligent, demonstrates a "literary" consciousness as highly developed as, but different in nature from, that of the madrigalists (see chapter 8). In this essay I aim merely to propose one instance of the musical vitality of the Chapel Royal, an example of a composer's responding to the demands of a particular occasion with some brilliance by weaving a new and fresh musical tapestry out of diverse threads spun inevitably in the recesses of his own creative imagination, but colored through and through by the assumptions and traditions of the institution to which he belonged.

The primary duty of the Chapel Royal was to provide daily religious services for the monarch and his court in any of the palaces in the London area, and occasionally (as we shall see) on progresses further afield. It was not a fixed body like the royal chapel at Windsor, but part and parcel of the sovereign's retinue. Its sphere, however, extended beyond the daily religious office into the ceremony and entertainment which constantly surrounded and supported the Crown. Besides the great occasions such as coronations, and the more domestic ones such as christenings, weddings and funerals, there were the masques which in their own way celebrated the ideals of kingship and the role of the court; and music also had its function in political events such as the occasion in 1611 when the king and the French ambassador swore to the maintenance of a league between the two nations, taking the oath in chapel where the organs played and anthems were sung to solemnize the event.[4]

On one occasion in the reign of James I, however, the Chapel Royal rose above a generally supporting role to become a veritable instrument of royal policy. This happened in 1617, during the king's first and last return to his native land after ascending the English throne in 1603. Clarifying his intentions to the Scottish Privy Council, James wrote of "a salmonlyke instinct . . . a great and naturall longing to see our native soyle and place of our birth and breeding."[5] He went on in the same letter to deny rumors that he desired to reform Scottish government civil or ecclesiastical, but his protestations cannot have cut much ice with the Scots, who had good reason to fear for the continued independence of their Presbyterian church.

To James, who embraced the Anglican faith as a natural adjunct to his elevated notion of kingship, the Scottish kirk was not merely a thorn in the royal flesh but a threat to his sovereignty, as he made clear at the famous Hampton Court conference of 1604 to the unfortunate Puritan dean who had dropped the word "presbyteri." If his party aimed at a Scottish presbytery, the king exclaimed, it "as wel agreeth with a Monarchy, as God and the Devill. Then *Iack & Tom, & Will, & Dick* shall mete, and at their pleasures censure me and my Councell and all our proceedinges." And after more of this kind, he turned to the bishops and said, "if once you were out and they in place, I know what would become of my *Supremacy. No Bishop, no King*, as before I said."[6] And so, having established firm political control over Scotland through the Duke of Lennox and a body of trusted councillors, James began from England to reduce the power of the kirk. By 1605 he had virtually overthrown the General Assembly, and the year following summoned eight of its most vociferous troublemakers to England from whence only two returned.

The notorious Andrew Melville, who caused a notable stir by plucking at the sleeves of the archbishop of Canterbury's white lawn surplice and calling them "popish rags" was incarcerated in the tower and later banished abroad. Meanwhile the king completed his domination over the kirk by forcing bishops upon it, and by gradually increasing their status and powers over the years.

Had it ended there all would have been well, for the Presbyterian system was far from destroyed, the Scottish bishops were moderate men of good sense and above all, ordinary churchgoers detected no change in the accustomed pattern of their worship. But whether out of growing zeal, or owing to that schoolmasterly temperament that would never leave well alone, James determined in his fiftieth year to teach the Scots to imitate better English customs (as he remarked) than drinking healths, wearing gay clothes and taking tobacco. To bring the churches of the two nations into line upon matters of ceremony and ritual was, then, to be the major and scarcely concealed purpose of the Scottish progress. And toward this end James ordained, in a characteristically didactic stroke of policy which exercised the traditional function of music and the other arts to persuade through delight, that throughout his stay the Anglican rite should be celebrated in all its glory at Holyrood by the English Chapel Royal.

It should be pointed out at this juncture that summer progresses were held annually throughout the reigns of Elizabeth and James. They took the court away from town when plague was apt to flare up, and they gave Elizabeth in particular a chance to inspect local government and also to beggar any families rising above their station by giving them the expensive pleasure of entertaining her royal majesty and retinue. James's interest ran more to the country pleasures of hunting and hawking; and there was plenty of that on the way up to Scotland in 1617. Indeed, the journey took over two months to the exasperation of the nobility commanded to attend; so many of them defected on the way that at one point, according to the Earl of Dorset, there was only a single lord left.

It is a tribute to the king's enormous tenacity of purpose that the Scot-

tish journey was ever undertaken. It called forth a storm of protest, including an earnest plea for postponement from the reigning favorite,
young George Villiers, newly created Earl of Buckingham, whom James
turned on so roundly that it is said he was glad to get away. The major difficulty was finance, with the Crown, as usual, heavily in debt. Finally the
London merchants were prevailed upon to lend £100,000 on security of
the crown jewels, and the tax farmers £50,000. Those who arranged the
loan had the consolation of a knighthood on the day of departure; one
who refused to pay was made to follow on foot until he complied.

Meanwhile the Scots had been busy for a whole year sprucing up the
streets of Edinburgh, ridding the city of vagabonds, and providing lodg-
ing for an estimated 5,000 men and horse. Some Englishmen reported
well on arrival: "the entertainment very honourable, very general, and
very full," wrote John Chamberlain to Sir Dudley Carleton, "every day
feasts and invitations. I know not who paid for it" (Nichols, 3:347). But
the sophisticated English attitude is perhaps better reflected in the scur-
rilous prose of Sir Anthony Weldon, who took the occasion to write what
must be one of the classics of racial invective. Peppered with remarks
such as "there is great store of fowle, as Fowle houses, fowle sheets and
shirts, fowle lynnen, fowle dishes and potts, fowle trenchermen and nap-
kins," it concludes with the scandalous opinion that "the men of olde did
no more wonder that the great Messias should be borne in so poore a
Towne as Bethlem in Judea, as I do wonder that so brave a Prince as King
James should be borne in so stinking a Towne as Edenborough in lousy
Scotland."[7]

Such schoolboyish petulance pales into insignificance, however, beside the anger of the Scots at the doings in Holyroodhouse. "The Kings
palice was reformit with all expiditoun of maissons and wrycht wark, his
chappell royall was decorit with organis, and uthir temporall policie," reports an anonymous Scottish historian somewhat tersely.[8] A considerable
instrument costing above £400, the organ arrived by sea from London
accompanied by its builder, Thomas Dallam, who on returning confessed
he had been better used among the Turks (whom he had visited with an

organ for the sultan in 1599). Worse was to follow. The refurbished chapel designed by none other than Inigo Jones included gilded images of the patriarchs and apostles. On the arrival of these statues the workmen at Holyrood simply downed tools, and people murmured, it is said, "that the Organs came first, now the Images, and ere long they should have the Mass." The Scottish bishops negotiated the removal of the offending statues, but only at the expense of a theological lecture on the nature of pictures and images from His Majesty, who made the telling remark that no one would have minded had the figures been of "lyones, dragones and divells."[9]

The day after the king arrived in Edinburgh many months later, as one Presbyterian historian reports, "the English service was begunne in the Chappell Royal, with singing of quiristours, surplices and playing on organes."[10] The Scots commanded to attend, more than annoyed at having to kneel for Communion, considered it "staining and polluting the house of religion by the dregs of popery."[11] Indeed, the general perturbation was so great that it led Anthony Weldon to remark, "I am persuaded that yf God & his angells should come downe in their whitest garments they would run away and cry, 'The Children of the Chappell are come agayne to torment us; let us fly from the abomination of these boys, & hide ourselves in the mountaynes' " (Nichols, 3:340).

Major incidents seem somehow to have been avoided, and the king pursued his aims by presenting to an informal gathering of clergy at St. Andrews five proposals: that Communion should be received kneeling not sitting (which to many Scots involved the doctrine of the Real Presence); that private Communion might be administered in cases of necessity (which smacked of the last rites); that private baptism might be administered; that the great church feasts should be observed (which contravened the self-sufficiency of the Sabbath); and that the bishops should conduct confirmations (which increased their limited powers). Nothing was decided on these scores during the visit, but the following year a General Assembly of the Kirk, summoned at Perth and subjected to outrageous pressures, accepted the Five Articles, as they came to be known. It was a Pyrrhic victory, though, for James realized that they could not be enforced. Indeed, they were generally unobserved until Charles and his stiff-necked Archbishop Laud adopted a less conciliatory approach to the same issues and thereby precipitated the so-called Bishops' War, the first open hostilities in a civil war that rent the nation and led eventually to the temporary eclipse of the monarchy.

A remaining question about the royal visit is why it was not the Scottish Chapel Royal that provided the services at Holyrood. Charles Rogers, author of A *History of the Chapel Royal of Scotland* (Edinburgh, 1882), assumed it did, without quite showing how. The native establishment had once flourished, of course, but since 1603 its revenues had gone to line the pockets of royal favorites, in particular a faithful Scots servant named John Gib; and it had declined in spite of the efforts of the dean and the Scottish Parliament to preserve it as a national institution. It is true that a few sung services appear to have been held in the wake of the king's visit, but the organ soon broke down (Dean Galloway wrote that it had been "too commonlie visited" [Rogers, 127]), and all fell once more into decay. Indeed, the situation that Rogers and other Scottish historians outline makes it extremely unlikely that a choir could be found in the whole of Scotland to do justice to the English choral service. The actual evidence that the English chapel was present comes, first, from a petition addressed by the gentlemen to King Charles in 1633 before they embarked on a similar journey: "when they attended the late King into Scotland there was delivered to the Dean of the Chapel towards their charge £400 and there was also allowed them a good ship well victualled."[12] And Sir Anthony Weldon corroborated their method of transport in his own manner:

> the skipper that brought the Singing-men with their papisticall vestments complaines that he hath beene much troubled with a strange singing in his head ever since they came aborde his ship, for remedy whereof the Parson of the parish hath perswaded him to sell that prophane vessell, and distribute the mony amongst the faythfull brethren. (Nichols, 3:340)

By far the most rewarding evidences of the visit, however, are two works specially written for the occasion by Orlando Gibbons, chief organist of the chapel, who must himself have been in attendance. One of these pieces, designated "for the King's being in Scotland" in one source (Christ Church 21), has long been known from the *Tudor Church Music* edition.[13] Its opening lines confirm the designation:

> Great King of Gods, whose gracious hand hath led
> Our sacred sovereign head
> Unto the place where all our bliss was bred,
> O send thine angels to his blessed side
> And bid them there abide,
> To be at once his guardian and his guide.

These words may seem at first sight more pagan than Christian, until we recall the manner in which James was accustomed to refer to the monarchy: "For kings are not only God's lieutenants upon earth and sit upon God's throne, but even by God Himself they are called gods."[14]

The other Gibbons piece was brought to my attention years ago by Thurston Dart, who on a visit to the United States found it in the manuscript collection of the New York Public Library. It occurs in Drexel manuscripts 4180–85, a set of early seventeenth-century part books which came from the library of Edward Rimbault, according to whom they had once belonged to the diarist John Evelyn; it is also conceivable that they were among the books Rimbault removed from Christ Church Library.[15] I was myself subsequently able to identify the original scribe, John Merro, by comparing this set with another (BL Add. 17792–96), which shares the same hand and some of the same repertory, and which had been included by Pamela Willetts among the group of manuscripts, many of them associated with Oxford, that she had shown to be the work of this copyist, whose name she uncovered.[16] Arnold Ashbee has since pointed out that Merro was a singing man at Gloucester Cathedral mentioned in a visitation of 1609 and in subsequent years; he died on 23 March 1636 and was buried in the Lady Chapel.[17] Craig Monson in his recent study of the secular manuscripts of the period argues convincingly that the part books were begun around 1615 and probably completed in the years shortly after 1625; they constitute one of the largest and most interesting collections of the time, even exceeding in size and scope of repertory Thomas Marl's *Tristate Remedium* (Add. 29372–77, begun in 1616), with which they are roughly contemporary.[18]

How the only extant copy of one of these occasional pieces comes to be found in a set of manuscripts inscribed by a Gloucester lay clerk (and otherwise including Gibbons only as the composer of the "Cries of London" and the three-part fantasias) is a mystery. One tentative clue, however, arises from the career of the author of the poem. Since publishing an edition of the piece, it has come to my attention that the words also occur in another manuscript (Harleian 1423, fol. 102) attributed to a certain Dr. Hall, who may safely be identified with the English divine Joseph Hall (1574–1656).[19] Having been chaplain to the ill-fated Henry, Prince of Wales, Hall was pressed into service on the Scottish progress as a moderate Puritan who might help to win over the Scots to the king's point of view. Something of a vicar of Wakefield, it seems, he was suitably rewarded by preferment. On return from Scotland he went to the deanery of Worcester (where Merro might perhaps have had access to a copy of Gibbons's setting?), in 1627 to the bishopric of Exeter (having turned down Gloucester in the meantime), and finally to the illustrious see of Norwich. In his earlier days up at Cambridge round the turn of the century he had gained some attention as a poet, being mentioned by Francis Meres as one of the foremost English satirists on account of his *Virgidemiae*. There are three poems for the Scottish visit, the first two of which Gibbons set with great resource as a continuous whole. The third, addressing James as Phoebus, begs him to return to England ("Turne the[e] agayne o Phebus Fayre"), no doubt indicating the mind of the poet, who petitioned to leave at the earliest moment. The poems Gibbons set are reproduced below as they appear in the Harleian manuscript.

Though perhaps fulsome to our ears, the verse is in the best Jonsonian manner, and the invocation of the spirits of the plain and the music of the spheres is genuinely delightful.

Cearten veerses written by Doctor Hall
upon the kings coming into Scotland.

Doe not repyine fayre sun to see these eyne
   welcomer far then thyne
To see the beames of a moore glorius face
   Shine one his native place
And overrun the to his Northerne lyne
   fayre sonn doe not repyine
And yea thrise blessed bowers wch longe agone
   His cradle rocked one
W^{ch} at the first that vitall breath did geve
   whereby our worlde doth live
Doe not invie the spheres of heaven above
   In his deare lyght and love
whose presens under Arthures seate can frame
   An Eden both indeede and name

                     finis Dr Hall

2

Ioye that Alone wth better bayes
and mirtle bowes and highest dayes
   Crownest thy kinglie browes
Come come alonge to day wth me
welcome the flower of Royaltie
   Home to his native howse
Now doe thy best and more then all
To make a merry festivall
   Oh now or never doot
All the day longe feast dance play and singe
And Spend upon this revalinge
   Thy nimblest handes and feete
Call to thee all thy lightheeld trayne

Nimphes and phares of the playne
  And bid them trip it round
And cause the cirkles of the Skyes
Answare the cherminge melodyes
  In there consorted sounde
Still may the burden be welcome
welcome greate king to thy first home
  Then add unto the rest
Good speede home to thy other home
That count the hower whilest thou art gone
  And use to love the best.

finis Dr Hall

Gibbons's setting of this and of the other text, "Great King of Gods," both call for countertenor and bass soloists, a vocal chorus and a quintet of instruments, presumably viols which as usual are not specified. "Great King of Gods" appears in the recent edition of Gibbons's verse anthems presumably because it refers to the deity;[20] "Do not Repine, fair Sun" is excluded, presumably because it does not: but they obviously both belong to the same genre of composition. It was most generally known, then as now, by the term "verse anthem"; but a designation less ecclesiastical in implication might help to make the secular origins of the form, and its inclusive nature, more widely appreciated. Its distant forerunners, to be sure, are the medieval English carol and motet, the one with its alternation of verse, refrain and burden, the other with its insistence upon changes of texture. But the immediate ancestor is the solo song for voice and viols, always secular in context and function if not in sentiment, which arose out of sixteenth-century court entertainment, particularly the Elizabethan choirboy theater, and which reached its artistic peak in the works of William Byrd. Consort songs with spiritual texts could be—and were— adapted for church (where viols were not allowed) by the substitution of the organ for the obbligato consort part; and the increasing number of such arrangements in Jacobean times was matched by a growing tendency to bypass the consort version and write for organ from the very start.

It is becoming increasingly clear that the verse anthem or consort song form occupied a leading position in Jacobean vocal music, not only by a mere head count—it has a considerable edge numerically over both full anthem and madrigal—but also as regards composers' attitudes toward it. Evidently Jacobean composers of differing outlooks and persuasions all found in this medium a challenge to their ingenuity and a stimulus to their originality. It was above all a flexible form, less dependent than the madrigal or full anthem on the musical portrayal of verbal imagery, and less restricted than the lute song to strophic arrangement. It could be written along the established lines worked out by Byrd; on the other hand it could absorb a good deal of madrigalian technique such as pictorial word setting, expressive harmony or even contrasts of scoring. At the same time it presented some intriguing problems of overall design and of the relationship of chorus and solo passages which prompted an enormous variety of solutions. And it could span the whole range of taste and decorum from the flimsy trifles of Ravenscroft's publications to the most ambitious and serious compositions of the period, among which are Gibbons's own works.

Gibbons, of course, was no less alive to the possibilities of the form than Weelkes, Tomkins, Ward, Peerson or a host of others. David Brown in his monograph on Weelkes sees Gibbons's work as conservative by comparison,[21] but in fact his sense of expressive nuance and of formal design is a good deal more subtle than that of the Chichester composer, who favored the dramatic gesture and the schematic plan. Gibbons's works in this idiom, indeed, stand second only to the songs of Byrd as monuments to the sturdiness and vitality of the native tradition. It is true, however, that one of the two Scottish pieces, "Great King of Gods," represents the Gibbons who is most restrained and ecclesiastical in style and simple in organization. The most notable event in this sober piece is the repeat of the last seven bars of the first chorus in the final chorus, serving to tie the piece together musically, and perhaps to make a flattering connection between "the place where all our bliss was bred" and "Thy celestial state." "Do not Repine, fair Sun," though it belongs to the same

Example 7.1. Gibbons, "Do not Repine, fair Sun"

genre, projects a rather different atmosphere or "decorum," which is reflected most immediately in the notation in smaller values—the point is
obscured of course by the wanton halving of note values in modern editions of church music of the period. The piece relates to "Great King of
Gods" in much the same way as Purcell's court odes relate to his verse anthems, the difference being that Gibbons, so far as I can discover, had no
really established tradition to fall back on in composing this extended
work which, because it refers personally (not allegorically) and directly
(not ambiguously) to the monarch, anticipates in a remarkable manner
the Restoration welcome song.

Some of the purely musical aspects are also interestingly prophetic.
Instead of the customarily more immediate entrance of the solo voice or
voices after a short, often imitative, introductory passage that flows right
into the vocal passage, there is here a seven-bar instrumental "Preludium" (as it is labeled in the manuscripts), separated both by its musical material and by a cadence and rest from the ensuing vocal duet (example 7.1).

The musical material is different, to be sure, but in emphasizing stepwise movement in parallel thirds and tenths, quasi-canonic writing with
overlapping figures at the unison, and in introducing the rhythmic figure × that plays so important a part later on, the composer clearly establishes the whole mood and texture of what follows. This embryonic ri-
tornello, moreover, prefaces both parts of the first poem, which Gibbons
treats as two stanzas, each being first enunciated by a pair of soloists and
then repeated in different but related musical terms by the chorus—the

one literal repeat consists merely of the last two bars of the second "stanza" (bars 90–93, 113–16),[22] which are the same in both solo and chorus versions. On the other hand, in setting the poetry strictly in couplets, which in the first chorus, for instance, take precedence (judging by the main cadences) over the syntactical reading that would seem to demand a break after the fifth line, Gibbons follows the age-old tradition of embodying poetic form rather than searching for prosaic sense, a principle he undoubtedly learnt from his master, Byrd.

There is a novel feature about the music for the second poem that also forecasts a later development in the verse anthem. To set the first eight lines Gibbons adopts a rhythmic, chordal style that might even vaguely invoke the Restoration to some ears. The composer takes his cue, however, from later lines of the poem and here refers to the dance—not merely in spirit, moreover, but specifically to a type of branle, which the English called "brawls." In order to have his dance, though, Gibbons is obliged to alter the meter and structure of Dr. Hall's poem (turning three lines into a quatrain and repeating a two-syllable word in each third and fourth line) in a way that Byrd might not have countenanced. The whole of this second section of the work is full, with no verse passages, but Gibbons aims for a different kind of textural contrast in this predominantly homophonic style by isolating high or low trios from time to time. After a repeated strain and an extra half strain of the brawls (bars 125–36), the music breaks into galliard rhythm, which lasts up to exactly halfway through the second poem. Here the original time signature is resumed, together with a fully polyphonic manner reminiscent of the very opening of the piece; there also appears the rhythmic figure that is one of the elements which bind the work together, and in this appearance it also recalls the opening melodically (example 7.2). This figure occurs for the last time just before the climax of the work at the actual word, "Welcome!" where again the verse form is disrupted, and the music breaks into an extremely fast *tripla*—an unusually dramatic gesture for Gibbons (example 7.3).

To cap this and to create an even greater sense of musical unity with-

Example 7.2. Gibbons, "Do not Repine, fair Sun"

out resorting to the oppressively schematic or mechanical, Gibbons takes up all the threads in the last section in an interesting and masterly way. After plain chords for "Then add unto the rest," there is first a setting of "Good speed home" that in its falling stepwise progressions in thirds and tenths suggests an inversion of the initial idea of the "Pre-

Example 7.3. Gibbons, "Do not Repine, fair Sun"

ludium." "To thy other own" wittily rearranges the rhythmic pattern of "Do not repine," which has figured so largely in the piece. Then, at "that count the hours whilst thou art gone" we are momentarily back in the world of the branle before the literal repetition of the music of "Oh now or never do't" (bars 137–40) for "And vie to love thee best" (bars 198–201),

Example 7.4. Gibbons, "Do not Repine, fair Sun"

a repetition which gives the ear a nudge, so to speak, toward hearing this last section as an imaginative recalling of various strands of the composition to satisfy the claims of overall coherence which Gibbons, as a pupil of Byrd, always acknowledges even when he does not quite do justice to them. The final peroration, preceded by a dramatic rest in all the voices, is a bar shorter than the "Preludium" (example 7.4). It does not of course employ the same material. But it does move in a similar manner, if a little more grandly across a larger tessitura; in focusing attention on the chords on E, C and A, with G and D as subsidiary, it covers in miniature the main harmonic gestures of the piece; and in falling away from a melodic peak of G, to which the "Preludium" had first aspired (an octave lower of course), it makes a very satisfactory closing melodic gesture. In short, it concludes the business of the work in every possible way; more important, it does so with verve and artistry.

The piece, then, is a remarkable and novel attempt, firmly rooted in the verse anthem tradition established by Byrd, but stretching the conventions of the form in a way the older master would perhaps not have countenanced. More than anything else, it testifies to the vigor and flexibility of the native idiom in the hands of one of its greatest proponents. A decade or so earlier, at the beginning of the reign, the Italian vein would have been considered more appropriate for such a composition.

Indeed, both Gibbons and Weelkes wrote madrigalian settings of the text "Hosanna to the Son of David" presumably to welcome the king on some occasion, if not his entry to London in 1603. And in 1613 nearly everyone wrote elaborate Italianate settings of David's lament for Absolom when the nation mourned young Prince Henry. By 1617, however, the long-lived and enduring form of the consort song or verse anthem was coming back into its own, and was asserting an independence that would support it throughout the musical and political vicissitudes of the next half century.

The more mundane question of when the piece was actually performed still remains. The most appropriate occasion seems to be at some point during the first great event of the progress which is graphically recounted by an anonymous Scot in the records of the High Court of the Justiciary (Nichols, 3:317–18)—see figure 7.1 for a view of Edinburgh which, though dating from the eighteenth century, is based on a view of about 1650.

> The saxtene day of May 1617, the Kingis Majestie enterit at the Wast Poirt of Edinburgh, quhair the Provest, the four Bailyeis, the haill Counsell of the Toun, with ane hundreth honest men and mae, war all assemblit in blak gownes all lynit with plane velvet, and their haill apparrell was plane black velvet. At quhilk tyme first the Proveist, William Nisbet maid ane Harrand, welcoming his Majestie to his awin Citie; thareafter ane Harand was maid be Mr John Hay in name of the haill Citizens; ane purse contening five hundreth double angellis laid in a silver basing double overgilt, was propynit to his Majestie, quha with ane myld and gracious countenance resavit thayme with thair propyne, come tharefor throw the Citie to the Kirk, quhair ane Sermone was maid be the Archbishope of St Androis, Spottiswood; tharefter come directlie doun the streit towardis his awin Palice in Halyrudhous, being conveyit be the honest men of the Toun to the Corse callit St Johne's Croce, quhair be the drawing of ane sword his Majestie knychtit the Proveist.

A General View of the City & Castle of EDINBURGH, the Capital of Scotland.

Figure 7.1. "A General View of the City & Castle of Edinburgh, the Capital of Scotland." Print by Morris and Hogg (ca. 1765), based on a print by Van Hoyen (ca. 1650).

At the gate of the Inner Court of Holyrood, the king was presented with a book of verses by the College of Edinburgh, one of whose members made a speech, in Latin. After this, James presumably entered the palace—pleased with his "five hundredth double angellis" no doubt, but fatigued by the "harrands" that might have reminded him uncomfortably of his youth. "Do not Repine" must surely have been designed for performance during this latter part of the day. Its musical style is suited to the chamber not the open air; its verse refers to Arthur's Seat, the hill that broods over the palace; and the choir itself would scarcely have been welcome outside Holyrood. Whatever the truth of the matter, musical history would be a dull affair if we could not linger for a moment to imagine the king's pleasure at seeing the familiar faces of his own chapel, and his delight on hearing the music of its distinguished organist and composer. And imagination may perhaps extend so far as the hope that he took upon himself the part of Maecenas, and matched both pleasure and delight with an accustomed liberality.

NOTES

1. Based on a paper delivered to the national conference of the American Musicological Society at Toronto in 1970.

2. British Library Add. 29372–77, fol. 8v.

3. Harleian 7338, fol. 2v; quoted in J. A. Westrup, *Purcell*, 5th ed. (London, 1965), 199.

4. See W. R. Woodfill, *Musicians in English Society from Elizabeth to Charles I* (Princeton, 1953), 174.

5. J. Nichols, *The Progresses, Processions, and Magnificent Festivities of King James the First* (London, 1828), 3:309.

6. From an account of the conference by William Barlow, dean of Chester, printed in *James I by His Contemporaries*, ed. and introduced by R. Ashton (London, 1969), 183–89.

7. Harleian 5191, printed in Nichols, 338–43.

8. *The Historie and Life of King James the Sext*, Bannantyne Club Publications 13 (Edinburgh, 1825), 395.

9. John Spottiswoode, *The History of the Church of Scotland* (1655), ed. M. Russell and M. Napier (Edinburgh, 1847–51), 3:239.

10. David Calderwood, *The True History of the Church of Scotland from the beginning, unto the end of the reign of James VI* (Rotterdam, 1678), ed. T. Thomson (Edinburgh, 1842–49), 7:246.

11. Robert Johnston, *Historia rerum Britannicam* (Amsterdam, 1655), 518, trans. in Robert Chambers, *The Domestic Annals of Scotland* (Edinburgh, 1842), 1:476.

12. *State Papers Domestic 1633–34*, 38.

13. *Tudor Church Music* (Oxford, 1925), 4:197–202.

14. From a speech to the House of Commons, quoted by D. Harris Wilson, *King James VI and I* (London, 1956), 243.

15. See W. G. Hiscock, *Christ Church Miscellany* (Oxford, 1946), 127–33.

16. See *Consort Songs*, Musica Britannica 22 (London, 1967), 173; and Pamela Willetts, "Music from the Circle of Anthony Wood at Oxford," *British Museum Quarterly* 24 (1961): 71–75.

17. In *Music & Letters* 48 (1967): 310–11.

18. In "Voices and Viols in England, 1600–1650: The Sources and the Music" (Ph.D. diss., University of California, Berkeley, 1974), 226–49.

19. They are included in *The Collected Poems of Joseph Hall*, ed. A. Davenport (Liverpool, 1949), 150–55.

20. Ed. D. Wulstan in *Early English Church Music*, vol. 3 (London, 1964), where it appears with words written by Bramley for Ouseley's edition of 1893. Granted the original words are unsuited to modern use in church, there are several seventeenth-century adaptations, involving changes merely in the first three lines, that will serve. Two of them are as follows:

> Great King of Gods, whose gratious hand hath led
> our Sacred Soverain Head
> out of their hands, our ruine that would have bred (etc.)
> (Bodleian Rawl. poet. 23, p.168)

> Great God of Kings whose gracious hand hath led
> our sacred Sovereign Head
> Unto the Throne from whence our bliss is bred: (etc.)
> (A Collection of Private Devotions . . . published by
> Autoritie of Queen ELISA, 1560 [London, 1655], 210).

21. *Thomas Weelkes: A Biographical and Critical Study* (London, 1969), 170, 174.

22. The bar numbers refer to my edition of Gibbons's *Do not Repine, fair Sun* (London, 1961).

CHAPTER EIGHT

Word Setting in
the Songs of Byrd

The vocal music of William Byrd consists of the Latin masses and motets, a comparatively small amount of Anglican church music and a substantial body of "secular" compositions. Among the latter, settings of psalms and spiritual texts abound, but they were designed for a secular context and rarely taken over for church use; their musical style confirms their non-liturgical character. The numbers of works involved, though approximate on account of doubtful attributions and incomplete sources, are nevertheless instructive: there are three masses and about 180 motets; the Anglican works comprise two complete services, two evening services, some smaller liturgical items and probably no more than twenty anthems; the secular vocal music amounts to almost 160 pieces. Often extending to two or more sections, the motets generally dwarf the songs, many of which are single-stanza settings. Even so, this last number indicates a degree of involvement sometimes not appreciated by those who comment on Byrd's music.

Originally published in *Proceedings of the Royal Musical Association* 98 (1971–72): 47–64. This paper was illustrated by the songs "What pleasure have great princes," "Ye sacred Muses," "O Lord, how long," "With lilies white," "Wretched Albinus," and Psalm 15, "O Lord, within thy tabernacle," from Maurice Frost, *English and Scottish Psalm Tunes, ca. 1543–1677* (London, 1953), 80–81. The performers were James Bowman, countertenor, with a viol consort: Francis Baines (treble), Elizabeth Baines (alto), Peter Vel (tenor), and Jane Ryan (bass).

The vocal music for secular use may conveniently be divided into two main categories, the smaller of which comprises fully vocal items. These range from the severely contrapuntal settings of the seven penitential psalms in *Songs of Sundrie Natures*, 1589, to the brilliant English motets of *Psalmes, Songs and Sonnets*, 1611, and from part songs that have little in common with the currently fashionable madrigal to the two pieces that were expressly "composed after the Italian vaine" at the request of Thomas Watson for his *Italian Madrigalls Englished*, 1590. But a majority of the secular pieces, about one hundred compositions in all, are consort songs—songs, that is, for solo voice or voices with an obbligato accompaniment for three or more (but usually four) viols.[1] The progressively diminishing number of consort songs in the printed collections of 1589 and 1611 might suggest that Byrd increasingly lost interest in this traditional native form, but the manuscript sources reveal his continued attachment to it. Among a group of songs recently attributed to Byrd and now included in the collected edition, there are four that can definitely be dated after 1600 and three others equally mature in style.[2] What may be considered, then, a lifelong concern with the consort song produced, as one might expect, a body of works worthy of the composer and hardly surpassed in the secular music of the time. That the critical acclaim accorded to the finest madrigals and airs has so far eluded Byrd's songs is due less to their musical content than to certain conventions they observe, particularly with regard to the setting of words. A misunderstanding of this aspect of the songs has determined the nature of a good deal of subsequent comment, and it is this problem that must be examined first, in order to clear the way for a better appreciation of the composer's aims and methods.

Byrd himself contributed to the misapprehension of his consort songs when, in 1588 and 1589, presumably to encourage wider circulation, he published almost half their total number with words added to the instrumental parts, in the same format as madrigal prints. The fact that some confusion between the two genres had arisen before the composer's death we learn from Henry Peacham's well-known remarks, which conclude:

being of himselfe naturally disposed to Grauitie and Pietie, his veine is not so much for light Madrigals or Canzonets, yet his *Virginella*, and some others in his first set, cannot be mended by the best *Italian* of them all.[3]

Almost all the items in the first set are in fact consort songs, including *La Virginella*, the original solo version of which is preserved in Robert Dow's authoritative manuscripts (Christ Church, Oxford MSS 984–88). Of recent writers, E. H. Fellowes was the most influential to persist with this confusion between Byrd's songs and the madrigal proper. Anxious to maintain Byrd as a leader of his "English Madrigal School," Fellowes was a little exasperated to find the composer he most respected "tied hand and foot to his ideas of song-form"; he therefore retrenched to a stout critical position in which he claimed Byrd as "the originator of the art-song," excused many of his efforts as being "of historical rather than aesthetic interest" and loyally attributed some instances of "his comparative failure" to the quality of the words.[4]

A historically more accurate view was adumbrated by Burney in a footnote to his withering attack upon English madrigal verse: "those genuine English songs, set and published by Bird, must be excepted, in some of which there is not only wit, but poetry."[5] It was Edward Dent, however, who in a masterly essay, "William Byrd and the Madrigal,"[6] laid the foundations for the historically more enlightened approach to Byrd's songs that is reflected now in such major works of reference as *The New Oxford History of Music* and Gustav Reese's *Music in the Renaissance*. Historical enlightenment does not automatically engender critical sympathy, however, and the two books most influential in shaping the newly accepted view, Bruce Pattison's *Music and Poetry of the English Renaissance* (London, 1948; 2nd ed. 1970), and Joseph Kerman's *The Elizabethan Madrigal* (New York, 1962), both adopt critical attitudes which, though more sophisticated than those of Fellowes, are perhaps equally damaging to the music. They proceed on the largely unspoken assumption that the new poetry and the madrigalian aesthetic constitute the major artistic issues of the period;[7] and while allowing Byrd his anomalous position, they continue at least partly to judge his efforts by the madrigalian standard. Thus Pattison, overemphasizing a point made by Dent, writes:

> Compared with his immediate successors of the madrigal school Byrd is a very unliterary musician. His inspiration is entirely musical, as was that of the Netherlands masters and the early church school in which he learned his art. If there were no words at all to his songs, the effect would be just as great: one cannot imagine the same of Marenzio's madrigals. (86)

The questions begged by the term "unliterary," had they been raised, might have led to a real discussion of words and music in Byrd; but eager to promote the perfect union of golden verse and expressive music he found in the madrigal, Pattison gave Byrd a pat on the back for his desire to learn from the Italians and his subsequent improvement in the 1611 volume, and passed on. Unfortunately, the label "unliterary" has stuck.[8]

Kerman gives the songs a more sympathetic and perceptive hearing, and leaves as an open question whether "Byrd and Gibbons . . . are more successful with the native style than Weelkes and Wilbye with the imported one" (254). Yet adopting the madrigal as a standard similarly leads him into describing Byrd's style as one of "abstract composition," which he stigmatizes as "old-fashioned," "archaic" and "antiquated"—terms as inappropriate to the songs of Byrd as to the cantatas of Bach or the symphonies of Brahms.

At the time Kerman wrote, Byrd's relation to his predecessors could not be assessed with any accuracy; now that almost the entire pre-Byrd repertory of consort songs has been published,[9] the enormous extent of his advance can be more fully appreciated. As with so many other forms he adopted, Byrd observed the conventions of the consort song, but at the same time transformed its style and intensified its musical content beyond anything previously attempted or imagined. And it is not the music itself that has caused difficulties, but its conventions of word setting, which bear little relation either to Morley's rules for "dittying" or to

Example 8.1. Byrd, "What pleasure have great princes"

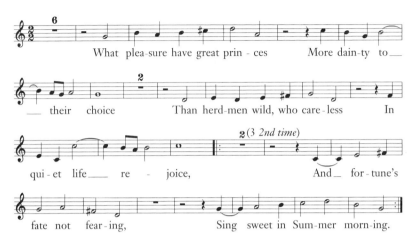

modern listeners' expectations. For an explanation of the basic principles, however, we have only to turn to the penetrating discussion of words and music—far wider in its implications than the title suggests—in John Stevens's *Music and Poetry in the Early Tudor Court* (London, 1961). The conventions Byrd observed, as opposed to the style he developed, are very much the same as those that governed Fayrfax, Cornish and Newark, and survived even in the work of Campion and Ferrabosco the younger. If Byrd is viewed as the greatest exponent of an ancient courtly art and his practice is seen as normal rather than eccentric, then the rationality of his treatment of words and the boundless originality of his music will at once be appreciated.

Byrd's approach to word setting may be observed at its simplest in those lighter songs which Peacham confused with the Italian forms. In the 1588 volume there are a number of songs, mostly settings of pastoral or satirical poetry, that replace the usual *alla breve* either with minims and crotchets, or with triple time in minims: a typical example is "What pleasure have great princes" (no. 19). The poem runs to five stanzas [the first shown in example 8.1 and the next two quoted below], each consisting of six lines rhyming *ababcc*—the form most commonly encountered in the songs. The lines are characteristically iambic and (but for the extrametrical feminine endings) regular in length. The verse is typically plain in language, impersonal in mood and sententious in tone; its proverbial themes return again and again in the poetry Byrd sets, the main distinguishing features here being the pastoral context and the shorter lines, both of which prompt Byrd to adopt a lighter style:

> Their dealings plain and rightful
>   Are void of all deceit;
> They never know how spiteful
>   It is to kneel and wait
> On favourite presumptuous,
> Whose pride is vain and sumptuous.
>
> All day their flocks each tendeth,
>   At night they take their rest
> More quiet than who sendeth
>   His ship into the East,
> Where gold and pearl are plenty
> But getting very dainty.

Like a large majority of Byrd's settings, "What pleasure" is strophic; the opportunity for pictorialism or dramatic declamation therefore never arises. More surprising is the lack of concern for sense and syntax that results from the separation of the poetic lines in the musical setting. The antithesis between the first two pairs of lines, unremarked by the melody, loses its syntactical thread in the intervening void and becomes virtually incomprehensible. Another long interlude after the fourth line endangers the listener's sense of how the subsequent phrases and clauses relate to the earlier part of the stanza—a situation the repeat of the couplet only exacerbates. The melody pays less than sedulous attention to "just note and accent": weak initial syllables (or words) in lines 1 and 3 and penultimate ones in lines 2 and 4 all receive emphasis from the comparatively long notes to which they are set; and there is a particularly strong accent on the unimportant word "to" in the second line of the first stanza.[10] It can perhaps be appreciated how from the page alone such a song might seem a purely musical composition, an abstract fantasy upon a vocal cantus firmus that happens to be pegged to words.

Once the song is heard, such matters seem of strictly academic interest. Immediately striking is Byrd's melodic invention: the piece has a genuine tunefulness rarely found in madrigals, and of greater substance than the ear-catching pleasantry of many lutenist airs. This quality, moreover, conjuring up a generalized image of the carefree rustic life, is arguably more suited than a detailed madrigalian commentary to the setting of a poem containing so many impersonal moral statements. What word in the first four lines of the second stanza would, in any case, be susceptible to word painting? How could any musical imagery or elaboration leave the central idea of the poem intact? How better could Byrd have expressed the generalizing effect of the poem than by stressing the form it gives to its moral assertions? And what compensation would the ready comprehensibility of a declamatory setting offer for the loss both of the formal structure of the syntax and of the rich and engaging substance of the musical accompaniment? It is from asking questions like these that we begin to see how appropriate is Byrd's response, and therefore, in at least one important sense, how literary.

It is the relationship of musical to poetic form that should capture our further attention. A most remarkable feature of the setting is how the rhyming lines are matched by musical rhymes, an age-old device of medieval song gaining new meaning here from the careful balancing of sequence, variation and cadence in a readily intelligible tonal order. Each line end coincides with a cadence, the one most strongly articulated, other than the final close, occurring at the end of the quatrain. (A fine stroke in this particular example is the avoidance of a potentially strong cadence at the end of the second line by means of overlapping instrumental entries which combine the vocal melodies of the first two lines.) The final repeat is a device common to many types of sixteenth-century vocal music and traditional in English song; in setting this kind of stanza, Byrd uses it to emphasize the final couplet, thus underlining what is usually the main point of the stanza by a musical effect comparable to, and indeed prompted by, the change in the rhyming pattern.[11] Here then is evidence of Byrd's literary concern at another level. An elaborate madrigalian treatment tends to reduce verse to a prose reading. In this case the music is not merely a reflection of the shape of the stanza: it actively represents, it " expresses," the poetic form.

Granted the differences in musical and literary style, these observations could be made—indeed they have been made—equally well of early Tudor songs.[12] Like his predecessors, Byrd observed the traditional decorum of forms, and it is this which makes his songs appear "abstract," "purely musical" compositions. The trouble with these epithets is that while stressing the composer's undoubted professional skill they tend also to imply that his music is virtually independent of the words and therefore, by further implication, in some real sense "inexpressive." On the contrary, Byrd generally extracts deeper feeling from a poem than composers more dependent for their effects on vivid images or on elaborate parallels between the contents of one stanza and another.[13] It is doubtful, for instance, whether Weelkes or Campion could have made so much out of the list of moral precepts from which "Care for thy soul" is compiled.[14] Yet there is no profit in speculating whether or not, or to what degree, Byrd's emotions were involved, for the nonrepresentational tradition in which he worked takes the pressure, so to speak, off the composer's subjective responses. As John Stevens remarks, "the suitability of a particular musical style to a particular poem is not a matter of emotional fitness but of convention" (107).

These points may be illustrated by a song written for an occasion that we may suppose had a considerable effect upon Byrd's personal feelings—the death in 1585 of his friend and colleague Thomas Tallis:

> Ye sacred Muses, race of Jove,
>   Whom Music's lore delighteth,
> Come down from crystal heav'ns above
>   To earth, where sorrow dwelleth,
> In mourning weeds, with tears in eyes:
> Tallis is dead, and Music dies.

The words lack any inspiring poetic quality, yet Byrd's setting is undeniably expressive. The declamation seems more careful than that of "What pleasure," and the melody, relieved of any obligation to further stanzas, indulges in what appears to be word painting in the third line. Strictly syllabic and nonrepetitive setting is relaxed, particularly in the final couplet, where a long and exquisite melisma on "Music" provides a climax to the piece. But all these expressive features, though they spring to new life in Byrd's music, find precedents in the elegies and dramatic laments of his predecessors;[15] and it is likely, in view of current aesthetic principles, that Byrd intended to honor Tallis's memory by a triumph of skill within the conventions of the elegy, not by a mere display of personal grief, which he would have considered inappropriate and unworthy. At any rate, there is no loosening of formal bonds under the stress of emotion, such as modern assumptions about the relation of content to structure might lead us to expect. Lines 3 and 4, which might have been run together, remain separate, and the whole of the final couplet is repeated in defiance of sense and syntax. Naturally, Byrd turns the formal requirement to his musical advantage, allowing the fifth line, with its soothing and slow-moving harmonies, to provide an essential contrast to the contrapuntally active and directed statements of the final line, which in turn find their release in a short but perfectly judged coda.

A comparison of "Ye sacred Muses" with the serious songs of the 1588 volume will reveal differences of degree, not of kind. Most restrained in their treatment of words are the metrical psalms, whose combination of biblical words and "common meter" dictated the use of a plain style, free of all superfluous ornament. Some writers have detected the influence of the tunes of the Anglo-Genevan Psalter upon these pieces, but the connection is limited to a common ancestry in medieval song. Byrd's interest in the psalms is more likely to have centered upon the sanction they gave to the arts of music and poetry than upon their role in Reformed worship; and a comparison of his melody with one of the "church tunes" will show how differently it is shaped (example 8.2). The length of the

Example 8.2. Byrd, "O Lord, who in thy sacred tent"

"fourteener" prompts Byrd always to observe the caesura, which he employs optionally in shorter lines but always places correctly. In the second couplet of this example the composer gains a broadened effect by inserting another caesura in the first " eight," and intensifies the musical interest by means of sequence, both for the two parallel verbal statements at the opening of the couplet and for all parts of the final line. It is noticeable that patterning of this kind, less straightforward than that of the rhyming pastorals, usually occurs toward the end of the serious songs. The tension it generates Byrd normally releases either in a melisma, or more often in a coda (example 8.3). Conspicuously lacking in the strophic settings of Byrd's predecessors,[16] these codas may perhaps be traced back to early Tudor court song by way of the customary extension of the final line in the midcentury "death-songs." There are certainly precedents in both earlier forms for Byrd's repeated invocations ("O Lord, O Lord") and his simple pictorial gestures (e.g., in line 3 of "Ye sacred Muses"). In writing musical similes rather than metaphors, to use John Stevens's useful distinction, Byrd merely acknowledged a tradition older to England

Example 8.3. Byrd, "O Lord, how long"

than humanism, the Reformation or the madrigal; he never let them expand unduly—even in the purely vocal songs—and they never override the strophic principle or interfere with the clear presentation of the poetic form.[17]

While his writing for the solo voice barely altered in style, Byrd increasingly found in the instrumental accompaniment another, and more subtle, means of making his songs "framed to the life of the words." The decisive advance of his early songs upon those of his predecessors lies in their contrapuntal elaboration; he was evidently concerned, as we might expect, to raise the form to a much higher musical level. After this had been achieved, probably by the mid-1580s, his further development of the solo song can be charted largely in terms of the increasing flexibility of the accompaniment. In place of the rigorously worked and sometimes crowded points that anticipate and enfold each vocal phrase in the songs (especially the serious songs) of 1588, there is a greater tendency for the viols to develop their own motivic material, to pursue some points to the exclusion of others, to arrive at cadences in more unexpected places and to change pace and rhythm with amazing variety.

This masterly later style is well illustrated by two of the recently published songs. They are anonymous in their source, the Paston group of manuscripts, and I have attributed them to Byrd on bibliographical and stylistic evidence, which cannot even be summarized here (see chapter 4); but the points arising from them could equally well be demonstrated from the five consort songs Byrd published after 1600.[18] "With lilies white" is a poem, possibly written by Edward Paston himself, commemorating the death in 1608 of Lady Magdalen Montague, the grandmother of the young lady who married Paston's eldest son in the same year:

> With lilies white those virgins fair are crowned
> > That wed themselves to our great Lord and Saviour,
> And never were in worldly pleasure drowned,
> > But solely liv'd in chaste and sweet behaviour,
> Expecting still with lamps of crystal shining
> The bridegroom's call to bid them to his dining.
>
> Among these maids, fair Mawdlyn, late deceased,
> > May well be plac'd in virgin's weeds attired,
> Who as in years in virtue still increased,
> > And was a flow'r of beauty most admired,
> Whose corpse in earth in marble tomb reposes,
> And soul in heaven crown'd with sacred roses.

But for an increase in the number of melismas and the fitting of syllables to shorter notes, the design of the vocal part runs along much the same lines as that of "Ye sacred Muses"—though for once in a strophic setting Byrd appears to have noticed the needs of the second stanza in the figure he devised for the fifth line. But the accompaniment flows more freely and unifies the piece with material developed out of the countersubject to the opening point. It is the accompaniment, moreover, that maintains the mood of exalted contemplation, which is not disturbed by occasional excursions into pictorial or symbolic commentary. The end of the first vocal phrase, for instance, is indeed "crowned" by the first viol's entry with the point, postponed until this moment with obvious intent; and the bass viol sinks most convincingly into the "worldly pleasure" of division in accompanying the third line. The customary cadence after the quatrain is replaced here by a more affirmative one at the end of the third line, presumably to effect a change of mood suggested by the words of the first stanza.

In these later songs, Byrd's matchless technique rises to the portrayal of the most difficult and intangible moods. Among the Paston songs occurs a droll verse upon the fall in 1601 of the queen's favorite, the Earl of Essex, who is identified here with a Roman governor of Britain defeated in his attempt to overthrow the emperor who raised him to power:

> Wretched Albinus, thrall to heavy hap,
>> How could the stars such angry fate afford?
> Did'st thou not lie e'en now on Pleasure's lap,
>> And had sweet Fortune chained to thy word?
> How comes it then, on good, evil should attend,
> And that a silly woman works thine end?

Everything about the setting is, in terms of Byrd's style, a little exaggerated, a little overwrought: the false relations that strike a lugubrious note at the end of the first line and lend a surprisingly voluptuous air to the end of the third; the teasing, ambivalent figure in the treble viol that announces the cadence at the end of the quatrain with an ingratiating leap to the unprepared seventh; the syncopated declamation and shifting tonalities of the fifth line in unusual contrast to the even flow and static harmonies of the previous line; and finally, the languorous suspended falling figure in the treble viol which suggests the earl's fate throughout the second line and which also literally "works" the end of the piece, closing in an unusually drawn-out decorated suspension. From the opening plunge of its first vocal phrase to the progressively diminishing repeats of its last, the song quietly and affectionately parodies not only the old "death-song" but also Byrd's own elegiac manner.

The increasing importance and flexibility of the accompaniment in the later songs tend to draw attention away from the shape of the stanza, but there is never any question of its being undermined or ignored. Poetic form is also a major concern in the part songs of the 1589 and 1611 sets, even though the purely vocal conception and Byrd's predilection for counterpoint make its apprehension more difficult. It is this concern, and not merely conservative reaction to a newfangled musical idiom, that explains the persistence of certain features such as predominantly syllabic underlay, priority for the articulation of the poetic line over the projection of the sense of the text, a careful proportioning of line lengths and an avoidance of pictorialism or of vivid contrasts of style and texture. With no such firmly established form as the consort song to start from, Byrd experimented more widely in his part songs. He naturally adopted those madrigalian features he could use— mostly textures or turns of phrase, rarely harmonic or cadential formulas; but in view of his secure sense of style and of formal values it is difficult to agree with Kerman that many of his part songs "seem to strive uneasily for some kind of compromise between the native and the imported musical idiom" (iii), or to accept his label "transitional" for them.

The full extent of Byrd's respect for poetic form, however, is revealed most strikingly by comparing his songs, either consort or fully vocal, with his settings of prose, whether in Latin or English. So far from exhibiting any of the kinds of restraint or control described so far, the prose settings expand freely and tend to embrace every suitable opportunity for pictorial display. The *Cantiones sacrae* of 1589 and 1591 take this process to its furthest limits. The greater restraint of *Gradualia* and the masses was most likely prompted by their liturgical intent, for the exuberance bursts out again in the magnificent English motets of the 1611 secular set. There are of course good reasons other than their prose texts for the grandiloquence of the motets—Latin still outranked the vernacular as a language of eloquence, and the composer was consciously emulating a great Continental tradition; but it is noteworthy that when Byrd encounters Latin verse, either quantitative *(Laudibus in sanctis)* or accentual (as in *Ave verum corpus*), he generally modifies his style in one way or another to emphasize the poetic structure.

In the dedication of the first book of *Gradualia*, 1605, Byrd expressed his own views about the relation of words and music in a passage that is subject to a variety of interpretations.[19] Fellowes at one point explained it as "Byrd's own statement that beautiful words inspired him inevitably with suitable musical ideas," and proceeded to attribute what he considered the "comparative failure" of the psalm settings of 1588 and 1589 and the pieces in Leighton's collection to their "wretchedly poor verbal text."[20] Pursuing this line of argument, can we explain the relative austerity of the songs as a whole by the notion that Byrd responded half-heartedly to the predominantly plain-style verse he either chose or was commissioned to set? The examples already discussed firmly contradict such a notion, which, it should be added, involves a misunderstanding both of the composer's statement and of some basic artistic principles of the period. It is not the words themselves, but the hidden power of the thoughts behind them to which Byrd refers in *Gradualia*, and far from dwelling on the mechanics of his own response to the words, he implies, in a variation upon a well-known medieval theme, that all his "fittest numbers" *(aptissimi quique numeri)* are but echoes of a greater harmony caught from a profound contemplation of the First Composer. Moreover, to think that Byrd needed "beautiful words" to fire his imagination betrays anachronistic assumptions about the lyric and music's relation to it. We are dealing with an age in which poetry was a branch of rhetoric, a form of argument:

> The function of poetry both Sidney and Dryden, a hundred years apart, assume, is not to express the feelings but to move or persuade the reader or listener. The crucial feelings involved, the emotional experiences to which the poem must be true, are those of the reader, not the poet.[21]

Poetry's sister art has a complementary role in this scheme: music adds delight to the argument, and makes the mind more receptive by "ravishing" the ear (to use the contemporary metaphor). Even the musical "imitation" of words and images, which we interpret as subjective pictorialism and consequently call "word painting," is more properly considered a figure of musical rhetoric aimed at not so much portraying as amplifying the theme to make it more pleasing and more persuasive.[22] Whether using this device or not, Byrd focuses his art, not on his own process of interpreting the text, but on the listener's mind. He seeks to project, or to create an easy passage for, the ideas behind the text, and the style of his setting is therefore determined by deeper considerations than merely the inspiration of "beautiful words"—Fellowes's conception of which he would in any case not have shared.[23]

We need to look more closely at the music itself and at the artistic context in which it was created to explain discrepancies of style in so great a composer as Byrd. The governing aesthetic principle during the period was fitness or decorum, and its importance in music cannot be too greatly stressed, for it explains many things that elude our ready comprehension. It was this principle which promoted the composer's concern for poetic form, and which caused the stylistic differences between the prose and verse settings. Poetic form is certainly a major concern of the literary theorists: George Puttenham, writing during the earlier part of Byrd's career, devoted a third of his *Arte of English Poesie* to "Proportion Poeticall" which, he wrote, "holdeth of the Musical, because . . . Poesie is a skill to speake & write harmonically" (64).[24] What is implied in the term "harmonically" is a beautiful and measured order. This is the quality, then, that music is most fitted to represent. A musical setting should above all retain the "proportion poeticall" and second, add from its own rhetoric a figurative quality Puttenham calls "Enargia"—"because it geueth a glorious lustre and light" (143)—which fulfills an age-old requirement of the property of beauty referred to by Thomas Aquinas as "the shining forth of the *form* of a thing, either of a work of art or nature . . . in such a manner that it is presented to the mind with all the fullness and richness of its perfection and order."[25]

Whether Byrd himself thought in such philosophical terms cannot of course be known, but his remarks on style and propriety in the *Gradualia* of 1605 show a certain familiarity with the terms and ideas of the rhetorical handbooks. And in the differences of style among the songs themselves can also be detected a sense of decorum that cannot have been entirely intuitive; the avoidance of musical rhyme in all but the lighter songs, for instance, reflects Puttenham's stricture, "so . .,. doth the ouer busie and too speedy return of one maner of tune, too much annoy & as it were glut the eare, vnlesse it be in small & popular Musickes" (83). Similarly, the cadential melismas and codas of the serious songs show an equally decorous concern on Byrd's part "to follow the nature of his subject, that is if his matter be high and loftie that the stile be so too" (149).

It is decorum, then, not simply conservatism, that lies behind Byrd's rejection of the madrigal as a viable means of setting poetry. He cannot have approved either of the destruction of poetic form to which the madrigal is prone, or of the employment for light matter of a style Morley describes as "next unto the Motet, the most artificial." It is significant that the two pieces in Watson's collection, Byrd's closest approach to the madrigal, share a verse in honor of the queen, whose praise warranted the employment of a lofty style to convey "a simple toy." Morley's single-minded pursuit of the lighter forms of Italian music, and the perfect grace of his settings, may perhaps explain why his publications were countenanced under Byrd's monopoly of printed music. But if Ben Jonson considered Donne's *First Anniversary* "profane and full of Blasphemies" because it addressed a thirteen-year-old girl in terms appropriate, in his judgment, only to the Virgin Mary,[26] might not Byrd have been equally censorious about the towering musical monument erected upon the triviality of "Thule, the period of cosmography"? Viewed like this, Weelkes's failure to achieve a permanent post in the Chapel Royal appears perhaps a little less inexplicable.

As the most respected composer of the age, Byrd had considerable influence upon his younger contemporaries. Kerman has attributed various features of the English madrigal to the persistent native idiom of which Byrd was the chief representative, and it is conceivable that his views on poetic form and musical decorum had greater effect than has so far been recognized.[27] Byrd's greatest direct successor was Orlando Gibbons, who seems in his *Madrigals and Motets* of 1612 to have taken the older master's purely vocal song style as a point of departure, and who found a form so congenial to his talents in the verse anthem, Byrd's extension of the consort song to composition on a larger scale.[28] But the true inheritor of the native tradition of solo song was John Dowland, whose setting of verse places him closer to Byrd than is generally realized, despite stylistic and textural differences.

Among the songs of this splendid triumvirate, those of Byrd have proved the most difficult for a later age to understand and enjoy. It is after all an adverse musical judgment that lies behind Fellowes's apologetics and behind the critical responses, "unliterary" and "old-fashioned," now paraded as historical facts. But Fellowes in particular never appreciated the necessity of performing the consort songs in their original form, with "instruments to express the harmonie, and one voyce to pronounce the dittie," and later critics have never quite managed to separate the works themselves from the expectations they bring to them. Performed by their proper medium and heard without invidious comparisons, even the sober psalms, so forbidding on voices alone and so different in their rhetoric from Dowland's spiritual songs, are suddenly transformed into rich musical tapestries in which the contrapuntal strands of the accompaniment weave an engaging pattern upon the plain but expressive stuff of Byrd's sturdy melodies. The later songs, moreover, are revealed as small masterpieces of the highest order, equal to Dowland's finest efforts, and as finely wrought as the Hilliard miniatures or the Shakespeare sonnets.

In order to gain the full measure of Byrd's song idiom, it is desirable to approach it, as we have seen, not in retrospect from the madrigal and air, but looking forward from the earlier triumphs of English song. It is not alone among Elizabethan art forms to benefit from such an approach, for it shares some place in that curious side of Elizabethan culture described by Roy Strong in his illuminating remarks about Nicholas Hilliard—an almost exact contemporary of Byrd—and his followers:

> The late Elizabethan court . . . reveled in a neo-medievalism, whether it manifested itself in spiky gothicism of dress, building great castles, jousting in fancy dress as knights before the Queen or devouring interminable romances of chivalry of the type of Sidney's *Arcadia* or Spenser's *Faerie Queene*.[29]

Byrd's first printed songbook, with its occasional poetry and echoes of the courtly game of love, breathes this atmosphere quite strongly, but it would be as dangerous to suggest that he was consciously influenced by court fashion as it would be wrong to imply that he deliberately cultivated an antique manner. The independence of his genius, reflected in the whole immense range of his musical endeavor, is nowhere more apparent than in his songs. An inspired blend of his own highly individual musical language with strong traditional formal principles, they are not only one of the most original artistic achievements of the age, but also among the most musically satisfying contributions to the art of song.

NOTES

1. For an account of the form, see my article "The English Consort Song, 1570–1625," *Proceedings of the Royal Musical Association* 88 (1961–62): 73–88.

2. Nos. 34, 38, 40, 41, and 35, 36 and 39 in *Consort Songs for Voice and Viols,* ed. Philip Brett (*Collected Works of William Byrd*, rev. ed., vol. 15), (London, 1970), later incorporated into the Byrd Edition.

3. *The Compleat Gentleman* (London, 1622), 100.

4. Fellowes 48, 153, 244, 161 and 133.

5. *A General History of Music* (London, 1789), 4:122n.

6. *Festschrift für Johannes Wolf* (Berlin, 1929), 24–30; Dent's findings also appear, much condensed, in "Musical Form in the Madrigal," *Music & Letters* 11 (1930): 230–40.

7. Literary critics, however, have for some time differed on the question of the "mainstream" of English poetry; see Yvor Winter's review of C. S. Lewis's *English Literature in the Sixteenth Century*, reprinted in *The Function of Criticism* (London, 1957); and his articles on "The 16th Century Lyric in England," *Poetry* 53–54 (1939), reprinted (somewhat revised) in *Forms of Discovery* (Denver, 1967); also Douglas L. Peterson, *The English Lyric from Wyatt to Donne* (Princeton, 1967).

8. E.g., in *The New Oxford History of Music* (London, 1968), 4:200.

9. *Consort Songs;* see note 2.

10. Features of this kind, common in the strophic settings (see also exx. 8.2 and 8.3), make it difficult to agree that Byrd's voice parts either concentrate "on

following the sense and intonation of the words" or are "an expression of their meaning," views expressed by Richard J. McGrady in his literary and musical survey, "The English Solo Song from William Byrd to Henry Lawes" (diss., University of Manchester, 1963), 34 and 51.

11. Two exceptions prove the rule: in "Though Amaryllis dance in green" only the last line of the couplet is repeated, because it is a refrain; in "Come, pretty babe" the opening words "Come lullaby" prompt an unusual sixfold repeat. In a thoroughly misleading discussion of the songs (in *The Technique of Byrd's Vocal Polyphony* [London, 1966], 263–66), H. K. Andrews claims that Byrd "seems to make little effort to match poetic structures with comparable musical forms" largely on the grounds that the repeat of the final couplet in settings of the English type of sonnet turns the sestet into an eight-line section, "thus destroying the essential 'octave/sestet' construction." So it may appear on paper; but in performance the listener has no difficulty in hearing it in its proper function as a repetition, reinforcing rather than extending or destroying the poetic form.

12. See Stevens, 17–18, 37, 100–101 and 104–5.

13. See Pattison, 150–54, concerning this last feature, which is characteristic of the lutenists' poetry, but not of that set by Byrd.

14. *Psalmes, Sonets & Songs* (1588), no. 31. Francis Pilkington's setting of the first stanza in his *Second Set of Madrigals* (1624), no. 19, emphasizes by comparison the "literary" nature of Byrd's approach. Pilkington's version is madrigalian in a superficial sense, with chromatic passages thrown in for good measure, but it bears no discernible relationship, expressive or formal, to the words, which appear to have been slapped beneath the notes as an afterthought.

15. *Consort Songs*, nos. 1–2.

16. *Consort Songs*, nos. 17–23.

17. This preoccupation with poetic form throws into question the relationship of the consort song to humanist theories about the expression of sense and emotion that Edward Doughtie briefly proposes in the introduction—the best recent essay on music and poetry of the period—to his authoritative edition of *Lyrics from English Airs, 1596–1622* (Cambridge, MA, 1970), 19. Byrd's quantitative settings (the 1588 set, nos. 23 and 34) raise more precisely the question of humanist influence. They are isolated examples, probably undertaken as a result of Byrd's contact with the Sidney circle, and they did not alter his preference for a more rhythmically flexible vocal line.

18. *Gradualia*, book 1, 1605, no. 26, and *Psalmes, Songs and Sonnets*, 1611, nos. 25, 28, 31 and 32.

19. Porro, illis ipsis sententijs (ut experiendo didici) adeo abstrusa atque recondita vis inest; vt diuina cogitanti, diligenterque ac serio peruolutanti; nescio

quonam modo, aptissimi quique numeri, quasi sponte accurrant sua; animoque minime ignauo, atque inerti, liberaliter ipsi sese offerant.

20. Fellowes 48, 133.

21. Stephen Orgel, "Affecting the Metaphysics," *Harvard English Studies* 2 (1971): 238.

22. See Frank Kermode's review of Pattison's book in *Review of English Studies* 25 (1949): 266.

23. My guide on this subject has been Rosamund Tuve's scholarly study, *Elizabethan and Metaphysical Imagery: Renaissance Poetic and Twentieth-Century Critics* (Chicago, 1947).

24. *The Arte of English Poesie*, ed. G. D. Willcock and Alice Walker (Cambridge, 1936); the book is thought to have been drafted up to twenty years before its publication in 1589.

25. Quoted in K. E. Gilbert and H. Kuhn's *A History of Esthetics* (New York, 1939), 141.

26. *Ben Jonson*, ed. C. H. Herford and Percy Simpson (Oxford, 1925), 1:133.

27. See chapter 6.

28. Gibbons's approach to his texts is discussed in an important but little-known article by John Stevens, "The Elizabethan Madrigal: 'Perfect Marriage' or 'Uneasy Flirtation,' " *Essays and Studies*, n.s., 11 (1958): 17–37.

29. *The English Icon: Elizabethan and Jacobean Portraiture* (London, 1969), 14–15.

CHAPTER NINE

William Byrd:
New Reflections

As a musician, Byrd was both a product and a shaping force of the Elizabethan age—"Brittanicae Musicae parens," as one eulogist put it. "He belonged to the generation of Sidney, Hooker and Nicholas Hilliard, not that of Shakespeare, Dowland and Bacon," Joseph Kerman has said. "He was as impervious to late Elizabethan elegance, Euphuistic or Italianate, as he was to the subsequent Jacobean 'disenchantment.' "[1] An equally important Elizabethan literary figure with whom Byrd can be compared is the poet Edmund Spenser.

Spenser and Byrd played important roles in building and enhancing the culture of the Elizabethan court, the one with elaborately devised poems and romances that created an almost Arthurian atmosphere in this Tudor setting, the other with settings of her courtier's verses, anthems and services for the Anglican Church of which she was head, music for the queen's own instrument, the virginals, and "Latin songs" in effect praising the monarch to whom they were dedicated. Both consequently received significant royal favors in addition to the court-appointed jobs

Abstracted from a lecture given at the annual William Byrd Festival at Portland, Oregon, in September 2001, also given as a roundtable paper for the Center of Medieval and Renaissance Studies at UCLA in May 2002.

they landed when they were still young. Byrd got a music-printing monopoly granted to him and his aging teacher in 1575, Spenser a royal pension of fifty pounds a year in 1591.

Both needed these favors because, although the Byrds claimed to be a step or two above Spenser, who was a "poor scholar" at Merchant Taylor's School, both were determined seekers of the Elizabethan path of upward mobility. There was also an artistic bond, or at least a connection that may be more obvious today than it was at the time: both Byrd and Spenser clearly had a historical sense, and were involved to one degree or another with the work of their predecessors. We should not think of that historical sense as equivalent to present-day canonic or intentional concerns, of course. Yet Byrd's pointed reference, at the opening of the Sanctus in his first mass, the one for four voices, to the same place in a mass by John Taverner, the leading composer of King Henry VIII's reign, is surely a symbol replete with significance; and Spenser's archaisms were actually a matter of complaint from his contemporaries and immediate successors.

At a certain point, comparisons break down, as they always do. Byrd never set Spenser's verse: they were not at all in collaboration. Recent researches have shown that Byrd was born earlier then we thought, in 1540 rather than 1543, and that makes him a good twelve years older than the poet. Spenser was a Cambridge man who gravitated to the Protestant circle around the Earl of Leicester; Byrd never got a degree, remained a Roman Catholic all his life and looked for protection to powerful Catholic nobles like the Earl of Worcester. He also outlived his time, dying at the age of eighty-three with little to mark the fact. Spenser died before the Elizabethan age had outrun its course: his burial at Westminster Abbey was attended by a public display of grief, and in the title of his posthumous collected works, published in 1611, he was entitled "England's Arch-Poet," a prototype for poets laureate to come. Byrd's stubborn recusancy makes the composer an interesting case of the insider who is in one respect on the outs with authority: his relation to the established order was clouded with what seem increasingly subversive—if not treasonable—involvements with the Jesuit priests who invaded England. In any case, admiration for his queen was not his major project. He could never have been the recipient of a remark like Karl Marx's unsubtle reference to Spenser as "Elizabeth's arse-kissing poet."

Louis A. Montrose has recently challenged the modern tendency to see Spenser as "an unequivocal celebrant of Elizabethan political and social orthodoxies." In an eloquent manner he argues "against an understanding of Spenser's relationship to royal authority as either wholly assenting or wholly oppositional, and in support of one that allows for the multiplicity, discontinuity, and inconsistency of Spenserian attitudes toward the monarch, the courtly establishment, and the state without assuming that he was either merely hypocritical or merely muddled."[2] The quotation is one that might guide our footsteps in approaching William Byrd also, for neither Edmund Fellowes's view of him as a pillar of the Anglican Church who had a slightly embarrassing "association" with the Catholics, nor the whole appropriation of him as an enemy of the state by eager latter-day Catholics, will quite do.

Drawing attention to a material issue about Spenser that also bears thinking about in relation to Byrd, Montrose writes: "We may understand Spenser's own publication process, unfolded over the last two decades of the sixteenth century, to have been as calculated as [Ben] Jonson's in its appropriation of the resources of the printed book to shape a distinctive and culturally authoritative authorial persona" (83). Contrasting Spenser with courtier-soldier-scholars like Sidney and Raleigh, Montrose demonstrates the need of the socially subordinate Spenser "to construct and to sustain an authorial persona in a corpus of generically varied printed poetry books" (84).

Constructing and sustaining an authorial persona is a very different thing in music than in poetry. Byrd could not project himself as a Colin Clout, nor adopt any other direct autobiographical persona. But there are other ways of asserting authority, and Byrd was the first English musician to realize the power of print as a decisive factor in doing so. With the grant of a monopoly over printed part music and music paper to Byrd and Tallis a new era dawned. Byrd, who must have been the driving force behind the enterprise, immediately designed an elaborate publication dedicated to the queen, the *Cantiones* of 1575—partly in gratitude, partly with a view to establishing himself, his aged teacher and English music on a new footing, as the highly patriotic prefatory matter makes clear. . . .

The later *Cantiones*, published in 1589 and 1591, reflect an altogether different strategy from that of Byrd's English songbooks of 1588 and 1589, with their expressive ethos based aesthetically on medieval ideas and musically on the work of his English predecessors. This is not to say that there are no connections to earlier styles or forms—there are some retro gestures included here too. But the main foundation of the style of these motets, which must mostly represent the work of the years between 1575 and 1591, is the sophisticated Continental imitative style that Byrd had learned a great deal about as a result of his contact with Alfonso Ferrabosco, one of Elizabeth's several foreign musicians. To the texts of these motets Byrd brings an energy, poignancy and commitment different in degree rather than kind from the style of his songs. The "voice heard on high" in *Haec dicit Dominus* from the 1591 collection is brought excessively low as the word "lamentationis," the property of that voice, is pictorially and effectively adumbrated in another, more somber, key. Examples could be multiplied. . . .

There seems to be little doubt as to the cultural, political and purely human reasons for this development in Byrd's work, stemming as it undoubtedly does from the status of Roman Catholics within a Protestant state, even one so equivocal as Elizabethan England. The scenes of Jesuit priests being hung, drawn and quartered—that is, eviscerated and butchered—their heads placed on poles above the city gates as a warning, and their burned body parts displayed elsewhere must have acted powerfully upon the imaginations of an entire generation. Such scenes adorned the English College in Rome as a constant reminder, and books printed for the Roman faithful also emphasized them. Craig Monson even goes so far as to claim that Byrd's work in his Latin songs is part of a Jesuit propaganda effort "to foster an English Catholic identity and ideology grounded on consensus."[3]

The work of uncovering this persecution story and revealing Byrd's music as a kind of counterdiscourse has largely been done, and done powerfully and well. It is perhaps time to move on to consider other issues that might move us closer to a more complex understanding of Byrd's position and its ramifications. The publications of the 1588–91 period as a group, like Spenser's poetry publications spanning a rather wider period, do indeed create a "distinctive and culturally authoritative authorial persona," to borrow Louis Montrose's words again (83). Here is the consummate courtly composer, writing songs of every conceivable kind, from the sprightly "Though Amaryllis dance in green," to the lyrical and heart-warming setting of Sidney's "O dear life." Byrd is involved in every national event—a song celebrating the great victory over the Spanish armada in 1588 was not published but presumably known at court—and he was right on the mark politically and socially with his commemorations of Sidney the great Protestant hero. Byrd's reputation for skill (as well as, in Peacham's words, for gravity and piety) was greatly enhanced by the publication of his Latin songs, which only a few would see as subversive, and all would acknowledge as representing European high art—the highest language set forth in the most complicated polyphony. It is arguable that no English composer ever again was able to rise to such a challenge on such a scale.

Yet in a sense this carefully constructed portrait of authority is undermined by the very expressiveness which for later generations gives it such power. The beauty of Byrd's English music shows that there was no need for him to develop a sense of interiority. He could and possibly should have stayed within the carefully chosen world of the indigenous lyricist, adventuring into Continental imitative polyphony only to create beautiful structures like the early works of Lassus.

Interiority, a sense of inwardness: it comes into Tudor and Stuart culture through a variety of means. One is the growing awareness of the body and its humors according to the theories of Galenic medicine. Another is religious meditation, and it is here that we meet Byrd's dilemma. I am proposing that the strength of his reaction to the persecution of his fellow Roman Catholics, and his identification with the Jesuit cause, drew him into modes of composition and expression that undermine his classical poise just as they make him intriguing for us today. It might be better to contemplate for a moment how dislocating all this must have been for a composer attracted on the one hand to the general, not particular, expressive values of medieval culture and on the other to strophic forms and abstract patterns. (Byrd was equally an instrumental composer for all his protestations about the superiority of the voice.) Looked at in this way, it is possible to assert that the crisis years, from the time his wife, Julian, and their servant, John Reason, were first cited for recusancy in 1577 until Byrd made the decision around 1593 to retire to the Essex countryside, produced a very different composer from the one he set out to be.

At Stondon Massey, close enough to the Petre establishment at Ingatestone, Byrd began a new project, that of adorning the Roman Tridentine liturgy with art that was clearly meant to attain liturgical decorum as well as to promote the cause of the Jesuits and their Catholic Reformation. As I argue in the several prefaces to my edition of *Gradualia*, decorum was largely kept while more subtle ways were found to inject political messages into the printed volumes, through such means as musical nuance or arrangement of contents. I spend some effort trying to contend with the theory that Joseph Kerman derived from the Catholic historian John Bossy that *Gradualia* and the masses represent an Augustinian retreat into some sort of acceptance and acquiescence.

I would like to suggest that Byrd turned away from the Continental expressive "motet," though he had imbued it with as much intensity as any of his peers, because it failed to satisfy some of his inbred aesthetic impulses and concerns. It had served as a catalyst, perhaps even in a cathartic manner, enabling him to process and produce his feelings in sometimes dramatic ways. Just as the keyboard pavan-galliard pair flowered because of their strophic limitations, and his grounds and other variations could build to expressive heights because of the constraints of the repetitive underpinnings, so in his vocal music Byrd also needed some real constraint in order to reach an even deeper level. The liturgy put him back into such a confining framework. Within the tension between form and content, a different sense of interiority could burgeon, the slightly repressed intensity that makes motets like *Justorum animae* and *Optimam partem elegit* even more powerful than *Vigilate, Exsurge, Domine* or *Haec dicit Dominus.*

Whatever view we take of the interesting inconsistencies in Byrd's output, there can be no doubt of the integrity with which he met the various challenges he faced. Had he not adopted the English song style and made it work through imbuing it with stronger contrapuntal values, we would have no way of assessing the appearance and effect of the Italian madrigal style in England and its results. If he had not allowed his reaction to his situation as a Roman Catholic to infect his music at such a deep level, we should presumably have had either more Renaissance polyphony of the slightly bland kind that assumes God is in his heaven and all is more or less right with the world, or a late refashioning of older English polyphonic values that would have been magnificent but similarly detached—there are hints of this in the earlier Latin music. Finally, had he not embarked on his retirement project to cultivate a musical flower garden (as he calls it in his dedication to Sir John Petre) both to adorn the liturgy and to provide for those moments of collective devotion that Roman Catholics cherished in the frequent absence of a priest, we would have little sense of the nature of worship in those clandestine circumstances.

In each of these cases, even in Byrd's failure to contain his work within the decorum he surely sought, he invites us to witness the strength of his feelings, never hiding behind any of the generalized formulas of his time. It is for this reason, of course, that his music is still so very much alive in our own troubled times.

NOTES

1. *The New Grove Dictionary of Music and Musicians*, 2nd ed. (London, 2001), 4:722.

2. "Spenser's Domestic Domain: Poetry, Property, and the Early Modern Subject," in *Subject and Object in Renaissance Culture*, ed. Magreta de Grazia, Maureen Quilligan, and Peter Stallybrass (Cambridge, 1996), 83, 121.

3. "Byrd, the Catholics, and the Motet: The Hearing Reopened," in *Hearing the Motet*, ed. Dolores Pesce (Oxford, 1997), 379.

CHAPTER TEN

Prefaces to *Gradualia*

Gradualia is primarily a collection of pieces proper to Mass at most of the chief feasts of the Roman Catholic calendar, as the composer emphasizes in rather precise descriptions of the contents in each unit of his great work, in book 1 of 1605 and book 2 of 1607. For the feasts in book 1 and the majority of feasts in book 2, Byrd provided settings of the introit, gradual, alleluia (or tract), offertory and communion. With few exceptions, the settings for each feast are all in the same clef-combination and mode; extra pieces, if supplied, usually consist of an important antiphon from Vespers or another office service of the same feast.

Introit settings include the verse—verses of all chants may be set for a reduced number of voices—and an indication for a da capo. Settings of the gradual and alleluia, which are sung consecutively in the service, are presented as two numbers comprising (1) gradual, gradual verse, alleluia, and (2) alleluia verse, alleluia—rather than (1) gradual, gradual verse (2) alleluia,

---

This monograph has been assembled from Philip Brett's prefaces to the five *Gradualia* volumes, *The Byrd Edition* (London: Stainer & Bell), with some reordering: vol. 5 (*The Marian Masses*), vii, iv–v, vii–xiii, xxvii–xix; vol. 6a (*All Saints and Corpus Christi*), vii–xi; vol. 6b (*Other Feasts and Devotions*), vii–xv; vol. 7a (*Christmas to Easter*), vii–xi; vol. 7b (*Ascension, Pentecost, and the Feast of Saints Peter & Paul*), vii–xii, xix, xii–xiii; vol. 5, xxiii–xxvii; vol. 7a, xii–xiv; vol. 7b, xvi–xvii, xiv–xvi, xx–xxiii.

alleluia verse, alleluia, as in the service books. Byrd's arrangement provided him with two pieces ending with "alleluia," a word he never tired of setting anew. The second alleluia in the gradual-alleluia unit is not a da capo.

In addition to the main sequence of music for the Mass, especially in book 1 Byrd includes a generous sampling of other music for liturgical use and for private devotions. The texts he uses throughout are not those prescribed by the service books of the Sarum rite, which predominated in England before the Reformation and apparently persisted in some Catholic circles during Byrd's time. Significantly, the composer followed the Roman reform initiated by the Council of Trent and enshrined in the revised Breviary and Missal authorized by the Dominican Pope Pius V in 1568 and 1570 respectively.

CONTENTS AND MEANING OF BOOK 1

Masses for the Blessed Virgin Mary / *page 129*   Context / *page 141*
All Saints and Corpus Christi / *page 145*   Music for Private Devotions:
The Primer / *page 157*   Holy Week and the Easter Season / *page 165*

Masses for the Blessed Virgin Mary (a 5)

The first section of *Gradualia* book 1 (nos. 1–5) consists of music for five voices, all in the D mode with one flat in the signature. Byrd attempted to cover the very many occasions when a Marian mass was required, either on feast days of the Blessed Virgin Mary or for the customary Saturday observance of a votive mass—a mass which changed several times over the church year.[1] The multitude of duplicate texts that characterize these occasions led Byrd to adopt a system in which ingenuity, economy of effort and paucity of direction to the user are so combined that not until recent years was the full majesty of the concept revealed, first by James Jackman and then more fully by Joseph Kerman.[2] The following description of some of its salient features may be more readily understood if "The Marian Masses: Liturgical Table of Contents" is consulted as it is read (pages 130–31).

THE MARIAN MASSES:
LITURGICAL TABLE OF CONTENTS

IV. EASTER TO PENTECOST

V. PENTECOST TO ADVENT

Feast of the Annunciation
of the Blessed Virgin Mary

Feast of the Assumption
of the Blessed Virgin Mary

Since all but two of the Marian introits share the same psalm verse, *Eructavit cor meum*, with the doxology, one setting (printed as a part of no. 6) does duty for most occasions. The same music for the doxology is, however, printed again at the end of no. 12, and a related, earlier version occurs at the end of no. 1.

THE TRANSFER SCHEME

Many texts from the Marian liturgy serve another liturgical function when slightly curtailed. Thus *Suscepimus Deus* (no. 1) sets seven short phrases of text that constitute the Purification introit; the first five of these phrases reappear as the gradual for the same feast. The printed music is made to suit both purposes by the provision of an internal cadence (usually with a fermata and a barline to mark it) at the requisite internal spot. These are simple examples of the unit approach Byrd adopts. A more complicated procedure occurs when, for instance, the first part of the verse of the gradual *Speciosus forma* (no. 17) has to be supplied from a different piece, no. 6, the singers returning to no. 17 for the second part of the verse and the subsequent alleluia. Some pieces are such a collection of units that they can never be performed exactly as they stand in the part books if they are to satisfy any known liturgical requirement. *Gaudeamus omnes* (no. 23) is the head of an introit joined unceremoniously to the rump of an alleluia. *Diffusa est gratia* (no. 22), also never performed in its entirety if it is viewed liturgically, serves three separate occasions: one of them, the gradual of the Assumption, requires the performers to begin at a point well into the piece (at "Propter veritatem").

One might ask why Byrd adopted such a complicated method at all. Not surprisingly, he abandoned it in book 2 (except in the six-part music) by writing separate settings for liturgical items with duplicate texts. Jackman had the answer, I believe, when he related Byrd's system to a principle of economy often found in liturgical books (21), though he did not pursue the point. A model cannot be found in the polyphonic collections of the age, but it can indeed be discerned the contemporary chant books. While Sarum Graduals had tended to reproduce a chant every time it was needed, the printed *Graduale Romanum* in the late sixteenth century capitalized on the Tridentine abbreviation of that formerly vast liturgical collection by printing each chant rarely more than once and by referring to it in a rubric whenever it was needed in another context. This was the text Byrd followed. With characteristic doggedness and ingenuity, he merely extended the principle of this transfer scheme (as I shall call it) to a certain logical extreme—without following his model in the meticulous application of rubrics. Not dependent on the chant (a point that his method of operation emphasizes), he was at liberty to transfer from one liturgical situation to another the setting of any duplicate text, whether or not the original chants were identical. The contemporary Roman Gradual, however, illuminates not only the general features of Byrd's scheme but also its specific problems.[3]

It is the proliferation of alleluias, as Jackman first pointed out, that gives away Byrd's intention to cater for the whole Marian liturgy, not merely the elements indicated (or implied) by the headings he himself supplied. Alleluias have no place, for instance, in the introit, offertory and communion of the Nativity (nos. 6, 10 and 11), or the offertory and communion of the Advent votive Mass (nos. 14 and 15). Byrd supplied them because they were needed when these texts were sung at the votive Mass in Paschal time (the fifty days from Easter to Pentecost) or at the Annunciation when it falls after Easter. All these alleluias are of course detachable: they are set off by barlines or rests. This is the same procedure as that of the Venetian Graduals of the printers Liechtenstein and Giunta. Byrd omits the post-Paschal rubric that they supply, but is more thoroughgoing in supplying the alleluias themselves, which they sometimes omit (e.g., in *Salve sancta parens*). In some cases (e.g., nos. 9 and 18), Byrd makes the alleluia detachable even though it must always be sung.

Byrd's print is arguably more obscure about masses for the actual Marian feasts than it is about the votive masses. Once again the contemporary Graduals clarify the issue. The Pian scythe that in 1568 cut such a swath of saints' days from the Roman calendar, unchecked in its growth since the ninth century, left feasts of Christ and Mary relatively untouched. The single exception was the Presentation of the Virgin (21 November), based on a legend and not widely observed in the Western church until the fourteenth century.[4] Though it was reintroduced under Pope Sixtus V as early as 1585, and raised in status by Clement VIII in 1604, it is left out of some service books of the time. We know that it was celebrated, at least in the Jesuit circles in which Byrd moved, from a letter of Father Henry Garnet, superior of the English province, written on 21 November 1604 from his headquarters at White Webbs in Middlesex: "Today, being the feast of the Presentation of Our Lady, there happened to be here together by good fortune John [Gerard], Blunt, Percy, Hungerford, Cornforth . . . and Batley and Taten and two priests etc. High Mass was sung."[5] Since Garnet was a keen musician, it is in exactly such a context that one would expect Byrd's settings to have been used.

The four Marian occasions named in *Gradualia*, then, are the oldest and most important feasts of the Virgin:

the Purification (2 February)
the Nativity (8 September)
the Annunciation (25 March)
the Assumption (15 August)[6]

In addition the calendar in 1605 prescribed the following:

the Visitation (2 July)
Dedication of Our Lady of the Snow (5 August)
Vigil of the Assumption (14 August)
Octave of the Assumption (22 August)
Octave of the Nativity (15 September)
the Presentation (21 November)
the Conception (8 December)[7]

Of these the Visitation and Conception share the same Propers as the Nativity. The Vigil of the Assumption has the introit *Vultum tuum deprecabuntur*, with verse *Eructavit* (instead of the feasts' *Gaudeamus omnes*), and takes its alleluia verse from the mass of the day. Our Lady of the Snow (S. Maria ad Nives) differs from the Nativity only in substituting the alleluia verse *Post partum Virgo* and offertory *Ave Maria*, thus becoming identical with the votive Mass of the Pentecost-to-Advent season in which it falls. Though Octaves occasionally require different texts at Mass, those of the Assumption and Nativity have the same Propers as the feasts themselves. The Presentation is a special case: owing perhaps to its reintroduction after the initial Tridentine reform, there is confusion about its Propers among the Missals and Graduals which include it. Some books (especially those printed in Venice) specify the Nativity texts, while the others, anticipating what later became universal practice, assign to it the Propers of the votive mass of the season.

It is fair to assume that Byrd envisaged the use of his Marian music on all these occasions. The reason he chose to group the series of Propers known as the *Missa Salve* under the heading of the Nativity may be because of the importance of the feast, or because he initially composed them for that occasion, or because the feast had some special significance for him. The simplest answer, however, is once again that he was following his text source. The Venetian Graduals—those printed by Liechtenstein (1580), Gardano (1591) and the Giunta firm (1602, 1606, 1613)— all give a full set of chants under the Nativity and refer to them by the rubric "omnia ut in Nativitate eius" for the Visitation, Conception and (in Giunta alone) the Presentation.[8]

MUDDLES

It is not surprising that in juggling the pieces of this complicated jigsaw puzzle Byrd occasionally got into a muddle. Sometimes it is simply a matter of the omission or insertion of a word or phrase.[9] Slightly more serious is his attempt to get *Ave Maria gratia plena* (no. 14) to do double duty as an alleluia verse and offertory for Advent without making the provision to curtail it in the first of these two guises—to end after the word "mulieribus" and proceed directly to the alleluia. The intention for no. 14 to serve as both alleluia and offertory is confirmed by one of the rare rubrics in *Gradualia;* in any case, an alternative possibility—that the end of the preceding gradual *Tollite portas* (no. 13) could lead into the beginning of the alleluia verse in its other appearance in *Gradualia* as part of the double or greater alleluia, *Alleluia. Ave Maria. Alleluia. Virga Jesse* (no. 20)—is not musically viable.

This double alleluia is perhaps the most problematic component of Byrd's scheme. The order of the verses *Ave Maria* and *Virga Jesse* is correct for the Annunciation Mass when it occurs in Paschal time. But the piece is placed among the cycle of votive masses, where it is presumably meant to serve as the greater alleluia for Lady Mass in Paschal time. For this purpose, however, its two verses are in the wrong order—and the music does not allow one to solve the problem simply by reversing them. A further complication arises from its placement before the tract *Gaude Maria* in the following context:

Post Septuagessima[m]

20 Alleluia. Ave Maria. Alleluia. Virga Jesse
21 Gaude Maria

In Annunciatione B. Mariae Virginis

22 Diffusa est gratia. Audi filia.

The logical order for the first two is the other way round—tract followed by alleluia—and it is likely that Byrd intended it to be so. "Post Septuagessima[m]," the phrase in the headline above *Alleluia. Ave Maria,* does not signify a feast or common liturgical unit like most of the headings in *Gradualia.* It can only be explained as a shortened form of the rubric "Post Septuagesimam, omissis Alleluia et versus sequenti, dicitur Tractus" (or more simply "Post lxx. Tractus"), which refers to the tract *Gaude Maria. Alleluia. Ave Maria* must therefore have been moved at some stage of the planning or printing of *Gradualia.* It is tempting to suggest, moreover, that it was moved not one but two places. In its correct and possibly original position as the alleluia for the Annunciation it would have occurred after no. 22, comprising the gradual and tract for that feast.

The suspicion remains that Byrd took this one fairly notable wrong step in the labyrinthine ways of the Marian section of book 1 as the result of a tidying-up operation. Having mistakenly assumed that the Annunciation alleluia could complete the Lady Mass cycle, he may have moved it in accordance with a general principle, observed in all but the first mass, of referring back (*ut supra*) but not forward (*ut infra*) for transfers; in the process the heading for *Gaude Maria* was presumably left behind.

One can see how Byrd may have been misled about the order of the verses of *Alleluia. Ave Maria. Alleluia. Virga Jesse* if he took one of the Venetian Graduals as his model. They all specify transfers for the alleluias of the Paschal votive Mass. Giunta prints the alleluia *Ave Maria* under the Advent votive Mass and the alleluia *Virga Jesse* under the Purification-to-Easter votive Mass, and refers to these two places both in the Easter votive Mass and the Annunciation. Liechtenstein and Gardano print both alleluias on the same folio under the Annunciation (in the correct order for the feast) and refer back to them from the Easter votive Mass, where the order is correct but the procedure even more likely to cause confusion.

Besides the liturgical difficulties described above, musical problems arise whenever Byrd did not have the possibility of a transfer in mind when he wrote a piece, a matter which Kerman has explored in some detail.[10] As he points out, some apprehension about the transfer process can be read into Byrd's remarks in the book 1 preface:

> So that these songs might be arranged each in its own place according
> to the various parts of the office, I have appended at the conclusion of
> the book a special index in which all [the songs] appropriate to the
> same feasts, though they differ in their number of voices, will easily be
> found listed together. (236)

The index as printed makes this promise appear extravagant, and yet it is careful to specify the internal verses, so that anyone with Missal or Gradual in hand and some knowledge of the liturgy might gain an immediate inkling of the possibilities. And though it does not repeat the liturgical headings that appear in the body of the books, it does indicate the categories they define by means of rules.

We may still wonder why no consistent attempt was made to provide direction for the transfer scheme, either here or in the body of the music. The rubrics are sparse indeed: there are only seven of them in the entire collection—five belonging to the Marian masses of book 1. Those that do occur cover some of the standard transfers and repetitions such as the da capo of an introit (no. 12), the repetition or transfer of a piece to provide the next link in the chain of Propers (nos. 14, 19) or the insertion of the ubiquitous *Eructavit* verse and doxology (nos. 16, 17). The more complicated situations are passed over in silence.

THE PRINTED ORDER OF THE MARIAN MASSES

After the Purification and the Nativity in the book's order, the concentration of these rubrics in the votive masses, beginning with the introit for Lady Mass in Advent, *Rorate caeli desuper* (no. 12), prompted Jackman to wonder whether

> what appears in the *Gradualia* as the third and fourth Masses *ought* to be the first and second, as Masses belonging to the Temporale, and beginning with the opening of the ecclesiastical year at Advent. Hence the appearance in these Masses of the explanatory matter, i.e., of the rubrics, is not only natural, but is further evidence of the liturgical thought behind the work. (30)

Tridentine Missals and Graduals do not support Jackman's view of the correct order, according to the usual arrangement of liturgical books on which this diagnosis is based; and votive masses, because of their special intention, are excluded from the Temporale, which represents the usual order of the day. Nor is Jackman convincing when he attempts to shift the blame to a notional editor or to the printer; Byrd must have been very closely involved in the printing of this as of all his published works. More persuasive on the order of the Marian music is Kerman at his most pragmatic, painting an attractively realistic picture of Byrd's progress from mass to mass, filling in gaps as the grand design neared completion.

> The order of publication may correspond by and large with the order of composition, which was not rearranged either because this order meant more to the composer than liturgical correctness, or because he did not wish to separate musical numbers that he thought of in conjunction. (251)

The demonstration of this is persuasive, though the tiny musical elaboration and adjustment to underlay in the medius of the doxology of the Nativity introit (no. 6, bars 55–59) compared with that of the Advent Lady Mass (no, 12, bars 50–54) of which it is otherwise a literal reprint, thinly suggests (but does not prove) that the latter was written first.

The order of Marian masses is the same in all contemporary editions of the *Graduale Romanum* and the Missal. First come the feasts by date (the Sanctorale matches the Temporale in starting at the beginning of Advent). Much later in the book—after the Common of Saints and other votive masses (such as those of the Holy Cross, the Angels and the Holy Ghost) and just before the occasional votive masses and the Mass of the Dead—occur the votive Masses of the Virgin Mary (set out in five temporal categories, not the three usual in Sarum books). This means that the Conception, on 8 December, is the first specifically Marian occasion in the book. As explained above, however, the chants for that feast have to be transferred from the Nativity in the Venetian Graduals, leaving the Purification as the first Marian feast with a full (but still not complete) quota of chants.

And it is with the Purification that Byrd evidently started.[11] He might then have written all the music for the feasts in the order they are presented in *Gradualia* (adding onto his curtailed Purification offertory to make the Annunciation gradual), or alternatively he might have turned to the votive mass cycle early on, completing the Nativity Mass by the addition of the alleluia verse, *Felix es sacra Virgo Maria* (no. 9). We cannot know why Byrd decided to place the Nativity and the votive masses in the middle of the complex before the Annunciation and Assumption. (They

would have fallen after these two feasts at the end if he had been following the Gradual literally.) He might have been trying to achieve the
method, expounded earlier, of turning backward rather than forward
whenever a transfer is needed. And perhaps rubrics first appear in the Advent votive Mass simply because their need first becomes seriously apparent there. Indeed, "Ave Maria: ut supra" at the end of no. 14 may reflect a last-minute realization on Byrd's own part of having made a
liturgical error in identifying the alleluia verse with the offertory; and the
other four rubrics may have followed as illustrations of general principles.

The *ut supra* theory, however, leaves a notable exception in the Purification offertory. Again, Byrd's general dependence on contemporary
editions of the *Graduale Romanum* suggests a plausible explanation for
the fact that the very first mass in *Gradualia* is incomplete and requires
one of the more awkward transfers in the book. All these Graduals print
under the feast the introit, gradual, alleluia, tract and communion only—
precisely those items which Byrd sets as nos. 1–5—and refer the user to
the Common of Virgins for the offertory *Diffusa est gratia.*[12]

Byrd's setting of this text, at the opening of no. 22, omits the concluding words "et in saeculum saeculi"; and this small error suggests that the
Gradual he was working from was one of the Giunta editions. When one
turns in any of them to folio 142v, the place specified for the offertory
transfer, one notices that the words missing from Byrd's setting are
printed at the top of the next page (fol. 143v) where he might easily have
overlooked them. The coincidence is almost too good to be true, but it
does indicate one way in which Byrd could mistakenly have decided to
allow the Annunciation gradual to do double duty as the Purification offertory. More important, Byrd's literal adherence to the Gradual in the
matter of the Purification transfer prompts one to wonder whether, after
all, he did not conceive the whole transfer plan independent of any individual mass. It is not beyond the bounds of imagination to envisage such
a tenacious and zealous composer setting out on a twenty-five-piece series, a scheme and a Gradual to hand, and simply writing away each night
until it was finished.

There are other reasons why the Purification might have been chosen to open the collection. Its words (unlike those of the Nativity) are biblical, and sensitivity on this matter caused the composer to omit words altogether from several nonbiblical Propers and antiphons of the six-part St. Peter music of book 2. Second, the feast was carried over into the Book of Common Prayer and its presence at the beginning might reassure the casual Anglican observer.[13] Third and most important, its climactic and musically extended statement—God's answer to the aged Simeon that he should not die unless he had seen the Christ (no. 5)—mixed personal vision with a symbolic message of hope for the English Catholic community under a Scottish monarch from whom much was expected on his arrival in England in 1603.

Context

It has become customary, following the methods of art history, to seek in music of this period features that can be attributed to the will of its patrons. The Earl of Northampton, dedicatee of book 1 of *Gradualia*, can have had little or nothing to do with the contents; yet Byrd took the opportunity of the dedicatory letter to such a learned man to make an articulate and revealing statement of his aesthetic position.

> For just as in the art of construction it would be base to fashion a rough work out of a very precious material, so too nothing surely will be fitting for the Sacred sentences in which are sung the praises of God himself and the Citizens of heaven except some heavenly harmony, to the extent that we can attain it. Moreover, in the very sentences (as I have learned from experience) there is such hidden and concealed power that to a man thinking about divine things and turning them over attentively and earnestly in his mind, the most appropriate measures come, I know not how, as if by their own free will, and freely offer themselves to his mind if it is neither idle nor inert.

Nearly all commentators quote only the second of these sentences, which is an undeniably moving statement from an aging composer about a universal phenomenon, the nature of the creative impulse. But without its preliminary rider it can be mistaken for the Romantic doctrine of inspiration. The first sentence addresses one of the primary aesthetic concerns of the period. In an expression reminiscent of the rhetoric books, Byrd emphasizes the need for high matters to be treated in high style, and expounds the doctrine of decorum central to Renaissance aesthetics. There is a logical difficulty, however, in the notion that only heavenly harmony will do, for the question is not to what degree (as in Byrd's qualifying clause) but how we may attain it. The second sentence, then, emphasizes the process by which the mortal mind may become receptive, by *divina cogitanti, diligenterque ac serio pervolutanti.* The emphasis here is, of course, not on the composer but on an *afflatus* coming wholly from without.

Byrd's sentiments seem to echo thoughts expressed in the preface to the Roman Catholic translation of the New Testament, published in Rheims in 1582, a book he would certainly have possessed and studied. We now know it as the third part of the Douay-Rheims Bible; the translation came out of the English College at Rheims, which later moved to Douay [now Douai], and was made under the supervision of William Allen, its president.[14] Explaining that the literalness of the translation from the Vulgate may seem "to common English ears not yet acquainted therewith, rudenesse or ignorance," the translators make the following appeal:

> but to the discrete Reader that deeply weigheth and considereth the importance of sacred wordes and speaches, and how easily the voluntarie [i.e., free] Translatour may misse the true sense of the Holy Ghost, we doubt not but our consideration and doing therein, shal seeme reasonable and necessarie.

And later,

> we presume not in hard places to mollifie the speaches or phrases, but religiously keepe them word for word, and point for point, for feare of missing, or restraining the sense of the holy Ghost to our phantasies.

It is this action to which Byrd refers in terms suspiciously like those employed in his Bible.

When setting sacred sentences earlier in his career for the motets published in 1589 and 1591, Byrd had been truly expansive, and had moreover freely adorned his work with illustration of the kind we call madrigalism, and rhetoricians of the time would have called *amplificatio.* This was high style with a vengeance, something Byrd did not apply to texts in the less elevated vernacular (except, in a modified way, to two compositions in honor of Queen Elizabeth—the first English madrigals to be published—for Thomas Watson's anthology of 1591, *Italian Madrigalls Englished*). The marked concentration of the musical style of *Gradualia* in comparison with that of these earlier motets is not simply to be explained by what one might call the late-period syndrome. Certainly Byrd's music grows richer in detail as he ages, but some pieces in *Gradualia* and the 1611 *Psalmes, Songs and Sonnets* (where finally there is some unbending toward the vernacular) show him to have been still enthusiastically capable of working on a large canvas with exuberant brush strokes. By and large, however, Byrd must have been responding in *Gradualia*, and especially in the portmanteau Marian section of book 1, to a different kind of decorum. The restraint comes from the liturgical context, surely, and is a response to the clarity and intelligibility urged upon composers by the reform of the Roman liturgy. What it emphatically does not include, of course, is self-effacement: these settings are every bit as rich in personality as the more extrovert works of the 1580s. From the moment in the early 1590s when Byrd began his settings of the Ordinary of the Mass, with their inspired amalgamation of Tridentine lucidity with a division of text based on that of the pre-Reformation English mass (a derivation highlighted by the reworking of musical ideas from the "Meane" Mass of Taverner), it is evident that the composer was working toward a personal solution of the problem of liturgical music, grounded in the old order, but purified and refreshed by the militant spirit of the Counter-Reformation (on the masses, see chapter 2).

However restrained and contemplative the music of *Gradualia* seems, then, it would be a mistake to underestimate the degree of militant sectarianism it represents. In this sense, the Rheims Bible offers more to those who would understand *Gradualia* than a model for its aesthetic theory.[15]

The translation was a child of its time, its aim not to have scripture read indifferently by all but to meet Protestant exegesis on its own ground and to keep Catholics in the faith. Its commentary reveals an understanding of certain scriptural passages, among them those set by Byrd in *Gradualia*, that would not be at all obvious to most modern listeners or readers. I am not referring to the passages concerning St. Peter in book 2, which of course prompt enormous marginal notes asserting the biblical authority for the primacy of the See of St. Peter. More unexpected is the allegorical interpretation of the psalms and other biblical passages occurring in the Marian music in a polemical manner which seems insupportable to the modern observer.[16] The very first line of *Gradualia*, "Suscepimus Deus misericordiam tuam in medio templi tui" (Psalm 47:10), for example, provokes the comment, "Grace and mercie is only granted to those that are within or come into the Catholique Church" (OT, 940); and the introit verse (from the same psalm), "Ierusalem, and mount Sion were most obliged to praise God, for greatest benefites received, so the Catholique Church therby prefigured, and having received farre greater, is most of al bonden to be gratful" (OT, 93). Psalm 44, the source of *Vultum tuum* and *Diffusa est gratia*, is characterized as "a mariage songue of the beloved bridegrome and bride: Christ and his Church" (OT, 78); the voluptuous sentiments of *Audi filia* signify that "Christ loveth the Church adorned with his giftes, and mutually his true children love and serve him" (OT, 89); and the verse *Adducentur Regi* prompts the politically suggestive statement, "By this means manie are converted to Christianitie: and one country inviteth and Draweth another" (OT, 90).

Finally, an extensive marginal note interprets the line "Optimam partem elegit" (Luke 10:43) as a debate on monastic life. Mary is preferred to Martha, the contemplative to the active life. The Protestants are castigated for having abandoned the religious of both sexes, "for there was never true religion without such vows and Votaries, and if there be none in their Whole Church that profess contemplation, or that vow anything at all to God voluntarily, neither in their bodies nor in their goods, God and the World know they have no Church or religion at al" (NT, 169). Byrd's setting (no. 25), the final piece in the Marian series and one of the most beautiful, can well be imagined as a tribute to the many people he must have known who had themselves chosen the best part, and had left the country to live out their lives in one of the several English religious houses in the Low Countries.

All Saints (a 5) *and Corpus Christi* (a 4)
ALL SAINTS

Three compositions form a nonliturgical zone between the Marian mass music which opens the five-part fascicle of *Gradualia* book 1 (1605) and the All Saints Propers which close the fascicle. Their presence ought not to be taken lightly, for they are an indication that although the collection is primarily liturgical, it also serves other purposes. Their tone seems calculated to reassure those familiar with the *Cantiones sacrae* of 1589 and 1591 that the composer's new project does not represent acquiescence or resignation to the political situation facing Roman Catholics in Protestant England. The opening twenty-five pieces covering the entire Marian liturgy constitute in themselves a mildly ideological gesture, since what Roman Catholics saw as the excellent prerogatives of Our Blessed Lady were one of the things which divided them from those "Heretickes which make her no better than other vulgar Women," to quote the commentary to Luke 1:28 in the Rheims Bible (NT, 138). The very first mass, moreover, with its emphasis on the fulfillment of God's promise to the aged Simeon in the context of purification, so suggestive of the aims of the English Roman Catholic mission in general and of the hopes of an aging recusant composer in particular, may have been equally encouraging—though its placement may also have been more an accident of Byrd's following the Gradual to hand rather than interpretive design.

GRADVALIA:

AC
CANTIONES SACRAE,

quinis, quaternis, trinifque
vocibus concinnatæ.

CONTRATENOR.

*Authore Gulielmo Byrd, Organista
Regio, Anglo.*

*Dulcia defectâ modulatur carmina linguâ
Cantator Cygnus funeris ipse sui.*   Martialis.
lib.13.Epigr

1605.

LONDINI,
Excudebat Thomas Este.

Figure 10.1. *Gradualia*, book 1, 1605. (Reproduced by kind permission of the
Dean and Chapter of York.)

GRADVALIA,

AC
CANTIONES SA-
cræ, quinis, quaternis, trinifque
vocibus concinnatæ.

LIB. PRIMVS.

Authore Gulielmo Byrde, *Organifta*
Regio, Anglo.

EDITIO Secunda, priore emendatior.

Dulcia defectâ modulatur carmina linguâ
Cantator Cygnus funeris ipfe fui.   Martialis.

SVPERIVS.

LONDINI,
Excudebat *H. L.* Impenfis RICARDI REDMERI,
Stella aurea in D. Pauli Cœmeterie.
1610.

Figure 10.2. *Gradualia*, book 1, 1610. (© The British Library Board. All Rights Reserved.)

GRADVALIA :

SEV

CANTIONVM SACRARVM

Quarum aliæ ad Quatuor, aliæ verò ad
Quinque et Sex voces editæ sunt.

Liber Secundus.

Authore Gulielmo Byrde, Organista
Regio, Anglo.

Musica Diuinos profert modulamine Cantus :
Iubilum in Ore, fauum in Corde, et in Aure melos.

BASSVS.

Excudebat Thomas Este Londini, ex assignatione
Gulielmi Barley. 1607.

Figure 10.3. *Gradualia*, book 2, 1607. (© The British Library Board. All Rights Reserved.)

GRADVALIA,

SEV

CANTIONVM SA-

crarum: quarum aliæ ad Quatuor, aliæ

verò ad Quinque & Sex voces editæ sunt.

LIB. SECVNDVS.

Authore Gulielmo Byrde, *Organifta Regio, Anglo.*

Ex Noua & accuratifsima eiufdem Authoris recognitione.

*Mufica Diuinos profert modulamine Cantus:
Iubilum in Ore, fauum in Corde, & in Aure melos.*

CANTVS Primus.

Excudebat H. L. Impenfis RICARDI REDMERI,
ad Infigne Stellæ aureæ in Diui Pauli
Cæmeterio. 1610.

Figure 10.4. *Gradualia*, book 2, 1610. (© The British Library Board. All Rights Reserved.)

The appearance of the All Saints Mass at the end of the fascicle, how-ever, is greater reason to look for allegorical meaning. For the recusant Roman Catholic community, still reeling under the increased persecu-tion of the later years of Elizabeth's reign, this feast was a celebration of its considerable number of martyrs.[17] For its Propers, Byrd abandons the contemplative, even-tempered mood of the Marian pieces: the brighter F fa ut key replaces D la re, a second soprano part (G2 clef) usurps the C4 tenor, and an almost reckless celebratory mood is engendered in the introit *Gaudeamus omnes* (no. 29), which opens ostinato-like in a way that suggests an ensemble containing three soprano parts.[18] The famous of-fertory *Justorum animae* (no. 31) avoids the elevated, static quality of Las-sus's well-known setting, which suggests that God and his saints are in heaven and all is right with the world, in favor of a searching mood typ-ified by the false relations that underscore the faulty vision of the unwise, and the bass's overshooting the dominant C for B♭ and then lingering on A just before the close of the piece.

Even more directly audible in Byrd's All Saints Mass, however, are two poignant moments in which simultaneous false relations splash across the texture of the music like bright white highlights on a rich painting. The first occurs in *Timete Dominum* (no. 30) where at bar 69 the tenor, on its only top B♭ in the piece, clashes wildly with the Superius's adjacent B♮ at the elaborate cadence on C depicting "onerati estis" (you who are bur-dened). The other is a veritable outbreak of C♮–C♯ simultaneities that cel-ebrate those "qui persecutionem patiuntur propter justitiam" (those who suffer persecution for the sake of justice) at the conclusion of the com-munion *Beati mundo corde* (no. 32). A musically sentient person of Byrd's circle could hardly fail to make a connection between these moments and the sufferings of the many Jesuits and seminary priests who had indeed carried a great burden and had been hunted down and often put to death at the hands of an exasperated government.

The three pieces that occur between the Marian and the All Saints music have already been mentioned. They lend substance to the militant outlook more discreetly indicated in the liturgical items themselves. Two of them can be directly related to the political genre familiar from the *Cantiones sacrae*. A note on the text of *Unam petii* (no. 27) in the Rheims Bible, Psalm 16:4, exclaims, "How special a benefite David esteemed it to be in the Catholique Church the only true house of God!" (OT, 56). Byrd enters into the spirit of wishful thinking indicated by so disarming an anachronism. His setting, cast in the same clefs as the All Saints music and in a similar key, C fa ut, ends with the two sopranos soaring at the height of the texture on an expressive melisma depicting the words "templum ejus": this brightly affirmative piece represents the idea of a converted England as a radiant possibility rather than a faint hope.

Plorans plorabit (no. 28) portrays the reverse side of the coin, dwelling on the actual condition of "the captive flock" in a motet that looks back to the Lamentations settings of White and Tallis, as well as to Byrd's own setting of those gloomy texts. Cast in the lowest set of clefs in *Gradualia* (elsewhere the C1 clef rather than the C3 clef is doubled), it is also one of only three pieces in the G la re key (with two flats) in the collection. The low clefs isolate the soprano as effectively as the legislation of the 1580s and 1590s was meant to isolate the Jesuits, seminary priests and those who harbored them. And the harmonic palette is so rich that though in some ways it recalls the 1570s, it also suggests—by means of an unusual concentration of expressive suspensions and such gestures as the move to a 6-3 or 6-5 chord over a raised bass note (bars 18, 73, 77 and 83)—an atmosphere that is positively baroque. The air of magnificent bleakness turns in the second half to one of political suggestiveness. The threats of the prophet Jeremiah against the occupants of David's throne are surely directed toward a Stuart king and his wife whose people had also turned from "the true religion," and who had also in 1605 begun to forfeit the trust of the Catholic minority, who had hoped for too much from them.[19]

Adoramus te Christe (no. 26) may seem out of place in this context. Not even a fully vocal setting, it is a solo song with instrumental accompaniment on a text consisting of the versicle and response at the Office of the Holy Cross, one of the "little offices" which occur in the Book of Hours, or Primer as it was called in England. A mechanistic bibliographical view would interpret its introduction as a means of filling up the space left on ¹E4r by *Optimam partem elegit*, the communion of the Annunciation. More likely it too had a symbolic purpose. The Holy Cross was "a particularly English devotion recalling St. Helena who, it is said, discovered the remains of the True Cross."[20] And as if to emphasize the native tradition, Byrd adopts the consort-song form he derived from his English predecessors. More than that, he took the motif for "redemisti mundum" from Tallis's *Sancte Deus* (where it occurs to the very same words at the end of the piece) and—unusual in his songs but more common in the looser technique of his predecessors—spread it about the whole setting; in the opening bars it functions as a countersubject to the main motif, occurring regularly each bar and alternating between entries on G and D. We may recall that in the masses Byrd alludes in a similarly self-conscious way to his English heritage by quoting and reworking motifs from Taverner's "Meane" Mass (see chapter 2). This perfect musical miniature, set like a Hilliard portrait in an imposing frame, turns our attention momentarily away from the Roman liturgy to the devotional and musical traditions of those to whom *Gradualia* was directed. Together with the motets of hope and grief that follow, it shows Byrd addressing the concerns of his own community with imagination and sensitivity.

"Adoramus te Christe" was one of the texts that Henry Garnet, superior of the English province of the Society of Jesus, recited immediately before he died on the scaffold at St. Paul's churchyard on 3 May 1606 for his alleged implication in the Gunpowder Plot. It happened to be the feast of the Invention of the Holy Cross. Twenty years earlier, in early July 1586, when Garnet slipped into England with his fellow Jesuit Robert Southwell, Byrd was among those who gathered to welcome him at Hurleyford, the house of a certain Richard Bold. William Weston, the Jesuit propagandist who reported the occasion, noted that the place

> had a chapel for the celebration of the Divine Mysteries, an organ
> likewise and other musical instruments, and, moreover, singers of

both sexes belonging to the family, the master of the house being singularly experienced in the art. Thus during the course of those days we celebrated, as it were, a long octave of some magnificent festival.[21]

Since in the next breath Weston makes the outrageous claim that for his religion Byrd had "sacrificed everything, both his office and the Court," there is reason to be cautious about such an account; but it indicates a context in which *Gradualia* and the masses would have been both needed and appreciated. Southwell, writing about the same visit to the Jesuit general Claude Acquaviva, corroborates the musical details, and indicates that an actual feast was to be observed:

> If all had fallen out according to our pleasure, we should have sung Mass with all solemnity, accompanied by choice instrumental and vocal music, on the very feast of St. Mary Magdalen [22 July]. This however was put off to the next day, and I could not spend it there, being called elsewhere.[22]

Garnet himself, who sometimes refers in his letters to singing Mass, was known for his "exquisite knowledge in the arte of musicke."[23] Byrd was making music in Garnet's company again in early 1605 when a certain Charles de Ligny, a man from Cambrai, observed them both at a house somewhere near London—White Webbs, Garnet's headquarters two miles north of Enfield in Middlesex and about fifteen miles west of Stondon Massey, Byrd's home.[24] It is likely that they met many times in the intervening years and that Garnet had some influence on Byrd's great liturgical design.

CORPUS CHRISTI

The choice of the Corpus Christ Propers ([4]nos. 1–4) to open the four-part fascicle of book 1 of *Gradualia* is perhaps an indication of this influence. (The book contains three fascicles, for five-, four- and three-part music. After 32 numbers in the first fascicle, numeration starts again from [4]1–20 in the next, and again from [3]1–11 in the next. In book 2 all the music in four, five and six parts is numbered consecutively from 1–46. In the present discussion, superscript numbers are added to specify references in book 1 where necessary.) The feast was traditionally important and marked by outdoor processions as well as a festival of mirth in pre-Reformation England. Robert Persons, who along with the other Jesuits was anxious to curtail the excessive feasting and fasting characteristic of English Catholicism, was ready to stomach a complete restoration of everything connected with Corpus Christi "with all solemnity of honoring that Divine Sacrament, which our Heretickes have sought so much to dishonour."[25]

The appearance, for the first time in Byrd's collection, of office antiphons, hymns and purely devotional texts (such as *Ave verum corpus*) is suggestive of the importance a contemporary Roman Catholic, especially one attuned to Counter-Reformation thinking, would have attached to the feast and the Sacrament on account of doctrinal differences with Protestantism. And the unannounced inclusion in book 2 of music for the votive Mass of the Blessed Sacrament leaves little room for doubt that Byrd had Jesuit views in mind. This mass became a prime ingredient of the Forty Hours Devotion, which was first heard of in Milan in the 1530s, adopted by St. Philip Neri with the support of Loyola himself and furthered by none other than Clement VIII, the Jesuit who was pope in 1605. Many Catholics thought that adoration of the Sacrament was undesirable; the Jansenists thought it idolatrous; but the Jesuits encouraged it as "the sign of a warlike confession of faith" and promoted it actively.[26] It is tempting to speculate that Byrd composed this votive mass, the Corpus Christi antiphons and also the Litany of Saints in book 1 for some Jesuit enactment of the Forty Hours—there was certainly enough reason to conduct such a special devotion on behalf of the missionary priests and their congregations in the early years of the seventeenth century.

There is a well-known record of a celebration with music of Corpus Christi itself in 1605, shortly after the publication of *Gradualia* book 1, and shortly before Garnet's capture. Writing on 24 June to an English nun at St. Ursula's convent in Louvain, the Jesuit superior reports:

besides the general affliction, we find ourselves now betrayed in both our places of abode and are forced to wander up and down until we get a fit place. . . . We kept Corpus Christi day [30 May] with great solemnity and music, and the day of the octave [6 June] made a solemn procession about a great garden, the house being watched, which we knew not till the next day when we departed twenty-five in the sight of all, in several parties, leaving half a dozen servants behind and all is well.[27]

It has been conjectured that the house, which Garnet does not name, was the home of Sir John Tyrrel at Fremland.[28] Since this is merely eleven miles from Stondon Massey, just beyond the Petre house at Ingatestone, it is tempting to think Byrd may have been present, as he was on the occasion in the same year that Charles de Ligny described.

The Corpus Christi Propers are written in the G sol ut key which seems to encourage Byrd's most melodious streak. The beautifully balanced phrases of the introit *Cibavit eos* (4no. 1), with its deftly managed alleluias, set a warm, even-tempered mood, intensifying into fervency, that is maintained throughout. There is none of the tension of the All Saints Mass here—a mild false relation at the beginning of the final alleluia hints at the consequences of taking the Sacrament unworthily, but the spirit is always one of confidence and devotion. It is one of the most attractive and satisfying of Byrd's works.

Though in book 2 Byrd included settings of sequences for Easter, *Victimae Paschali laudes*, and Pentecost, *Veni Sancte Spiritus*, he did not attempt to set the Corpus Christi sequence *Lauda Sion*, which with twelve stanzas is over twice as long as either of the others. The final alleluia in *Oculi omnium* (no. 2) is, however, preceded by a signum and barline so that the sequence may be sung in its correct position after the alleluia verse, *Caro mea*, and before the final alleluia.

The companion settings to the Corpus Christi Mass include the Magnificat antiphon for Second Vespers, *O sacrum convivium* (4no. 7), which also functions as a processional antiphon at the feast. Byrd provides a detachable alleluia presumably so that the piece can be used as a devotional motet at any celebration of Mass or Exposition of the Sacrament. The hymn *Pange lingua gloriosi* (no. 8) is another text prescribed for the procession (and for Second Vespers), and it also forms part of the Forty Hours Prayer. Byrd's setting suggests a modified form of antiphonal performance, with stanzas 1, 3 and 6 chanted and stanzas 2, 4, 5 and the Amen sung to the polyphony. A small fragment of the chant is alluded to by the tenor at the opening of stanza 2, and progressively shorter fragments by the soprano in the two other polyphonic stanzas— enough to indicate the right chant, not enough to involve the composer in cantus firmus composition, which he avoids throughout *Gradualia* except in two other instances (both in the same section of book 1). Setting the fifth rather than the sixth stanza meant that Byrd had on hand a setting of the *Tantum ergo*, often used on its own as a hymn of veneration to the Sacrament. *O salutaris hostia* (no. 6) is also an excerpt of a hymn commonly used at the Exposition of the Blessed Sacrament: it is the fifth stanza of Thomas Aquinas's six-stanza *Verbum supernum prodiens*, which is the hymn at Lauds on the feast of Corpus Christi.

Ave verum corpus (no. 5) is a text also associated with the Exposition of the Sacrament; furthermore, it had been recited by the faithful at the consecration during Mass in England from medieval times. Byrd's famous setting, however, ends with the personal invocation "miserere mei," lacking elsewhere (cf. the version at p. 1856 of the *Liber Usualis*). Its source was the Primer or *Officium Beatae Mariae Virginis*, the typical (i.e., authorized) edition of which was issued in Rome in 1571, following on the revision of the Breviary in 1568. In this book it forms part of the "daily exercise," and in Richard Verstegan's translation of 1599 (STC 16094) it is labeled "Unto the holy Sacrament of the Eucharist, A prayer." Byrd's highly personal, almost subjective setting is one of the few pieces of *Gradualia* to adopt the G la re key (*Plorans plorabit* is another). It marks a decisive turn from the hieratic mood of the Corpus Christi Propers into a devotional world where, for one rare instance in the composer's works, syntax overrules strict adherence to verse form in the setting of the first two lines, where Byrd also makes an important doctrinal point by placing declamatory stress not on "corpus" but on "verum" and intensifying the word even further by means of a cross relation.[29] Not surprisingly, the manuscript evidence suggests that the piece existed and circulated in an earlier state. For Byrd to take it out and revise it for publication shows that he not only esteemed it musically but also recognized the importance of the personal style of devotion which it represented and which was such a notable survival of medieval custom in recusant spiritual life.[30]

From this point in book 1 of *Gradualia*, it is the devotional, semiliturgical aspects of Roman Catholicism in general, and the Primer texts in particular, that push aside the liturgy itself. To the extent that this material compromises the ideal order that the collection encourages us to imagine (as it was intended to encourage Byrd's co-religionists), it reflects the complex reality of recusant worship.

Music for Private Devotions (a 3, a 4): *The Primer*

The remaining contents of book 1 of *Gradualia* correspond to the second half of its extended title, *Gradualia ac Cantiones sacrae*. Except for a single piece ([3]no. 8), they are not "graduals" or Propers of the Mass. They reflect instead a characteristic of Roman Catholicism in Byrd's England that has been the subject of as much comment as its liturgy: the intensity and all-embracing quality of its devotional life. Even a revisionist historian like Christopher Haigh, who minimizes the effect of Counter-Reformation ideals and emphasizes the continuity of English Catholicism, admits that "among the Babthorpes at Osgodby, the Montagues at Battle and the Wisemans at Braddocks, in Dorothy Lawson's house near Newcastle and in the partnership of John Mush and Margaret Clitheroe at York, there was an intense religious life which contrasts sharply with the superstitious magic of the pre-Reformation villages."[31] We may take as an example the Lady Magdalen Montague, whose biography was written by her confessor. The account of her chapel and its choir, where Mass was celebrated on solemn feasts "with singing and musical instruments"[32] (and also, apparently, a surfeit of priests) is well known. It is in just such circumstances that *Gradualia*

Propers might have been sung, though Lady Montague appears to have had no direct connection with Byrd.[33]

As important as the public worship she enabled, however, is the intense spiritual life she maintained:

> In her private devotions she did every day say three offices, that is of the Blessed Virgin, of the Holy Ghost, and of the Holy Cross, whereto she added at least three rosaries, the Jesus Psalter, the fifteen prayers of St. Brigit, . . . and the common litanies, and, finally, sometimes the Office of the Dead. Which prayers, when in her infirmity she could not say herself, she procured to be said by others, distributing to every one a part.[34]

The principal book which Lady Magdalen and her retainers and friends would have needed for this mortifying round of spiritual observance was the *Officium Beatae Mariae*. Of the various books of prayer and devotion, such as the Manual and the Jesus Psalter, the Primer had the highest status.[35] It generally contained the Offices of the Virgin Mary, the Holy Ghost and Holy Cross, the Litany of Saints, the fifteen gradual psalms, the Office for the Dead, the commendations of souls, a daily exercise and many other prayers for different purposes, the biblical Passion stories, hymns for the whole year, Vespers antiphons, as well as some informational elements such as the calendar, and an introduction to the Christian faith. The (Little) Office of the Virgin Mary which was its first and principal element and from which its Latin title was derived, consisted of the full complement of Hours: Matins, Lauds, Prime, Terce, Sext, None, Vespers and Compline.[36] The book, then, was a sort of substitute for the Breviary, and is "witness to the desire of the laity to have a form of devotion that was comparable to the Divine Office of the priest and was parallel to it."[37]

The Primer was not a new feature of Elizabethan Catholicism, for the book had been immensely popular in pre-Reformation times. Hoskins lists sixty-three Latin editions of the Sarum or York Primer, and a further twenty-six in English and Latin or English alone, and gives useful summaries of their contents.[38] Its status in Catholic devotion in general is indicated by the speed with which its revision followed that of the Breviary (1568) in the general revision of the liturgy that followed the Council of Trent. A typical (i.e., authorized) edition was issued in Rome in 1571. The need for an English translation of this official Roman Primer is mentioned by the two organizers of the English mission, Robert Persons and William Allen, in 1580. This was accomplished by the poet, Catholic propagandist and publisher Richard Verstegan. Published abroad in 1599, it proved a staple of Catholic worship, running into over forty editions between then and 1800.[39]

Some further idea of the importance of the Primer can be gained by its appearance in court cases and in lists of confiscated books. When Henry Norwich, a Northamptonshire man who informed against Catholics, brought his nephews Edward and Simon before the Star Chamber in 1578, along with Sir Thomas Tresham and servants of Lord Mordaunt, he accused Simon of importing bulls, pardons and other superstitious devices, of supporting a popish scholar at Louvain, and of using *Officium Beatae Mariae Virginis* and a Latin bible.[40] A list of books confiscated from Tresham's house at Hoxton, possibly during the raid of 1584, includes "*A little Prymer . . . Hymni et Collecte Latine* 16 . . . *A prymer English and Latin* 4 [and] *Foure Latine Prymers.*"[41] Part of the importance of the Primer for the Roman Catholic household was that it enabled the laity to maintain religious observances in the all too frequent absence of a priest. As Robert Persons put it, in those circumstances, "when no publick [office] can be said . . . at least wise the Service of our Lady may be said by some one or other" (85).

The step in *Gradualia* from public to private, from the Gradual to the Primer, is first taken with a particularly significant piece, *Ave verum corpus* (4no. 5). In its personal form with the supplication "miserere mei" (rather than "miserere nostri" of the Breviary), this eucharistic prayer is part of the "Dayly Exercise." The text of *Visita quaesumus* (4no. 11) is also found in this section of the Primer, and its single difference from the version in the Breviary, where it is the Compline prayer, hints that the Primer was its source; the contemporary Breviary omits "Christum" from the final petition of its version of *Visita quaesumus,* which is therefore much more concise than that of the modern service books quoted by Kerman (322n). Set in the bright C fa ut key of *Unam petii a Domino* (⁵no. 27), it also shares with that piece the same set of clefs from which the lowest part (in the F3 clef) has been as it were subtracted to produce a specially brilliant effect employed nowhere else in *Gradualia.* Like *Ave verum corpus* its phrases begin in homophonic style, but then open out in concise counterpoint. The difference in style may partly be owing to the fact that this is a prose not a verse text, and partly to an evident need to keep the effect untouched by the darker moods that tend to overtake settings in *Gradualia.* One might hear it as a prayer of thanks for protection during the night rather than the more usual supplication for deliverance from danger or oppression.

Another text which delineates the difference between the Breviary and Primer more dramatically is that of *Post dies octo* (³no. 9). Working from the Breviary, where the composite text appears as part of Vespers on Low Sunday, Kerman could write, "oddly, in Byrd's piece the *Magnificat* antiphon *Post dies octo* is *followed* by the versicle and response which *precede* it in the service ('Mane nobiscum Domine, alleluia. Quoniam advesperascit, alleluia')" (332). The two texts appear in the order Byrd set them in an appendix to the Primer entitled "Orationes Dominicales et Feriales, cum suis Antiphonis & Versiculis per Annum"—"The Prayers on Sondays and other dayes with their Antiphonaes and Versicles throught the year" in Verstegan's translation.

If the presence in *Gradualia* book 1 of extraliturgical devotion in general and the Primer in particular is indicated by these two pieces, *Visita quaesumus* and *Post dies octo,* then we might not be wrong to see the Primer as the source for other texts that are shared with either the Missal or Breviary. A most important group of these are the hymns from the Office of the Blessed Virgin Mary, the first and chief ingredient of the Primer. *Quem terra pontus* (³no. 1) is the hymn for Matins, *O gloriosa Domina* (no. 2) the hymn for Lauds, *Memento salutis auctor* (no. 3) the hymn for Prime, the little hours and Compline, and *Ave maris stella* (no. 4) the

Vespers hymn.[42] The concise style and quarter-note movement of the first three emphasize Byrd's sensitivity to decorum in setting pieces for these lesser offices in a vein far less ambitious and even more terse than that of any of the Mass Propers. *Ave maris stella*, as we might expect, gains a rather more expansive treatment, possibly because all or some of it was composed at an earlier date, or simply because it figures in a major service. The exchange of clefs (and therefore extension of range) in the middle voice in the fifth stanza is an extraordinary and puzzling feature which occurs again in *Gradualia* book 2 in the Christmas Propers, but only between pieces, not within them.

As advertised in Byrd's preliminary note, "the more solemn antiphons of the same Blessed Virgin," those sung at the end of Compline, are included in this last area of the book. They are divided, however, among the three- and four-part sections. The antiphon for the Paschal season, *Regina caeli* ([3]no. 5), occurs right after the three-part office hymns and serves as a kind of musical climax to them: the shapely text, articulated by four instances of Byrd's favorite acclamation, "alleluia," evidently challenged him to produce an elegant and expansive piece which even outlasts the four-part antiphons with their much longer texts. Indeed, the degree of compression Byrd achieved in *Salve Regina* ([4]no. 4) and *Alma redemptoris mater* (no. 5) can be gathered by comparing them to the setting of *Salve Regina* which occurs in the 1591 *Cantiones sacrae*.[43]

It is of course too easy to fall into the trap of interpreting the condensed style and pithy rhetoric of *Gradualia* as a "late-period" phenomenon, when it may simply be an expression of Byrd's sense of decorum. The "sacred songs" of the 1589 and 1591 collections are what Morley calls motets, compositions in the high style; whereas those of *Gradualia* are clearly written with their function, either in the liturgy or in communal devotion, foremost in the composer's mind; if so, their chronology is uncertain, for they could belong to any part of Byrd's maturity. In the case of the Marian antiphon *Ave Regina caelorum* (no. 6), however, a date of composition close to that of publication is indicated by the state of the text.[44] In the wake of revisions to the Vulgate in 1592, Pope Clement VIII caused a revised Breviary to be issued in 1602 and a revised Missal in 1604. In almost all instances where there is any difference at all in the texts, *Gradualia* settings are of the earlier version of Pius V, not that of Clement VIII (cases in point are *Felix es sacra Virgo Maria*, the Alleluia verse for Mass at the Nativity of the Virgin, the All Saints offertory, *Justorum animae*, and *Unam petii a Domino*). The considerable differences in text of *Ave Regina caelorum*, however, show that it was copied from the later Breviary, and thus the setting cannot have been written before 1602. It is a remarkable composition, standing apart from the other Marian antiphons; perhaps Byrd was particularly anxious to produce a striking setting to make up for his rather characterless six-part *Ave Regina* from an earlier period, found only in manuscript sources.[45]

Marian devotion was clearly important to Byrd, who endeavored, as we know, to provide for the entire Marian liturgy in the opening twenty-five numbers of his collection. It was, indeed, important to the recusant community as a whole.[46] It is no surprise, therefore, to find among this last section of *Gradualia* book 1 a number of other pieces devoted to the Virgin. The idea of including the Magnificat antiphons of the Purification must have occurred to Byrd after having planned and completed the five-part mass music. Though the running head in the print does not mention the feast, it does indicate that *Senex puerum portabat* (no. 18) is for first Vespers and *Hodie beata Virgo Maria* (no. 19) for second Vespers. In musical style, moreover, these pieces shun the exuberance of the four-part Compline antiphons for the contemplative, even ruminative manner of the Marian masses—again a matter of decorum and sense of occasion, perhaps, rather than the date they were composed.

There is yet another piece for the feast of the Purification, happily added as an afterthought to fill up the extra half sheet of paper needed because the two-page index exceeded merely by one page what would otherwise have been the last gathering in the Superius, Tenor and Bassus books of the original print. Another composer might have responded to these technical difficulties by cutting something. Quite apart from a characteristic streak of stubbornness, however, Byrd may not have become aware of the situation until printing was well advanced, and he would have had good reason not to sacrifice any of the Easter pieces in the last gathering, as we shall see. The added piece, *Adorna thalamum tuum Sion* (^{3}no. 11), is an antiphon for the Procession of the Blessing of Candles—the event for which the Purification became known as Candlemas. We have already mentioned the report of a group of Jesuits performing the Corpus Christi procession in 1605 round the garden of a house, one that was probably not too far from Byrd's village. Candlemas, in damp February, would have taken place entirely indoors, and would no doubt have been celebrated with special warmth in recusant households, where the cycle of feasting and fasting was fervently maintained. Byrd's setting, an elegant example of his restrained liturgical manner, would have added its own luminosity to such an occasion.

The remaining Marian music is a mixture of devotional pieces designed for a variety of occasions. *In manus tuas Domine* (^{4}no. 15) is the well-known Compline verse to which has been attached an invocation to the Virgin. This composite text is strung beneath the notes of what was first conceived as a four-part instrumental fantasy.[47] Only one voice of the original has survived, but it is enough to show the sort of adjustments made for the words, adjustments which are similar to, though perhaps a bit more radical than, those made to instrumental lines of consort songs for their publication as part songs in the collections of 1588 and 1589. The Marian invocation coincides with a homophonic section (beginning at bar 35) in which the three melodies supporting the rest of the piece are first heard simultaneously. This is characteristic of several fantasias, consort or keyboard; yet highly unusual in Byrd's vocal music is the fairly haphazard distribution of the two verbal phrases, "Sancta Maria, mater Dei" and "ora pro nobis," between the three musical ideas. The general effect, however, is of that lovely, tuneful, easy manner so beautifully projected in the Corpus Christi introit, which is in the same key.

Compared to *In manus tuas Domine*, *Salve sola Dei genitrix* (no. 17) appears a darker and more rhetorically inclined cousin. In G, but with two flats (the same key as *Plorans plorabit* and *Ave verum corpus*), it turns dramatic for the final invocation concerned with death, which provokes expressive pauses and declamatory rhythms. This is an unusual piece most likely composed near the date of publication, and possibly for the same singers as *Visita quaesumus*, for its voices are disposed similarly.

Sandwiched between *In manus tuas Domine* and *Salve sola Dei genitrix* in the Marian heartland of the four-part fascicle occurs the Litany of Saints (no. 16). A feature of the Tridentine Primer, where it is directed to be said kneeling after reciting the seven penitential psalms, and almost every other Roman Catholic devotional book, as well as the Missal, Processional and Breviary, the litany had a multitude of purposes. One use, suggested by the context, is in Marian devotions. Another, suggested by the presence of a large number of eucharistic texts earlier in the fascicle, is for the Exposition of the Sacrament or the Forty Hours Devotion, mentioned above (pages 154–56; see also pages 174–77). The piece alternates chanting with polyphony, and what is puzzling about Byrd's setting is that the cantus firmus, easily identifiable in his polyphonic segments, is not exactly like any of the several versions of the chant found in the many contemporary liturgical books of all kinds that I have consulted, including the Sarum Graduals and Processionals as well as their Roman counterparts.

Close in function to the litany, but rather more expansive in its setting, is the response *Deo gratias* (no. 20). This is not based on chant and can be sung on any occasion, such as the end of Vespers, following the acclamation "Benedicamus Domino." A similarly unattached piece is the psalm motet *Ecce quam bonum* (no. 9), which has no liturgical or paraliturgical function. Calls for unity must have been needed among the recusant communities and their leaders from time to time: the annotations to the psalm (Psalm 132) in the Rheims Bible make this clear, and also take the opportunity to capitalize on the metaphor of hierarchy implicit in Aaron's anointment, "who being head of the Church, unity and concord descended from him to other priests, and so to the people, even to the lowest and meanest in God's Church" (OT, 245). Byrd's gently sententious setting is calculated to put a glow around every aspect of the text, from the persuasively inviting motive for "habitare fratres in unum" even down to the ample expanses allowed for the portrayal of Aaron's beard. The divine command, when it manifests itself toward the end in telling homophony, is also gently bestowed rather than laid down in this splendid work.

Holy Week and the Easter Season (a 3)

The final category in Byrd's own description of the contents of *Gradualia* book 1 consists of "various songs for three voices set appropriately for the feast of Easter." We have already met one of these pieces, *Post dies octo* (³no. 9), as a fugitive text from the Primer. This immediately suggests a similar derivation for *Haec dies* (no. 7), which may be the verse of the Easter antiphon to which Byrd has simply attached an alleluia—the words are not found anywhere in the contemporary service books in exactly the form Byrd presents them. *Alleluia. Vespere autem Sabbathi* (no. 6) was another less than obvious choice, for it consists of the two antiphons from the tiny truncated Vespers service incorporated in the special service on Easter Saturday, the Paschal Vigil. Because the setting of the second antiphon does not include its intonation, the implication is that this and the psalm verses should be supplied from the chant books. *Angelus Domini descendit* (no. 8) is the only straightforward text of all the pieces in this group: it is the offertory for Easter Monday and Low Sunday.

On the face of it the choice of these Easter texts seems rather arbitrary, and their presence as settings therefore the result of a search in Byrd's portfolio for suitable unpublished material. But it appears more likely that, owing to their common key, common clefs and shared motives in (at least) the alleluia sections, these four pieces were conceived as a set.[48] The rationale behind the choice of texts appears to be based on chronological sequence: the dawn of the first day of Easter week; the day itself ("*haec* dies"); the angel's response to the women who are the subject of the first piece; and the octave of Easter, ending with its evening, and the clinching plea for Christ to "remain with us." There may even be a doctrinal point in the composer's mind which links Christ's resurrection (and birth) with the miracle of his arrival in a closed room: in the words once again of the Rheims annotators, "such Heretikes as deny Christs body to be, or that it can be in the B. Sacrament, for that it is in heaven . . . be invincibly refuted by Christs entering into the Disciples, the doores shut; and by that that his true natural body . . . was in the same proper place that the wood was in, and passed through the same; as he also came out of his mothers Wombe, the clausure not stirred: and passed through the stone, out of his Sepulcher" (NT, 275–76). The various annotations on John 20:26, elaborating this main point, are unusually extensive.

The two remaining pieces in the volume, *Christus resurgens* ([4]no. 2) and the Passion according to St. John (*Turbarum voces in passione Domini secundum Ioannem:* [3]no. 10) are also both for Easter or Holy Week. They throw into relief a question that has not so far been raised in any detail—the relation of Byrd's music in *Gradualia* to the chant of the liturgical books he consulted for his texts. Discussing the transfer system that originated with the Marian masses, I pointed out that Byrd was able to extend it further than the Gradual on which it was modeled because he ignored the chant and was therefore able to use the same music whenever the same text occurred, whether or not it was associated with different chants in the liturgical books. If Byrd's setting of the Propers stand notably aloof from the chant—an initial allusion in the Christmas introit, *Puer natus est,* seems to be an exception—he evidently invited the participation of chant in certain traditional circumstances. No doubt daunted by the eighty lines of verse which constitute the Corpus Christi sequence, Byrd slapped a *signum congruentiae* over the final notes of the alleluia verse cadence (in [4]no. 2) in the expectation (surely) that *Lauda Sion* would be chanted before the singers took up his final alleluia. In his setting of the Corpus Christi hymn, *Pange lingua gloriosi,* Byrd cheated on the *alternatim* scheme in order to make sure of providing a setting of the important stanza *Tantum ergo,* which could be used on its own in devotions to the Sacrament. The expectation here must also have been that chant would fill in the gaps: once again a *signum* and barline provide for the insertion of the sixth stanza in chant between *Tantum ergo* and the Amen; and furthermore, the openings of the polyphonic verses make fleeting allusions to the chant as if to encourage the performer to choose the right tune. *Alleluia. Vespere autem Sabbathi* ([3]no. 6), as we have seen, invites the insertion of chant and again appears to make a shadowy allusion to it. The litany ([4]no. 16) is predicated on chant participation.

These are slim pickings in the professedly liturgical collection of a composer brought up to sing plainchant in church and to write cantus firmus compositions in his music lessons, a method of training that he put his own students through, to judge from Thomas Morley's singing and composition treatise. Yet there is in *Gradualia* a single link with that old tradition, a deliberate reference to a distant past in Byrd's own as in the nation's life. It is the setting of the Easter processional antiphon, *Christus resurgens* ([4]no. 10). The text suited *Gradualia* because it shares the same function in both Sarum and Roman uses. Byrd's setting, however, or at least its first part, is written in an archaic style with the Sarum chant (which is different from the Roman) disposed as a cantus firmus in the traditional whole-note style much practiced by Byrd's immediate predecessors in their ritual polyphony.

Byrd drew his version of the cantus firmus not from the manuscript tradition, as Kerman assumed, but from the printed Sarum Processional, whose various editions often exhibit small variants.[49] These variant readings show that Byrd was not responsible for the "two errors in the cantus firmus" which "never occur in genuine liturgical items" (Kerman 81, 62–63); the composer, it turns out, was not fudging, he merely lacked bibliographical discrimination. Since the "errors" are not found in the earlier chant sources, the piece cannot have been written before 1558. Everything points to its having been conceived in Byrd's late teens in the spirit of a technical exercise, as Kerman proposes; and all the reasons he adduces for a later dating for the *secunda pars* are convincing. Perhaps the piece was refurbished for *Gradualia:* this would explain both why the cantus firmus is abandoned in the *secunda pars* and why the two allusions there to the Sarum tune are made in the same manner as the other references to chant in the collection. If Byrd did rewrite the second part for publication, however, it is amazing he let slip the opportunity to sweeten the alleluia refrain, its opening a candidate for the sourest passage he ever allowed into print.

This one problematic concession to old Sarum in the whole of *Gradualia* raises its own issue. In the masses of the 1590s, Byrd was at pains to emphasize (even to create) his English Catholic lineage by means of the structural frame of his settings, and more especially by a series of quotations from Taverner's "Meane" Mass, the chief of which is a critical reworking of the opening of Taverner's Sanctus in the Four-Part Mass. Whereas the symbolism of old Catholicism purified by reformed zeal is not hard to extract from such a situation, the thought behind the inclusion of *Christus resurgens* is harder to discern. To conclude that it has no meaning at all is, in view of the careful arrangement of the rest of the collection, scarcely an option. Perhaps, placed next to *Ecce quam bonum*, a psalm motet, a genre also cultivated by Byrd's immediate predecessors, it constitutes simply one part of a twofold gesture or reference to the past. *Visita quaesumus*, which follows, seems almost self-consciously to reestablish Byrd's most contemporary mode of musical thought.

And it may not be going too far to suggest that the distancing of the polyphony from the chant that is so notable a feature of *Gradualia* is in itself connected with what Byrd understood to be reformed Catholicism. Did he understand something of the process of attrition and corruption whereby, for example, the responsibly edited chant of the first Gradual printed by the Giunta family in Venice in 1500 degenerated into the minimalist melodies of their late sixteenth-century editions? Did he know of the concerns in Rome which were leading to a musical revision of the Gradual by Palestrina and Zoilo in the wake of its liturgical renovation under Pius V—the results of which would not be available until the Medicean edition of 1614? Was literal quotation of the chant in whole notes within polyphony judged by Byrd, and possibly by his musical Jesuit friends, to be an unworthy remnant of a more talismanic era, to be replaced by intelligent and critical allusion in the new and purified Catholicism of the seventeenth century?

In the light of these questions the remaining piece, the St. John Passion (³no. 10), takes on special interest. Coming at the end of the Easter pieces, with which it shares clefs, key and even some music,[50] this would have been the last item of the collection had not the exigencies of printing urged the addition of the Candlemas processional antiphon, as discussed above. Polyphonic choruses such as these are of course dependent for their effect and meaning on their context in the recitation of the Passion in special tones pitched at three levels, one at middle range for the actual narration, that is, the voice of the Evangelist, one in a lower range for the words of Christ, and one pitched higher for the words of all the other characters—the crowd, Peter, Pilate, the maidservant, centurion and so on. Many versions of the "Passion tones" exist, as Bruno Stäblein's article in *Die Musik in Geschichte und Gegenwart* ably demonstrates without exhausting the possibilities. Byrd could have gained access to a number of them, though a natural choice would have been the Sarum tone used by several of his English predecessors. Alternatively, he could have ignored the chant altogether as he appears to do in the sets of Propers, and as he has so far been thought to have done in this music also.

In fact, his choruses refer constantly and pointedly to the Roman version of the chant codified by Giovanni Guidetti and published for the first time in the *Cantus Ecclesiasticus Passionis* of 1586.[51] Guidetti is one of the Roman chant reformers of the late sixteenth century who had greatest effect upon the choral part of the liturgy in the ensuing two and a half centuries. A singer in the papal chapel and chaplain to Pope Gregory XIII, he was a friend and pupil of Palestrina. His most effective publication was the *Directorium Chori*, first published in 1582. It was the standard work for precentors and choirs for a long time, reprinted many times. Even George Abbot, the Anglican archbishop of Canterbury (1611–33) "whose theological views were distinctly Calvinistic," saw fit to include a copy in the Lambeth library.[52] In fact, Guidetti's Roman chant versions were not eclipsed until the nineteenth century and the onset of yet another reform of the chant, that of Solesmes.

The references to the chant in Byrd's choruses are, significantly, allusive rather than exact. These are not cantus firmus settings. Indeed, Byrd focuses on one feature alone, the descent from F to B (which he interprets as ♮) and thence to a cadence on C with which the regular uninflected statements of the *verba turbarum* conclude. In his single-mindedness over this figure—note how firmly it re-enters in choruses 5 and 12 after momentary absences—Byrd uncharacteristically misses the opportunity presented by the interrogative ending of the chant with its heady E♭s. Should this raise any doubt about the Byrd's knowledge of Guidetti's print, however, it should be emphasized that the composer sets precisely and only those parts of the *verba turbarum* Guidetti marks as suitable for a *chorus musicorum*—a good deal less than was customary for responsorial settings of the Passions.

That Byrd got his hands on an Italian liturgical source need not come as too great a surprise. We have already seen that his source for the transfer scheme of the Marian masses was a Venetian edition of the Gradual, probably the one repeatedly printed by the Giunta firm. The English mission depended to some extent on its good communications with Rome, a question which John Bossy has explored in some detail, showing the existence of three main routes, one through the Netherlands up the Rhine, a second through France, and a third by the roundabout way of Spain.[53] In a more direct way, the records of the English College in Rome reveal the names of two people who could and most likely would have brought books and music back for Byrd. A Thomas Bird, presumably William's son who lived in Middlesex, visited there in April 1600 for eight days; this is certainly suggestive, but perhaps too late for the St. John Passion choruses, which also turn up in a manuscript which seems earlier than 1600. The other candidate is a certain Gabriel Colford, who was there for nine days in August 1593. This man is surely the Gabriel Colford who was cited in 1605 as assisting Byrd in proselytizing John Wright of nearby Kelvedon; at the time of the indictment he was in

Antwerp, but his home at Navestock was about two miles from Stondon. Interestingly enough, he was also connected with the recusant poet, writer and publisher Richard Verstegan, for whom he appears to have smuggled books. What more likely person to bring Byrd the latest liturgical collections from Rome?[54]

Finally, the placing of the St. John Passion choruses at the end of this book of *Gradualia* helps to illuminate the nature and purpose of the collection. Derived from the Passion narratives, which were printed in the Primer as well as the Missal, they had a role in devotional exercise as well as in the liturgy. The connection of Byrd's settings with a recently published book of Roman chant emphasizes yet again the strength and degree of his commitment to the new order, to a religion centered firmly on Rome, revitalized by Jesuit fervor and purged of its native pre-Reformation trappings. The settings of these texts also indicated something of the composer's personal involvement. The Passion was a portion of the biblical account of Christ's life that held a special meaning for those close to the mission, many of whose priests followed all too literally in the master's footsteps to their own version of Calvary.

The choice of the Passion to conclude the book also underlines the doctrinal concerns of the collection. Though Byrd could have copied the words from his Missal or from his Primer, he also must have read them again and again in the translation of the Rheims New Testament.[55] As we have said, this translation, so literal as to be sometimes incomprehensible, was not designed to make the Bible understandable; its importance lay in its annotations, which met Protestant exegesis on its own ground and served as ammunition for the faithful and a cordial for the fainthearted. Peter's denial of Christ could be read as a comfort by "Church Papists" (i.e., nonrecusant Catholics like Sir John Petre), or by those who had broken under torture. Above all, the commentary upon the Passion in St. John's Gospel establishes through a series of biblical allusions the birth of the church and its sacraments from the piercing of Christ's side on the Cross, whose veneration it also promotes. This last piece of the 1605 collection, then, despite its modest dimensions, allowed Byrd to en-

capsulate in vivid flashes of music, as fragmented as the world of his religion, the essence of a faith which he had devoted his life and art to serving and promoting.

CONTENTS AND MEANING OF BOOK 2

Votive Mass of the Blessed Sacrament: The Forty Hours / *page 174*
Masses of the Yearly Cycle: Christmas, Easter, Ascension,
Pentecost / *page 177*   Saints Peter and Paul / *page 187*

The second book of *Gradualia* followed only two years after the publication of the first. Byrd had now fulfilled his obligation to that part of the
liturgy—the Marian masses, All Saints and Corpus Christi—most crucial
to the cause of the recusants and to the Jesuits with whom he was involved. His way was now clear to present music for the major festivals of
the Christian life.

   This second volume certainly seems as a result better planned and
more systematic, presenting very little other than music for the Masses
and Offices of "the solemnly observed Nativity of Christ the Savior, the
Epiphany, the Resurrection, the Ascension, and . . . the feasts of the
Holy Apostles Peter and Paul," as Byrd puts it in his Latin dedicatory letter—in all likelihood simply overlooking Pentecost. In contrast with the
first book, this collection presents the feasts in the order of the church
year, beginning in late November with Advent. Byrd also appears to have
accepted the principle of including antiphons or responsories of the Offices, omitting them only in the case of the Epiphany, a problem area of
the collection, as we shall see, and Easter, which had already been served
with a good deal of extra music in book 1. If when preparing the Corpus
Christi music for book 1 Byrd balked at setting the extremely long Corpus Christi sequence, *Lauda Sion*, he made royal amends in book 2 by
tackling *Veni Sancte Spiritus*, the Ascension sequence, and by lavishing on
the sequence for Easter, *Victimae Paschali laudes*, some of his richest and
most emotionally complicated music. Finally, his enthusiasm waned for

the cryptic system of transfers that haunts the first twenty-five numbers of the first book, at least until the final six-part section. Rather than taking the opportunity provided in both Christmas and Ascension Masses of writing one piece to fit two purposes, Byrd provided fresh settings for each occasion.

The appearance of the print itself confirms this impression of greater tidiness. As we will see in some detail later, the arrangement of the contents of book 1 in descending number of voice parts with three separate sets of signatures was so unusual in English music printing that it foxed a number of binders who ignored the efforts of the title page and index to make matters clear. Book 2 reverts to the customary arrangement of ascending numbers of voices, and the signatures indicating the gatherings are disposed in the usual arrangement of an unsigned half sheet ([A]) for the preliminaries, followed by a single sequence in fours from B to H in the Cantus primus, Contratenor, Tenor and Bassus part books. The collation of the Cantus secundus book, containing all but the four-part music, is [A]², B–E⁴, and that of the Sextus Book, containing only the six-part music and integrating the title page and preliminaries into the first full gathering, is A–B⁴. All the part books are in East's customary upright quarto format.

The impression of orderliness, however, is not sustained throughout. From *O magnum misterium* (no. 8) to *Jesu nostra redemptio* (no. 19) unwary users of the volume would undoubtedly have been plunged into confusion unless they possessed an intimate knowledge of the Tridentine liturgy. The print gives no indication that *Beata Virgo* (no. 9) forms the "secunda pars" of *O magnum misterium* (no. 8) to constitute the only Matins respond in *Gradualia*—even though one of the few rubrics to appear in either book is lavished on the correct repetition of "Beata Virgo" after the verse "Ave Maria." Perhaps Byrd was uncomfortably aware of the problem that arises from the very different rhetorical strategies of the two pieces. In any case, this is a minor puzzle compared to what follows. The heading "In Epiphania Domini" promises a set of Propers on as full a scale as those for the preceding Christmas Mass. But while the introit, offertory, and communion are present, the central and most important items, the gradual and alleluia, are not. *Surge, illuminare Jerusalem* (no. 16), placed in the original print on the other side of a double item (*Ab ortu solis* and its second part, *Venite, comedite panem meum*) that has nothing to do with Epiphany, looks like the gradual verse, but it is in fact the first verse of Isaiah 60—in other words, the scripture from which the liturgical text was partly derived, not the liturgy itself—with an added alleluia.

Votive Mass of the Blessed Sacrament: The Forty Hours

The intervening piece inaugurates an entirely different and unlabeled mass. *Ab ortu solis* and its second part (nos. 14 and 15) constitute the tract for the Mass of the Blessed Sacrament, a votive mass that takes many of its texts from Corpus Christi, the feast of the Holy Sacrament. The informed user of *Gradualia* would know that settings of the introit, gradual and gradual verse, offertory and communion for this votive mass were already provided in book 1. All that was missing, in fact, was the first of the Paschal alleluias, *Alleluia: Cognoverunt discipuli*, which book 2 provides after the intervening Epiphany text *Surge, illuminare Jerusalem*, thoughtfully reprinting the verse *Caro mea* and the final alleluia from book 1 so that the join should not be too awkward (no. 16). More music for Corpus Christi follows, the antiphons *Ego sum panis vivus*, for Lauds, and *O quam suavis*, for first Vespers (nos. 17 and 18). The first book had contained the Magnificat antiphon for second Vespers, *O sacrum convivium*, surrounded by two hymns associated with the Blessed Sacrament, *O salutaris hostia* and *Pange lingua*. The appearance of the Ascension hymn, *Jesu nostra redemptio* (no. 19), in the context of Corpus Christi antiphons at this point in the new book may therefore signal its use as one of the many hymns for the procession on that feast. It is in the same key as the Corpus Christi music, not that of Ascension, though its clefs and voicing are different. Its vision of the triumphant Christ conquering oppression and filling the faithful whom he spares with his countenance must have been particularly potent for Byrd and his Jesuit friends in the aftermath of the Gunpowder Plot of 1605.

Byrd's setting of the votive Mass of the Blessed Sacrament and the other pieces associated with it could all have derived from a particularly solemn occasion, such as the failure of the Gunpowder Plot, when the Forty Hours Devotion would have been deemed appropriate. This exercise, as we have seen, was a crucial part of Jesuit policy and practice well known in England; it was likely used by the Jesuits as part of the spiritual refresher courses that were occasionally held at various headquarters around London. It had evolved out of the special monastic liturgical events in the period between Good Friday and Easter morning. Though the ceremonies varied, they usually began with the Mass of the pre-sanctified Host, which included, along with the *Adoratio Crucis* and communion, the reading of the Passion from the Gospel of St. John (for which Byrd provided settings of *turba* choruses in book 1). The Cross or the Host, or both, were then carried in procession to a sepulchre and then watched over with constant prayer for forty hours. The event ended with the triumphal procession which instated the Host on the High Altar, the preceding period having represented the gloom from the time of Christ's death until this final act representing his resurrection.

The number forty had biblical connotations of penance: the Flood lasted forty days; the Children of Israel were kept wandering the desert for forty years before being allowed to enter the Promised Land; Christ's temptation occurred during his forty-day fast in the Wilderness (the basis for the Christian season of Lent); and the period from the Resurrection to the Ascension is also forty days. The sequence of Propers in the print—votive Mass of the Holy Sacrament, succeeded by Easter and then Ascension—appears all the more suggestive of the Forty Hours Devotion in this light; and the seemingly incongruous heading "Post Pascha" before *Alleluia. Cognoverunt discipuli* shows that clarification was thought necessary.

After Filippo Neri introduced it to Rome in 1550, the devotion focused more specifically on the Eucharist and became very popular. By 1592, the practice was so widespread in the city that a papal bull directed that the Forty Hours should be held in each of the major churches of

Rome one after another in order to form a perpetual prayer for the salvation of France from the Huguenots, the success of Christianity in its struggle against the Turks and for the unity of the Church. Frederick J. McGinness, explaining this phenomenon in terms of a reformed Rome, gives a hint of why it might also have been a potent symbol and source of encouragement for Jesuit priests and their flocks in England: "as the church, Christ's mystical body, found herself assailed by vicious men, so like Christ's physical body she would be victorious, for as truly as Christ was present in the Eucharist, so through his grace did he mysteriously lead his people to victory."[56] And as the Forty Hours called attention to Christ's body it also emphasized the authority of the priest who both consecrated and displayed it in the bread of the Sacrament.

Clement VIII set out basic rules for the ceremony to ensure its high standard and to prevent it from degenerating into a form of spectacle (as it was always tending to do).[57] Part of the exercise consisted of saying the litany, for which Byrd had also provided a setting in book 1. But the most significant part of the devotion, because of its focus on the Eucharist, was the frequent celebration of the votive Mass of the Blessed Sacrament; while this had often been omitted from post-Tridentine Missals and Graduals, it was now more often included. The involvement of English Jesuits in the practice is confirmed in 1602 by a secular priest, Giles Archer, in a testimonial recording William Weston's saintly activities while imprisoned in Wisbech Castle (1588–98):

> In all our devotional exercises he was the moving spirit. He introduced the practice of reciting litanies daily after dinner for the conversion of England and several times arranged for the Quarant' Ore before the Blessed Sacrament for the same intention. . . . Again when we had the Quarant' Ore, he swept the place out, arranged the altar and polished the candlesticks as if he were a paid servant.[58]

It is in this spirit of refined and humble devotion, as well as the palpable notion of corporeality, that the music Byrd wrote for these devotions to the Blessed Sacrament may be intended. There is a special quality to this music of Byrd's in the key of G that is elusive of analytical procedures. One can hear of course the transcendental effect of the triad of the flattened seventh degree when juxtaposed with its upper neighbor at particular moments, such as the significant portion of the text of the alleluia verse, "qui manducat." It also occurs in the book 2 setting of *Alleluia. Cognoverunt discipuli* at the very word "discipuli," where it surely indicates the moment of truth that dawned on the disciples as they broke the bread and were enabled to recognize their risen master. The chord on F is a further step in the direction always taken by pieces in this key in cadencing frequently on C. There is no suggestion that to a Jacobean ear such a direction was any less soothing, calming or satisfying than the subdominant proves to the ear trained on later tonal music. When to this device and the atmosphere it produces is added the more demonstrative music of the office settings—*Ego sum panis vivus* (no. 17) with its "indescribable shudder of muted joy and vivacity" on the key words "vivet in aeternum" (to quote Joseph Kerman [81, 292]), and *O quam suavis* (no. 18) with its unusually concentrated chromatic rendering of the word "suavis"—an overall dimension can begin to be sensed. It is probable that Byrd took seriously the topics of ingestion which Kerman finds "not ideally suited for musical setting" and tried to endow them with the qualities of tangibility and materiality. The bread and wine that expressed the body and blood of the Savior were clearly not destined for dramatic or restless treatment of the kind meted out to more obviously celebratory texts of the liturgy, such as those for Easter. This is interior, devotional music, well matched to the purpose of meditation such as was encouraged by the eucharistic practices of the time, as well as down-to-earth enough to reflect the common elements from which the divine may be sensed.

Masses of the Yearly Cycle:
Christmas, Easter, Ascension, Pentecost

The three other sets of Mass Propers in this portion of the second book—Christmas and Epiphany for four voices, and Easter for five—

more obviously inhabit the outside world of the recusant. Some bizarre accident, it has been suggested, could possibly explain the omissions and confusions surrounding the set for Epiphany, already described. (Only the introit, *Ecce advenit*, offertory *Reges Tharsis* and communion *Vidimus stellam* are set: nos. 10–12.) It seems to me unlikely, however, in view of the care exhibited in the reform of text and underlay throughout book 2, which is one of the most accurate prints of the entire period, that an accident at the printing house could have gone unnoticed, especially one of such magnitude. Equally bizarre, perhaps, but worth suggesting in view of Byrd's evident involvement in the printing process and significant arrangement of contents, is a symbolic explanation: the potentates of Europe, not to mention the rulers of the British Isles themselves, had not been so assiduous as the "Reges Tharsis et insulae" in coming to worship the true God or bringing gifts to his stable, and the wreck of the Epiphany set, not precluding some extraordinary music, may well have been Byrd's way of projecting the disruption of the present onto the timelessness of the liturgy.

CHRISTMAS

Christmas and Easter, the major Christian festivals, have prompted a great deal of celebratory music. The Roman Catholic community in England, as John Bossy and others have shown, tended to mark these festivals with special domestic observances in the absence of accepted public worship. Among the earlier records of Byrd's association with the Petre family are of his being brought down by one of their servants in 1589 to share in their Christmas festivities held, not at Thorndon, their major seat, but at the more secluded house at Ingatestone. He stayed as long as Twelfth Night.[59]

Something of the special nature of these secluded events enters into Byrd's music, which rarely adopts the purely celebratory point of view—the Magnificat antiphon *Hodie Christus natus est* (no. 6) is the closest to doing so, though it does not begin to approach the six-part English setting of the same words from *Psalmes, Songs and Sonnets* (1611) in madrigalian *jouissance*. Both *O admirabile commercium* (no. 7) and *O magnum misterium* (no. 8) probe the idea of God's taking on human form, the one from the more lofty theoretical view matched by Byrd with careful balancing of phrases and pacing of emphasis, the other with a human image that is imbued with music of extra warmth and immediacy—it was an inspired gesture to place each of the voices in its upper range for the beginning of the point "ut animalia viderent Dominum" as though to portray the animals craning their necks to gain sight of the baby lying in the hay, an image unforgettable in the last, lulling motive, infused at the final cadence with a false-relation dissonance that is not so much a painful reminder of circumstances as a moment of pure sensuous pleasure and joy. *Beata Virgo* (no. 9) makes a strangely ineffectual impression as the continuation required to complete the Matins respond, though it is a piece of gem-like perfection in its own right. But these pieces for the Office do not eclipse the Propers themselves, from the magnificent introit, with its reminder of the church's musical history in the form of an allusion, rare for Byrd, to the chant, to the visionary moment of the communion *Vidimus omnes fines terrae* (no. 5), a piece which, though barely a minute in length, sounds as though it does indeed encompass "the ends of the earth."

EASTER

For Easter, Byrd restricted himself to the music for the mass of the day, producing as a result one of the most intense and concentrated groups of pieces within *Gradualia*. In the introit, the rising motive for the key opening word from Psalm 138, "resurrexi," is conventional enough, perhaps; but the folding back downward in the midst of the quarter-note movement, and the delaying twist at the end of the opening Cantus secundus and last Bassus statements indicate a complicated emotional trajectory followed through in the juxtaposition of the major triads on D and F leading to the first cadence on A. The nervous thrust into another tonal area immediately after the terse pair of homophonic alleluias confirms the restless mood of this disturbing piece. The key to its mood is perhaps to be found in the opening verse of the psalm, "Domine probasti me," which follows in a musical style that leaves the earlier discontinuities behind, yet becomes more agitated as it proceeds. The personal stakes involved in this scripture are outlined in the annotation of the Rheims Bible: "God who knoweth all thinges most absolutely and perfectly, without discourse or searching, yet, as it were, maketh experimental trial of his servants, to make them in some sorte to know him, and to know themselves"(OT, 140).

A nervous note is again struck in *Haec dies* (no. 21), in which the need for confession, a personal commitment, interposes itself between the opening celebratory gesture and the final statement announcing Christ's sacrifice. The mood is intensified further in the frankly dramatic setting of the sequence *Victimae Paschali laudes* (no. 22). An exposed cross relation at the entry of the Cantus primus places the emphasis on "victimae" rather than "Paschali" and this dissonance appears to enfold the Christian community and the musical discourse throughout the magnificent opening paragraph. The dramatic renderings are concentrated in two duets, the first a warlike masculine exchange between the tenor and contratenor, the second the female duet representing the voice of Mary Magdalene (we are reminded that women were not excluded from singing this music as they were in more orthodox church circles in England and abroad). The energy generated by each of these is matched in the full choruses that follow them. The offertory, *Terra tremuit* (no. 23), takes Byrd's epigrammatic style in *Gradualia* to its furthest extent. It is simply constructed but doubly effective: as a musical interlude opening and closing on the fifth of the mode it achieves maximum instability in preparation for the following communion; and as an emotional gesture it is surely meant to echo the sentiment of the Rheims annotator, who writes "persecutors and others being terrified shal be astoni[sh]ed and silent. . . . God wil come to iudge the world, more especially for the iusts sake" (NT, 433–34).

The limpid quality of the opening of *Pascha nostrum* (no. 24) comes as a complete contrast. Kerman detects an indiscernible private association in the pointed setting of "sinceritatis" in block chords (81, 275). Perhaps there is, but the context of the liturgical text in Paul's first letter to the Corinthians (1 Corinthians 5) is certainly suggestive of a meaning Byrd would have been likely to ponder. The saint is castigating his Corinthian congregation for allowing one of its members "such fornication, as the like is not among the heathen," and bread is initially mentioned to illustrate how "a litle leaven corrupteth the whole paste." The Easter text drawing on this passage leaves out the exhortation to "feast not in the old leaven, nor in the leaven of malice and wickedness" but they are clearly the background to the "azymes [unleavened bread] of sinceritie and veritie" celebrated in the liturgy. Finally, the passage occurs after St. Paul has announced his *in absentia* sentence of excommunication on the offender. The annotator, gruesomely celebrating "this marvelous punishment Christ hath appointed the Priests to execute . . . specially upon the disobedient, as Heretikes namely," expresses the wishful thinking of a recusant community powerless against its enemies. The Petres harbored their own traitor in the early 1580s, a servant whose testimony helped to seal the fate of the family's priest, John Payne, who was executed in April 1582.[60] (Such dangers beset all recusant households: Thoda Pigbone, after all, may have precipitated the charges against Byrd's wife at the Essex Archdeaconry Court in 1605.)[61] The anxiety of the Easter music, then, may have something to do with the anxiety of this true congregation, and the absolute necessity of each individual's keeping faith if England were to be found worthy of reconversion. The mystical power of Christ's sacrifice, so vividly suggested at the beginning of *Pascha nostrum*, can all too easily be inflected or even disrupted by earthly alleluias not all of which are in the plain harmony, straightforward rhythm and block chords of sincerity and truth.

ASCENSION

The remaining five-part music, for Ascension and Pentecost, adopts a very different musical and emotional stance from the Easter music that precedes it. The neat three-whole-note opening cell of *Viri Galilaei* (no. 25), repeated four times with barely enough added interest to mask its schematic design, marks the decisive and significant transition to a world far removed from the anxious fervor of the Easter Propers. In the place of abrupt transitions and curious juxtapositions are neatly patterned musical paragraphs. Instead of complicated part writing that constantly gives rise to dissonance are solid progressions and deliberate consonance—it is surely no accident that the first cadence of *Viri Galilaei* (bar 6) lacks a preparatory suspension, that there are no suspended dissonances at all until those in bars 16 and 17, and no others until the four carefully placed ones in the final alleluia from bar 29 to the end. Even more striking is the lack of rhythmic complication and figural elaboration. A little exchanging of emphasis between *arsis* and *thesis* over the words "ita veniet" and a rather tame eighth-note flourish at the end of the doxology are reminders of what is missing here in comparison to the more intricate style of most of the rest of the collection.

That is not quite how things remain, of course. In the Ascension music as a whole there is a trajectory from the slightly stolid introit and equally down-to-earth celebratory gestures and modest trumpetings of *Alleluia. Ascendit Deus* (no. 26) through the more expansive though slightly shorter second alleluia verse, *Dominus in Sina in sancto* (no. 27), with its animated rhythms for the image of captivity led captive, to the remarkable *Psallite Domino* (no. 29), in which the bass twice makes the extravagant gesture of an ascension by steps in half notes or whole notes through an octave and a fourth or fifth. The composer seems to have wanted not merely to find a climactic matching gesture from a rhetorical point of view, but also to contrast, throughout the set, the materiality of the earth and its people with the miraculous event by which a man-god takes himself *super caelos caelorum ad orientem,* to that "other sphere" for which those on earth can find only metaphorical or musical expression.

This dual picture is beautifully elaborated in the more extensive closing piece of the set, the Magnificat antiphon, *O Rex gloriae* (no. 30). After a brief introduction from the top three voices, the bass immediately recalls its exertions in *Psallite Domino* by covering the octave by leap and

continuing up the ensuing fifth by step. But the reference to those left behind, "nos Orphanos," is wonderfully centered on the numinous F chord
(rendered more powerful by its context here at the end of a passage predominantly in G), easing itself gently onto a D dominant. This progression is itself lifted up in sequence (to G and E), to be followed by a striking passage which evokes the solemnity of promises and contracts in a
falling scale as firm (if not so demonstrative) as that of Wotan's spear. The
"spirit of truth" once again recalls F, and the alleluia gently recycles the
F–D juxtapositions before nonchalantly settling on C, the key of the set.

PENTECOST

The introit of Pentecost is again a modest introduction to what follows,
and the alleluia settings seem almost to model themselves on the techniques and procedures already found in those of the Ascension set. *Confirma hoc Deus* (no. 34), the offertory, is one of those perfect contemplative pieces of Byrd, its final alleluia wonderfully integrated into the
preceding musical argument.[62] It seems from the musical setting that
Byrd understood the syntax as presented by the literal version in the
Rheims Bible "from thy temple in Ierusalem, kinges shal offer giftes to
thee"[63] (NT, 295)—though here is a case where for once the Revised
Standard Bible offers a more plausible interpretation of the initial prepo-
sition, one that the composer might well have arrived at independently:
"Confirm this, O God, which you have worked in us; with regard to your
temple, which is in Jerusalem, Kings will offer gifts to you. Alleluia"
(Psalm 68:28). The communion *Factus est repente* (no. 35) marks the emer-
gence of a truly madrigalian style to portray the sudden and violent wind
by rhythmic devices that (as noted above) have been markedly absent in
this part of the volume. A final alleluia, with its *note nere* upper parts over
a solid augmented bass that descends step by step in sequence, not only
balances the opening but effectively creates the spectacle of the apostles
chattering away in their many tongues about "magnalia Dei," the great
works of God. The setting of the sequence *Veni Sancte Spiritus* (no. 36),
out of liturgical order in the part books, may have been an afterthought,

or intended as optional—a detachable alleluia occurs at the end of the second alleluia verse (no. 33) that should only be used, presumably, when the sequence is sung to chant. This long piece is another case in *Gradualia* (*Ave verum corpus* in book 1 is a notable earlier example) of Byrd's adopting special procedures on account of the words being in verse rather than prose. Lines are carefully restricted in length, set off from other lines by cadences that are often matched in threes or otherwise coordinated with the rhyme scheme, and only the last line is allowed to expand at all. The effect is measured and balanced but inevitably restricted by the need to enunciate so many words so quickly.

Once again it is the Magnificat antiphon which provides the keynote to the set by almost literally responding to the pleas of *O Rex gloriae*, its Ascension counterpart (a good reason why Byrd might have chosen for once to set the first Vespers text rather than the more important Magnificat antiphon for second Vespers). *Non vos relinquam Orphanos* (no. 37) takes the process of the musical integration of the alleluia a step further even than *Confirma hoc Deus:* quiet affirmatory alleluias accompany its very opening phrase and emerge effortlessly out of the ensuing discourse from time to time, to culminate in a final alleluia in which the bass, after steadying the pace by rising through an octave in slow notes, settles gently onto a long dominant before the final cadence. The tender quietness of the piece brings to mind some of the most radiant Marian music of *Gradualia* book 1, and its confidence recalls moments from Corpus Christi. Although Byrd may have been working at less than white heat, the calm glow of these embers is equally warming to the receptive listener.

The Pentecost introit, *Spiritus Domini* (no. 31), opens with the same phrase (to all intents and purposes) as that of the last piece in the Ascension set, *O Rex gloriae* (no. 30). Anxious to repudiate anachronistic or ahistorical notions of organic unity, Kerman imagines Byrd in the grip of "a momentary mental set" that "bespeaks hastiness in the composition of the Whitsun Mass as a whole." But owing to the historical dependence on Whitsun of Ascension, which was apparently celebrated with Whit-

sun or even Easter before becoming a separate feast in the fourth century,[64] a symbolic link between the music of these two sets would be neither anachronistic nor the sign of a rushed job. Their rhetoric might also
reflect a set of values that Byrd and his friends associated with these two
feasts in such close temporal and historical proximity. It can surely be no
accident that Byrd chose for them the same set of clefs and put them in
adjacent tonalities, the keys of C and G, so distinct from the D of the
Easter set, and so closely related to each other that the first of the Ascension alleluias can actually end on G, presumably to indicate its need
for completion.

In the Rheims Bible, the following annotation meets the eye of the
reader who turns to Acts 1:11, the source of the Ascension introit, *Viri
Galilaei.*

> By this visible Ascending of Christ to heauen and like returne from thence
> to iudgement, the Heretikes do incredulously argue, him not to be in the
> Sacrament. But let the faithful rather giue eare to S. Chrysostome saying
> thus: *O miracle, he that sitteth with the Father in heauen aboue, at the very same
> time is handled of men beaneath, Christ ascending to heauen, both hath his flesh
> with him, and left it with vs beneath. Elias being taken vp, left to his Disciple his
> cloke only: but the Sonne of man ascending left his owne flesh to vs.* (NT, 291)

An event that would ordinarily be interpreted as the triumph of Christ
and Christianity is linked more specifically here to the validity of the
Roman doctrine of the Sacrament and its effect on those here on earth.
Furthermore, the annotation to Psalm 46, verse 6, the source of the text
of *Alleluia. Ascendit Deus,* links Ascension and Pentecost in a decisive
manner around the very issue of those left behind, "nos Orphanos," the
topic to which Byrd devotes such attention in his musical settings of the
two Magnificat antiphons, one from each feast: "Christ God & man,
after his Passion, rose from death and ascended: not leauing his Church
desolate, but making her ioyful by an other comforter the Holy Ghost"
(OT, 92). The extensive annotation to Acts 2:4, the origin of the second

part of the Pentecost communion, develops this idea by promoting an understanding of Christ's "visibly powring downe the Holy Ghost vpon al the companie" as a means of giving them "al truth, wisedom, and knowledge necessarie for the gouernmente of the Church," and granting to them and all others present ("as wel our Ladie, as other holy women and brethren . . . to wit, al the 120 mentioned before") the "grace and effect of the Sacrament of Confirmation, accomplishing, corroborating, and strengthening them in their faith and the confession of the same" (NT, 95).

Out of this conglomeration of ideas Byrd might well have apprehended the deeper meaning for him and his community of the two festivals. As soon as Christ ascended, he fulfilled his promise not only to his disciples but also, in a manner to which the Rheims Bible draws unusual attention in this passage, to their extended community: "though the Heretikes fondly argue, for the desire they have to dishonour Christs mother, that neither she nor they were there present, nor had the gift of tongues, contrarie to the plaine text that saith, *They were al together*" (NT, 295). Rather than leaving them orphans, in other words, he gave them, all of them, a church and its sacraments to sustain them, and the strength and wisdom to maintain it through thick and thin.

This example, bolstered by the presence of Mary and the holy women, must be interpreted as encouraging contemporary (recusant) Christians, finding themselves in the midst of persecution, to cherish and maintain a full confession of the faith in confidence and joy. Belief in the Resurrection, requiring a major leap of faith, and incorporating belief in salvation and the resurrection of the body, must cause anxiety and fear in itself. But once accepted, that belief can only be bolstered by the events of Ascension and Pentecost, events that emphasize the ascendancy of Christ and the establishment of the church and its sacraments. No wonder from a symbolic point of view, then, that Byrd should choose tonalities and styles of expression close to those of the Corpus Christi and Marian music in order to emphasize the material and spiritual relevance of these two major festivals to the lives of true believers.

Saints Peter and Paul

The concluding section of the second volume of *Gradualia* shows Byrd revisiting six-part texture with new purpose, neither re-enacting the grandiloquent, almost oppressive effect of the very early multi-voice pieces, nor simply recapturing the extraordinary expressiveness of some of the six-part music in the 1591 *Cantiones*. At the very end of the section are two pieces that have no role in the liturgy itself, but are suitably symbolic of the purpose and origin of music in religious worship, for they are both psalms. *Laudate Dominum omnes gentes* (no. 45) may simply have been intended as a psalm motet to match the series of English settings to be published in the final songbook of 1611. It is a complete setting of the terse, acclamatory Psalm 116 (without doxology), and looks back over Byrd's range of motet techniques, employing them all with new forcefulness and vigor, culminating in a final point in double imitation, handled in a new manner, and brilliantly emphasizing the everlasting nature of God's truth. I suggest that in the context of *Gradualia*, with its barely concealed emphasis on the cult of the Holy Sacrament nurtured by the Jesuits, it is worth considering the role of this text as a psalm to be said or sung at the conclusion of Benediction of the Blessed Sacrament, a relatively recent "para-liturgical" event. Later formalized versions of the observance, it is true, prescribe the doxology which Byrd did not include; but at this time, when the service was still in the process of evolving from a mixture of the evening votive antiphon before the statue of the Virgin with special ceremonies surrounding the Holy Sacrament, it may have been informal enough to allow for such an omission.

Venite exultemus Domino (no. 46) has something of the same relation to the invitatory to Matins (the alleluia suggests the Paschal season), and this reversed *alpha et omega* of the religious day makes an appropriate conclusion to the collection as a whole.[65] Musically retrospective in a different way, this last piece reminds us that Byrd, through his motets, introduced madrigalian techniques into English music before the English madrigal itself had come into existence, or at least before it had been seen in print. The quiet moment for "in confessione," summoning up the specter of guilt, is as exhilarating in its demonstrative quality as the rhythmic adventures surrounding "jubilemus Deo" and "et in psalmis jubilemus." The extraordinary acceleration and deceleration achieved by metrical reordering against the tactus make the final "alleluia" a suitable peroration for the collection as a whole.

All but one of the remaining pieces are for the feast of the Holy Apostles Peter and Paul (29 June). The plural "festis" in Byrd's dedicatory letter is a clue to the only hidden element, the inclusion under the singular heading "In festo SS. Petri & Pauli" (posted above the music and in the index of the part books) of the Propers for the feast of St. Peter's Chains (1 August) as well as for that of SS. Peter and Paul (29 June). This is the oldest of saints' days, possibly dating from the actual translation, in A.D. 258, of the two bodies to a hiding place in a catacomb-like structure near the Appian Way in Rome. *Solve jubente Deo* (no. 40) is a text exclusive to the feast of St. Peter's Chains, which otherwise shares mass and office texts with the feast of SS. Peter and Paul. The story of St. Peter's being awakened in prison by an angel who caused the chains to drop from the apostle's hands so that he could escape is told in Acts 12:6–11. The origin of the feast, however, is the dedication in Rome of a church on the Esquiline Hill in honor of SS. Peter and Paul; by the fifth century it is referred to as St. Peter "ad Vincula"—St. Peter's where the fetters are.[66] These feasts both had special significance for Byrd for two reasons, one doctrinal, the other personal. On the various biblical texts surrounding the life of St. Peter depended the authority of the Roman Catholic Church he had clung to so steadfastly; and the name of the saint was also identified with (and pronounced in the same manner as) the surname of the Petre family to whom he looked for protection and employment and under whose auspices his grand liturgical project, beginning with the masses and culminating in this second book of *Gradualia*, had been undertaken and now successfully completed.[67]

The difficulty of reconciling either kind of six-part writing represented by the concluding pieces already discussed with the exigencies of liturgical propriety, so real a consideration throughout *Gradualia*, ought to be taken into account as a dilemma for Byrd in writing this particular set of Propers. Another dilemma is signaled, possibly, by the return to an economical practice found at the opening of book 1: the ingenious but complicated system of transfers used in the Marian masses makes its reappearance here after being rather markedly avoided in the many places that might have allowed it in book 2 (e.g., the Christmas gradual and communion, identical words for which Byrd provides separate settings). The situation in *Constitues eos Principes* (no. 39), which serves (for both feasts) as gradual and, with a short extension, as offertory, is comparable to that in the very first piece of book 1, the introit/gradual *Suscepimus Deus;* and *Tu es Petrus* (no. 41), an alleluia verse and communion, is akin to the alleluia verse/offertory, *Ave Maria gratia plena* (no. 14 in the earlier collection). Moreover, Byrd himself mentions what appears to have been some hiatus in the smooth progress of publication when he refers in his dedicatory letter to "these Songs, completed long ago by me and delivered to the Press" (using the Latin word for winepress, rather than the more usual Renaissance "typis" or a sentence constructed around the more usual flourish, "in lucem editas"). Out of these hints, and stimulated by a negative critical reaction to *Nunc scio vere* (no. 38) and *Constitues eos Principes* (no. 39), Kerman speculates with great ingenuity that Byrd might have composed a Mass of St. Peter's Chains for 1 August 1603 in order to celebrate Sir John Petre's elevation to the peerage by James I on 21 July of that year. A telling point here is that the alleluia for that mass, *Solve jubente Deo,* occurs in the print before *Tu es Petrus,* the alleluia for 29 June.[68]

This is an exceedingly attractive proposition of the kind Renaissance scholarship enjoys purveying to a world bereft of occasional pomp and circumstance; and it does no harm until someone forgets its entirely provisional and imaginative nature. In a similar spirit, I would suggest an added element to the scenario to explain what Kerman sees as "the awkwardness of Byrd's introit and gradual." Though *Nunc scio vere* belongs solely to the two feasts, the gradual *Constitues eos Principes* turns up a number of times in the Sanctorale: it belongs in fact to the Common of Apostles and is printed there in the Giunta Gradual that may have been Byrd's working model, at least for this element of liturgical economy.[69] It is possible that Byrd began his scheme for *Gradualia* as a whole with the idea that he might provide a Common, not only of the Blessed Virgin, but also of Apostles. This piece, then, might belong to the earliest layer of the collection, and reflect a certain struggle between the notion of liturgical propriety on the one hand and celebratory gesture on the other; Byrd would not have wanted to eclipse it with a brilliant introit setting when he began to design a set for the specific feasts of St. Peter.

After this hiatus (if such it is), Byrd seems to find no difficulty in adopting a frankly madrigalian style to fill out the masses with their separate alleluia verses and common communion; and he goes on to add not one but three antiphons from their Offices in a similar style. Most of the imagery is that of heavy metal, or stone, and Byrd does not fight shy of the challenge it presents. Peter's chains and keys (or the realms to which they gain access) are portrayed in lively madrigalian eighth-note figures, and his rock-like essence in long bass notes over which the exuberance of a church that could be imagined but not enjoyed is projected, sometimes almost frantically, sometimes with studied deliberateness. Embedded in these texts are the tenets and arguments that give sole authority to the Roman Church; on their behalf Byrd eschews the restraint imposed elsewhere in *Gradualia* and, writing in expansive contrapuntal periods reminiscent of the earlier *Cantiones sacrae*, goes all out to give them due weight. In *Tu es Petrus* (no. 41), the final phrase "et super hanc petram aedificabo Ecclesiam meam" is extended for an unbelievable thirty breves (as long as several entire pieces in the Ascension-Pentecost series), and the comparable "tibi traditae sunt claves regni caelorum" in *Tu es pastor ovium* (no. 43) stops short of that by a single bar. After the message of *Quodcunque ligaveris* (no. 44) is delivered in fifty-six breves ("Quodcunque ligaveris super terram erit ligatum et in caelis, et quodcunque solveris super terram erit solutum et in caelis") there are still another thirty-four devoted to the authority behind this statement, which for

Byrd must have been an equally important element ("dicit Dominus Si-
moni Petro"). These include a grand final peroration of nine breves, separated from the main body of the work by a general pause that conveys a
great deal of power, and concluding with a three-bar dominant pedal replete with 6–5 progressions that bring their own historical weight to the
argument in hand. H. C. Collins wrote perceptively that the entire passage "rings like a challenge to England's rulers."[70] Among all this affir-
mation of St. Peter's role as foundation of the true church the theme of
martyrdom, celebrated so poignantly in the music of book 1 for All Saints,
strikes a potentially disruptive note. *Hodie Simon Petrus* (no. 42), a text divided into three by alleluias, commemorates the deaths of the two saints,
and in the spirit of the surrounding terrain, Byrd, evidently under the
spell of the larger theme of the church militant and invincible, allows ambiguity no rein, even matching the declining melodies that signify Paul's
bowed head and martyr's crown with rising alleluias at the conclusion.

There are three instances in the Masses of SS. Peter and Paul which
go far beyond the omission of a single phrase of the text such as occurs
in *Beata Virgo* (no. 9) and *Jesu nostra redemptio* (no. 19) earlier in the book.
In *Solve jubente Deo, Hodie Simon Petrus* and *Tu es pastor ovium* the text dis-
appears after the title, not to appear again except in the "alleluia" section
of the first two. These three items do not take their texts from the Bible.
Although this is also the case with various other pieces in the book (e.g.,
the alleluia verse of the Christmas Mass *Dies sanctificatus*, the second Pentecost alleluia verse *Veni Sancte Spiritus*, both sequences and several Magnificat antiphons), the special status of texts arguing the claims of the
Roman Church must have persuaded Byrd to take these unusual precau-
tions, lest he seem to be advocating treason. The fact that the most important text of all—"Tu es Petrus, et super hanc petram aedificabo Ecclesiam meam"—derives from St. Mathew's Gospel, and was therefore
printable, must have seemed a special irony.

Matthew 16:18–19, the passage that provides the text for *Tu es Petrus*
and *Quodcunque ligaveris*, is perhaps the most heavily annotated of any in
the Rheims Bible, designed to meet Protestant biblical exegesis on its

own ground.[71] And in this instance no immense leaps of logic or imagination were required, such as one finds in the application of Roman Catholic allegory to psalm texts like "Constitues eos Principes," in which "pro Patribus tuis nati sunt tibi Filii" is said to show "perpetual succession of Byshops in place of the Apostles" (i.e., it is understood as a figure of the apostolic succession), and argument lapses into desperate, short-breathed pleas for unity/unanimity, not dissimilar from those of imperiled causes at other times in history (including our own).[72] It was necessary in the case of the passage from St. Matthew merely to reiterate the more straightforward meanings over and over again in various forms, citing St. Augustine and other early fathers in support, but mainly relying on the basic meaning of the words to dismiss as specious the more tortured arguments of the Protestants who here had to meet the real disadvantage of their having chosen the Bible as the ground of faith.

The argument proceeds roughly as follows: that Peter does indeed mean rock (in Hebrew, Greek and Syriac, as well as Latin); that Christ as the original light, priest and rock was entitled to create light in others, priests out of others, and to designate other rocks; that Peter was given his prerogatives on behalf of the whole Roman Church, not for himself, and they did not die with him; that it was Christ's own church of the New Testament that was promised here but "not perfectly formed and finished, and distincted from the Synagogue til Whitsunday"; that heretics, like the gates of hell, shall never prevail against the church built on Peter; that the keys are the symbol of the power and authority vested in Peter to "open and shut heauen"; and that "so the validitie of Peters sentence in binding or loosing whatsoeuer, shal by Christes promis be ratified in heauen." Similarly, Byrd's music reiterates the key words over and over again in paragraphs of unaccustomed length for *Gradualia*, in a mood of confidence and joy, and surely with the intent of showing the inevitability of the case.

The Rheims annotations, however, lack the extreme note of exegetical triumphalism. The opposition, for example, named "the Heretikes" elsewhere, are here characterized merely as "the Aduersaries." The concluding passage, moreover, fails to castigate the English monarch in person, but gets at her obliquely by challenging "any temporal potestate" to show on what grounds "they" might have ecclesiastical authority comparable to that of Peter's successor:

> If now any temporal power can shew their warrant out of scripture for such soueraine power, as is here geuen to Peter and consequently to his successors, by these wordes, *Whatsoeuer thou shal binde*, and by the very keies, wherby greatest soueraintie is signified in Gods Church as in his familie and houshold, and therfore principally attributed and geuen to Christ who in the scripture is said to haue the key of Dauid, but here communicated also vnto Peter, as the name of Rocke: if I say any temporal potestate can shew authoritie for the like soueraintie, let them chalenge hardly to be head not only of one particular, but of the whole vniuersal Church.[73]

For a composer as sensitive as Byrd to the nuances of English recusant thought and life, all this would have added to the ambiguity and strangeness of his position. Excused his fines by order of the attorney general, examined by the council "rather gently" in the wake of the Throckmorton plot, becoming increasingly recalcitrant with age about attending the English church, but never once becoming fully implicated (so far as we can tell) in a rash or treasonable action, he perfectly mirrors the position of the outsider on the inside, the man of conviction who lives with inconsistency and compromise at one level or another.[74] Technically proficient to a point beyond technique, yet never simply refined, and occasionally even uncouth, his music, especially in this final Latin collection, is puzzling as well as satisfying, for it always reflects the poignancy of his human dilemma, switching back and forth from contemplation to assertion, from "awkwardness" to brilliance, from materiality to sublimity.

PATRONS AND PUBLICATION

The dedicatee of book 1 of *Gradualia*, Henry Howard, was one of James I's closest advisers. He is also one of the villains of the Whig-biased history of the period. The captious Sir Anthony Weldon considered him "of so venemous and cankered a disposition, that indeed he hated all men of noble parts, nor loved any but Flatterers, like himselfe"—a judgment echoed in even more extreme terms by a modern historian who says that his life was "one long intrigue, as noisome and sinister as the ailment that carried him off."[75] Posterity has not forgiven him for working so assiduously and successfully to secure Raleigh's downfall; and his self-made fortune, donnish temperament, nonrecusant Catholicism and homosexual preference have not done him much good with British historians either.

Many of Northampton's actions may be understood in the light of the wholesale eradication of his family and their fortune under the last three Tudors to which Byrd alludes in the dedication. Both his father, the poet Surrey, and his elder brother, the fourth Duke of Norfolk, were beheaded for treason. He himself was imprisoned on suspicion of plotting with Mary Queen of Scots, but survived and somehow struggled through Elizabeth I's reign, stripped of his family fortune.[76]

His part in the secret correspondence between Queen Elizabeth's chief minister, Sir Robert Cecil, the later Earl of Salisbury, and the Scottish king set the stage for the dramatic reversal of his fortunes under James I, who shared many of his tastes. Made a Privy Councillor in May 1603, created warden of the Cinque Ports in January 1604 and Earl of Northampton two months later, he became a key figure in the administration. A recent study portrays him as a hard-working public servant, less imaginative than Cecil (whom James created Earl of Salisbury, of pavan fame) but not more ruthless; he tried in vain to reform such matters as Navy control, patronage and tax farming to the advantage of the king, to whom he was unfailingly loyal.

Nothing is known of any connection between Byrd and Northampton, who, though Roman Catholic, is unlikely to have had as much to do with the contents of *Gradualia* as Byrd's closer patron, Lord Petre, to whom he dedicated book 2. The letter of dedication stresses four things that are likely to have been of importance to the composer. One is

Northampton's learning and love of music; he was esteemed as the most cultivated courtier of his age. Second is the help that Byrd received (and hopes to receive again) from him in his "family's troubled affairs"—possibly the recusancy fines or perhaps the interminable lawsuits to which the composer was prone. Third is the increase in stipend for the gentlemen of the Chapel Royal that he urged upon the king, an event celebrated in an appreciative entry in the Cheque-Book (5 December 1604), and referred to in the dedication.[77]

The other is Northampton's closeness to and influence with the king, also stressed in the dedication. Catholics had reason to expect much from the domination of the Privy Council by an inner circle consisting of Salisbury, Northampton, Suffolk and Worcester (another of Byrd's patrons), since the last three belonged to the pro-Catholic party. In the event, Northampton was used by James to justify his policy toward the Catholics, and to police them. He was, the king is reputed to have said, "a tame duck with whom he hoped to catch many wild ones."[78] We may in any case overestimate the feeling of betrayal with which Byrd later learned of Northampton's role as a lord commissioner in the trial not only of Guy Fawkes and the other conspirators in the aftermath of the Gunpowder Plot, but also of his friend, the Jesuit father Henry Garnet.[79] Northampton was not alone in his loyalist, anti-Jesuit stance: Worcester also belonged to that party, and Byrd must have become resigned to the opposition of these and many other Catholic aristocrats to whom the Jesuits and their mission were an acute embarrassment.

Book 1

Book 1 of *Gradualia* was registered with the Stationers' Company on 10 January 1605, in the following words:

Master **Easte**   Entred for his Copie vnder the handes of [Richard Bancroft] the late Lord Bishop of LONDON and the wardens, *A sett of songes* called *Gradualia ac Canciones sacrae &c. Aucthore* GULIELMO BIRDO Organisto Regi[a]e Anglo vi[d].[80]

It was presumably published before 24 February, when Northampton received the Order of the Garter, which is not mentioned in his list of honors in the dedication. November of the same year brought with it the Gunpowder Plot, and around that time Charles de Ligny was arrested at an inn near the tower and thrown into Newgate prison "on account of certain papistical books written by William Byrd, and dedicated to Seigneur Henry Houardo, Earl of Northampton"—quite clearly *Gradualia*.[81] The only surviving set of part books with the original title page is in York Minster Library; a number of others remain from the reissue of *Gradualia* in 1610.[82] Interestingly enough, the York copy is also bereft of all prefatory matter other than the title page, leading one to wonder whether the book continued to be issued without the dedication, which Northampton may have wanted to disown, or whether the original owner (the name Jane Staunton is written on the Contratenor title page) decided that the best way of concealing the nature of the contents was to destroy Byrd's precise description of them.

Owing to their absence in the York copy, H. K. Andrews took the view that the dedication and epistle to the reader belonged to the 1610 reissue.[83] This is impossible, however, partly because of the testimony of de Ligny and partly because of the witness of one or two complete eighteenth-century manuscript copies in score that derive from a copy (or copies) of the 1605 issue no longer in existence (or circulation). British Library, R.M. 24.c.13 once belonged to Sir John Hawkins who wrote on it "This score I bought at Dr Boyce's Sale 16th April 1779 for 14s." It reproduces not only the 1605 title page (with the addition of the words LIB. PRIMUS) but also the dedication and epistle as we know them from the reissue.[84] The other is Glasgow University Library, Euing Collection R.d.78 copied by "M. Overend" and dated 1774, which also reproduces the wording of 1605 on its title page.[85]

The makeup of the part books must in itself have confused binders. Even though the set is in the usual upright quarto format, and the contents are grouped according to the number of voices required, it is unique among Thomas East's musical prints in one important respect.

The three main sections, containing music for five, four and three voices respectively, reverse the usual (ascending) order of voices found in all other English musical prints. Furthermore, the pieces are numbered in three separate sequences, and the gatherings of each section are signed separately. The collation of the Superius, Tenor and Bassus is 4°: A², B–E⁴, ²B–D⁴, ³A–B⁴, ³C²; that of the Medius 4°: A², B–E⁴, ²B–D⁴, ²E²; and of the Contratenor 4°: A², B–E⁴, F². The title page and other prefatory matter occupy the initial half gathering (A1v is blank), and as usual are not reset for each part book; the same is true of the index on the last half gathering.

Byrd seems to have anticipated difficulty by detailing the order very carefully in his epistle to the reader, and the index is equally specific. The triple series of signatures suggest that the composer planned the three sections separately, perhaps giving them to the printer one by one. Since the second series, coinciding with the beginning of the four-part music, starts again at B rather than A (a gathering generally reserved for the title page and preliminaries, printed last), the original intention may have been to issue the four- and three-part music in a separate volume. When it became apparent that the index would need two pages, and would therefore require an extra half sheet in the Superius, Tenor and Bassus books, Byrd evidently supplied the exquisite setting of the Candlemas processional antiphon *Adorna thalamum* to make use of some of the additional paper.[86] One may share the printer's apprehension at the size of the book. Requiring forty-three sheets for a single set, it is the largest English collection of the period (over twice the size of the *Cantiones sacrae* of 1589). It must have been as expensive, both to print and to buy, as the scholarly editions of today.[87]

Beyond the York copy of the original 1605 edition, all other known copies of book 1 of *Gradualia* belong to the reissue of 1610, save possibly the Cambridge Bassus, which is without title page:

British Library, K.2.f.7
British Library, R.M. 15.d.1[88]

British Library, D.101.b (Superius, Medius and Bassus only)[89]
Cambridge University Library, Syn 6.61.15 (Superius only)
Cambridge University Library, Syn 6.60.6 (Bassus only)[90]
Lincoln Minster Library, Mm.4.5–9
Christ Church, Oxford, 489–94[91]

It is worth emphasizing the term "reissue" here because even though most reissues, like this one, advertised themselves as a "second edition," "newly emended," and so forth, they represent a totally different phenomenon in the book trade of the time. Musical publications that sold well, like Byrd's *Psalmes, Sonets & Songs,* generally went through several editions with no announcement of their newness, but rather an attempt to imitate the first printing so closely that an untrained eye would not notice the difference. The unsold, unbound sheets of *Gradualia,* on the other hand, must have lain around East's shop until Byrd decided (or, perhaps, was approached and persuaded) to consider a reissue. The person who apparently paid for this was Richard Redmer, who has reasonably been identified with the Richard Redman apprenticed to both William Ponsonby and later to Matthew Lownes, the person who, together with Thomas Snodham, took over East's copyrights in 1611. Redmer (fl. 1610–32), a publisher and bookseller who never again dealt with music, had been made a member of the company of stationers only early in 1610, and it is not at all clear, until further evidence arises, how important his role was.[92] In any case, he got Humphrey Lownes, a well-known printer, to execute a new title page.[93] Since the printing form held four pages, Lownes set up the title page four times, changing the part names round until he had the requisite number of copies to match the sets of sheets. This explains the slight discrepancies between the title pages of the various part books in the 1610 issue, and further confirms that the other prefatory matter, which would normally be contiguous with the title page on ¹A2, belongs to the original sheets. The disjunction between the title page and dedication is apparent in some copies of the 1610 issue (e.g., British Library, D.101.b Superius).

A peculiarity in the Christ Church copy noticed by H. K. Andrews is the altered state of the inner form of the second gathering (B1v, B2r, B3v, B4r) of the Medius book.[94] Careful examination shows that not all portions of the form have been entirely reset: one side of the form (B1v, B4r) must have slipped out, probably during removal from the press for a small correction during the original printing run, but enough of the rest was left intact for the compositor to be able to patch it up.[95] I have detected only seven other press corrections in book 1, all but two of them also in the Medius book. Since each part book could be made up from sheets representing different stages of the printing process, press corrections are not a good basis for conclusions about the relation of one copy to another. It seems worth noting, however, that the Christ Church set stands out as either the sole corrected copy or among the sole corrected copies in all instances save two (both in this section of *Gradualia*).

The minute details of underlay or notation in the press corrections show to what lengths the printer was prepared to go to satisfy the composer's evident quest for perfection. There are perhaps nine questionable or wrong notes, fifty remaining instances of doubtful or careless underlay, and another twenty-five minor errors of one sort or another in this entire large collection. In these circumstances, and for the obvious reason that the composer would not have taken the risk of going into print with such material unless he were seeking a degree of definition, the print would have to be judged the most authoritative source in the absence of an autograph.

MANUSCRIPT COPIES

The paucity of contemporary manuscript copies is nevertheless surprising. Those that do exist come exclusively from the prolific scriptorium of Edward Paston (see chapter 4); they were copied either directly or at few removes from the print, often duplicating its slight errors. There are two types of extraction. One is of reduced-voice sections—verses—often without words, for the three-voice collections, Royal College of Music

2035 and 2036, and British Library Add. 41156–58. Between them these manuscripts contain the following excerpts:

from *Suscepimus Deus* (no. 1), "Magnus Dominus . . . in monte sancto ejus"

from *Salve sancta parens* (no. 6), "Eructavit . . . Regi"

from *Rorate caeli* (no. 12), "Benedixisti Domine . . . Jacob"

from *Diffusa est gratia* (no. 22), "Propter veritatem . . . dextera tua"

from *Diffusa est gratia* (no. 22), "Adducentur Regi . . . afferentur tibi"

The other is of whole pieces, the great majority of them in one set of books alone, Saint Michael's College, Tenbury 369–73, part of which is wholly given over to *Gradualia*.[96] One looks to such documents with interest, since it is precisely in a Roman Catholic household like Paston's, if anywhere, that Byrd's liturgical intent would have been understood. The grouping of the three introit psalm verses at the end of Royal College of Music 2035 and in an internal cell in Add. 41156–58 is promising in this regard. But the Tenbury anthology suggests little in the way of raised liturgical consciousness. On the one hand, the scribe knew enough to extract the Assumption gradual *Propter veritatem* from the composite number *Diffusa est gratia* (no. 22) at fol. 49v but showed no interest in completing masses or even liturgically discrete units: the same Assumption gradual lacks its verse.[97] The presence of two detached alleluias (from nos. 15 and 16) suggests a taste for this well-known *Gradualia* specialty. The Paston scribes were also, it seems, fond of the exquisitely meditative Nativity offertory, *Beata es Virgo*, for it appears in two other of their manuscripts, Tenbury 349–53 (fol. 48v) and Add. 34049 (fol. 48v). None of these sources preserves any interesting variant readings.

Book 2

Byrd made an obvious choice of dedicatee for book 2 of *Gradualia*, but one out of step with his usual practice of offering his publications only to the most high and mighty in the land, beginning with the queen herself in 1575, and working through a list—Sir Christopher Hatton and Sir Henry Cary in the songbooks of 1588 and 1589, the Earl of Worcester and Lord Lumley in the motets of 1589 and 1591, Northampton in *Gradualia* book 1—representing the most powerful or luminous men of the court. Sir John Petre was not one of these, but a rich landed magnate; it was evidently to live under the protection of an influential Catholic seigneur that Byrd moved to the village of Stondon Massey in Essex in 1593. Inevitably their lives became intertwined, and Byrd shared in the family's religious observances at their houses at West Thorndon (Thorndon Hall), about seven miles away, and Ingatestone, four or five miles further off, to such an extent that in his dedicatory letter he describes the contents as "Flowers culled mostly from your Little Gardens, to be rendered to you in all justice (like Tithes)." Book 2 ends with grand settings in six parts of Masses for feasts of SS. Peter and Paul, connected to Sir John by the quadruple pun of the saint's name, the family name (pronounced Peter), the rock (*petra*), and Ing-at-stone, their second seat.

The epigrammatic poem that occurs after the dedication shows Byrd as the modern Christian augur, rooting out by implication more than merely heathen superstition. Fellowes allowed himself to suggest that its author, who signed himself "G.Ga," was "possibly George Gascoigne." Since he died in 1577, it seems unlikely. Boyd's allusion to "George Gage, a fellow Catholic," as "a more likely guess" was alert in the complete absence of other candidates.[98] The George Gage to whom he refers was about twenty-five at the time, and highly educated; he was ordained secretly in Rome by the Cardinal Bellarmine in 1614 with his close friend Sir Toby Matthew, and cooperated with the latter in furthering King James's diplomacy with the pope over the intended Spanish match during the years 1621–22.[99] The presence of a cultivated court Catholic in the book is a tempting thought, but it is a shot in the dark giving a good impression only because the earlier attempt was so wildly wide of the mark.

Book 2 of *Gradualia* was registered with the Stationers' Company on 19 February 1607:

Master **Easte**   Entred for his copie vnder th[e h]andes of my lordes grace of CANTERBURY and the Wardens A booke called *Gradualia. Ac Cantiones sacrae Quaternis, Quinis et Sex vocibus Concinnatae. Liber Secundus. Aucthore* GULIELMO BURD . . . vj^d

This entry and other circumstances have recently been analyzed by Teruhiko Nasu (1995) in an article that argues the importance of the archbishop of Canterbury, Richard Bancroft—who also, as the "late Lord Bishop of London," gave his hand to the first book of *Gradualia* on 10 January 1605 (he was enthroned at Canterbury in December 1604)—in enabling what might have been a problematic licensing process. Since the accession of Elizabeth I, constant attempts had been made by the government to control the number of presses and to employ the bishops as censors of what issued from them.[100] Byrd's earlier prints had presumably been protected from any such interference under the terms of his royal privilege. To claim that Bancroft, for licensing *Gradualia*, "deserves to be numbered among the patrons of William Byrd" (as Nasu suggests) is overenthusiastic on so little evidence; the archbishop is more likely to have been responding to the influence of fellow members of the Privy Council, such as Worcester and Northampton, who really were patrons of Byrd. He may even have been directed by the king's chief minister, Robert Cecil, Earl of Salisbury, to whom Byrd wrote in the earlier part of the reign "to obtain from the Privy Council a letter to the Attorney-General concerning his recusancy, similar to that granted to him by the late Queen Elizabeth and her Council"—in other words to seek confirmation of an exemption from punishment granted only to the highest in the land.[101]

As with the 1605 set, only a single copy of the original issue survives: British Library, K.2.f.6, lacking the Tenor book and signature E1 of the Cantus secundus book. The Bassus part book, bound with the original blue gray wrapper, is inscribed "Mr Wylliam Byrd his last sett of songs geven me by him Feb. 1607 [= 1608]." On the title page occurs the signature of Ralph Bosville, dedicatee of Morley's *First Booke of Ayres* (1600).

Interestingly, Bosville also noted the original price, 6s. 6[d.]. This gives a clue to how expensive it was to print and buy music in parts of this kind. Philip Gaskell notes that "in 1598, when English production costs were characteristically in the range 0.15*d.*–0.25*d.* per sheet including paper, the Stationers' Company laid down maximum retail prices for ordinary books of 0.5*d.* a sheet for books set in pica and english type, and 0.67*d.* for those set in brevier and long primer."[102] The evidence, though not full, Gaskell says, points to a retail price something like three times the cost of production. The second book of *Gradualia* consists of a total of 36.5 sheets (three sheets larger than the sizable 1589 songbook, but quite a bit short of the 43 sheets required for book 1 of *Gradualia*, the largest music publication of the pre-1630 period). If Bosville's figure represents the cost of a complete set of part books, as it surely must, then the retail price was 2.4*d.* per sheet, more than three times as much as that of the more expensive kind of letterpress book. We have some idea of production and retail costs for a slightly different kind of music from the lawsuit over Dowland's *Second Book of Songs or Ayres* of which East printed 1,000 copies for its publisher, George Eastland.[103] Only 12.5 sheets per copy, this print required a total of 25 reams of paper (an extra quire to every heap of two reams for proofreading and for copies for Morley as patent holder were what caused much of the trouble). East's fee was £10, or 8s. per ream. Paper costs were in addition £7 16s. 6d. So basic production costs were £17 16s. 6d., amounting to about 35d. per sheet. But Morley and Heybourn (who was involved in the patent) demanded a fee of £9 10s., and Mrs. Dowland got an additional £20 representing the fee for the manuscript and half the dedication, and there were further expenses of 5s. 6d., bringing the production costs up to about 0.91d. a sheet (i.e., very close to the "twelve pence a peece" that East claimed Eastland paid for each copy). Eastland, the printer complained, "doth sell the sayd books for four shillings six pence a peece [i.e., 4.32d. a sheet]. . . . Albeit other musicke of as greate skill or knowledge is sould for two pence the sheete or vnder." We can see, therefore, that the price for *Gradualia* was not far out of line. Assuming that [Byrd's] long-standing partnership with East would involve much lower production costs, closer to (but not as low as) the 0.35d. representing paper and printing only, the profit could have been considerable (Gaskell's 300 percent if production costs were 0.6d. per sheet). Profit of this order, however, depends on a full sale of the production, and the market for such a publication was not strong.

However many copies were printed, enough were left unsold, together with copies of book 1, as we have seen, for Byrd to contemplate a reissue of both books in 1610. Though no copy of the Tenor book with the earlier title page survives (the Cantus secundus book of the set also lacks the first leaf of gathering E), there can be no doubt that the copies with the 1610 title page represent a later issue of the same sheets, not a new edition. As with the reissue of book 1, Lownes set the title page in four versions.[104] The extant copies are as follows:

British Library, K.2.f.8
British Library, D.101.c (Cantus primus, Sextus, Bassus)
Cambridge University Library, Syn 6.61.16 (Cantus primus)
Folger Shakespeare Library, Washington DC (Sextus)
Lincoln Minster Library, Mm.4.5–9 (lacking Sextus)
Christ Church, Oxford, 489–994
Westminster Abbey (Contratenor and Sextus lacking title page)

The care with which the text was printed and corrected is evident here even more than elsewhere in Byrd's output. There are very few questionable notes, and fewer adjustments to underlay than usually were necessary during the print run. In just one case a series of alterations occurs that involves both sides of the form of a single sheet, along lines found by Alan Brown in a more complicated instance in the 1589 *Cantiones sacrae*.[105] Like his example, this is found in the Tenor part book:

	BL K.2.f.8	Westminster Abbey and Lincoln	Christ Church
sig. B3r	fun^{ccc} -da^{ms} -sti^s	fun^c -da ^{ccms}-sti ^{s}	fun^c -da ^{ccms}-sti ^{s}
sig. B4v	prae^m -se^{mqq} -pi^m -o^s	prae^m -se^{mqq} -pi^m -o^s	prae^m -se^m -pi^{qqm} -o^s

The Christ Church copy appears to represent the final state, but since copies could be made up of sheets printed at various stages, this sheet tells us nothing about the status of other variant readings in the copy. There is, then, no "dating" of a copy such as can happen with manuscript versions.

MANUSCRIPT COPIES

The number of contemporary and subsequent (pre-1850) manuscript copies of *Gradualia* book 2 is extremely small. All were copied from the print, and none has any bearing on the text whatsoever. I have not, therefore, investigated them very far. Bodleian Mus. f. 17–19, one of the manuscript sets of the East Anglian Thomas Hamond, contains most of the four-part music—with a footnote to no. 20 making it clear that the print used was the 1610 reissue— and Mus. f. 1–6 contains most of the rest, that is, music for five and six parts.[106]

A note announces that "most of these latten & Italian songs, ware taken out of M^r kirbies blacke bookes," so they may be a copy of a copy; Kirbye was doubtless the madrigal composer who was in the service of Sir Robert Jermyn at Rushbrooke Hall near Bury St. Edmunds. Interestingly, Hamond supplies the final bass note of *Constitues eos Principes* (no. 39), a note is missing in all extant copies of the print. This could mean that he (or Kirbye) worked from a printed copy with a press correction for this note; but after all, he could also simply have put it in.

Fitzwilliam (Cambridge) MS 114, dating from about 1740, contains all the four-part music. Add. 35001, copied by Samuel Wesley from about 1801 to 1825, is interesting because for the first time it assigns to each piece a liturgical function (usually the correct one); like Mus. f. 17–19, it also contains most of the four-part music to which it adds, interestingly, a piece from the Corpus Christi set of book 1. British Library manuscript Lms C.29, from the Madrigal Society anthology, is a complete copy dated 1780 and advertised on its title page as having been "made into a score by Mr. Danby, from the MSS. Parts, in the possession of S^r. John Hawkins." The manuscript parts in question, as we have just mentioned, are British Library RM 24 f.7–9. A note inside the cover shows that John

Danby (ca. 1757–98), a Catholic organist and composer, was paid for binding as well as inscribing the manuscript.

The Paston group of manuscripts gives this area of Byrd's *Gradualia* an unusually wide berth: Tenbury 349–53 include all the Ascension Propers (but not the Ascension antiphon) in a version transposed up a fourth in the high clefs; the first section of no. 25 also occurs twice in Tenbury 359–63—once in the high clefs up a fourth, and once with the same pitch (and clefs) as the print. *Quodcunque ligaveris* occurs in another of the Madrigal Society's eighteenth-century manuscripts, British Library Lms A.16–11.

Finally, there is a slightly odd *contrafactum* in New York Public Library, Drexel MSS 4180–84 (fol. 83v in MS 4180), the early seventeenth-century set written by John Merro of Gloucester. It consists of an Englished version of *Alleluia. Ascendit Deus* (no. 26), beginning "All ye people, clap your hands" but ending closer to the sense of the original with "God is gone up with triumph, even the Lord with the sound of the trumpet," and substituting "Sing ye praises unto God our saviour" for the final alleluia. The piece concludes with the last eight bars of *Psallite Domino* (no. 29), continuity being managed by the exchange of the two cantus parts and a certain amount of juggling with the inner parts. Interesting though this may be as the attempt of an Anglican musician to press the most Catholic part of Byrd's output into the service of the Protestant repertory, it has (like the rest of these manuscript copies) no bearing on the question of establishing a text.[107]

Byrd and the Petre Family

With the final mass and office music of the second book of *Gradualia*, as we have seen, Byrd acknowledged for once in his published works a local presence in his life and a person he had reason to think of with particular warmth, John Petre. Since Byrd evidently moved to Stondon Massey in 1593 at least partly to be under his seigneurial protection and since, on his own testimony, he shared in the family's religious life at their houses at West Horndon and Ingatestone, such a gesture was perhaps overdue.

This may indeed be the reason for the remark in the dedicatory letter about "these Songs, completed long ago by me and delivered to the Press."[108] It was in any case an astute choice of patron. What Petre lacked in presence at court and power in national affairs he more than made up for in local influence and the authority that came from territorial possession—the Petres, in the words of John Bossy, were "cast-iron landed magnates."[109] They fit exactly into the pattern of "seigneurial Catholicism" that he discerned. The existence of such households was the reason, as Lawrence Stone had already pointed out, that Elizabethan Catholicism could not be suppressed.[110] They were the natural refuge of adherents of the old faith, and it is entirely characteristic of Byrd that he should have chosen to attach himself to one of the wealthiest of the lot.

Their family's prosperity had been assured by John's father, Sir William Petre (1505–72), who amassed a considerable amount of property in the late 1530s when he was one of the commissioners under Thomas Cromwell for the dissolution of England's monastic establishments. Successful in this early service, he went on to be secretary to Henry VIII, managing to survive the considerable political and religious vicissitudes of the midcentury to serve all three of Henry's crowned children, not retiring until old age and illness prevented him, and the increasing role of his friend Cecil made him redundant. He owed his survival and his reputation as a negotiator to his taciturnity and moderation. After the negotiations for the return of Boulogne in 1550, a French diplomat noted that his side would have got the town for half the price, "but for the man who said nothing." His most daring act was to insist in 1536 on sitting on the archbishop's throne at Convocation because he was deputizing for Cromwell who represented the king. An almost Byrd-like tenacity can be inferred from his securing a unique bull from Pope Paul IV in 1555 confirming him and his heirs forever in their possession of what had formerly been church lands.[111] In matters of religion he was enormously discreet, of course, especially since his wife, who lived on at Ingatestone ten years after his death, was a convinced Catholic and friend of Queen Mary.

His son John (1549–1613), Byrd's protector, did not seek limelight at court like his father, but as a magistrate followed his example of public service throughout his working life at the local rather than national level. Less is known about him as a result. His tutor was his private chaplain, John Woodward, and his education was completed with a three-year stint at the Middle Temple (1567–70) in which music figured large.[112] His parents, who gave him free choice, are said to have been delighted with his marriage in 1570 to Mary Waldegrave, another incorrigibly Catholic wife like his father's.[113] The young couple lived at Writtle until, a year after Sir William's death, John bought, and over the next few years remodeled, Thorndon Hall (an Italian visitor described it in 1669 as "an ancient structure built after the same plan as all the others in England, with a tendency rather to the Gothic & Rustic than to any chaste style of architecture").[114] In 1575 he became high sheriff of Essex, and was knighted at the end of his year of office. From 1578 to 1603 he was deputy lieutenant of the county. But it was as a justice of the peace from at least 1573 that he and his fellow magistrate, Sir Thomas Mildmay, dominated Essex justice during Elizabeth's reign.[115]

It is clear that recusancy was incompatible with such public activities, and that Sir John, like his father, was a moderate who upheld the law. But in naming him a "barely-conforming Anglican," his biographer A. C. Edwards surely starts from the wrong side of the equation.[116] A clue to his sympathies and methods comes from the complaint in 1583 of one of the fellows of Exeter College, Oxford, where his father had endowed a number of fellowships, that Sir John was favoring "suche as have byne most suspected amonge us," for example, Kenelm Carter, "his sonnes Schoolemaster, under whome many Popishe schollers have prospered," as well as others who were bringing the college into disrepute with the authorities.[117] An even more telling glimpse into Sir John's attitude toward religion arises from a statement made by George Elliot, a former servant dismissed for embezzlement and accused of rape, who became a notorious informant against Catholic priests in particular (he helped to seal the fate of the celebrated Edmund Campion) and those who resorted to them in general. It was over the case of John Payne, a priest who spent some time at Ingatestone as the Dowager Lady Petre's private chaplain (disguised in the role of household steward), that Elliot in the testimony he gave to the Privy Council in August 1581 identified "the names of all such Papistes as carry the countenance of gentlemen or gentlewomen," including both Lady Petres, and tried as best he could to implicate the lord of the manor:

> The said Sr John had many tymes before perswaded me to go to ye churche for fashion sake, and in respect to avoide ye dawnger of ye lawe; yet to keepe myne owne conscience. And . . . furder saithe he, do you thincke there are not that goe to ye churche that beare as good a mynde to godwarde as those y^t refuse, yes and if occasion serve wilbe able to doe better service then they wch refuse to go to ye churche. Yet would I not for anye-thinge wishe you to participate wth theim eyther in there prayers or communion. And I verylie thincke Sr Johne al-thoughe he goethe to ye churche dothe not receave the communion.[118]

Yet the power of the Petres was such that in 1582, only a few months after the trial and execution of John Payne at Chelmsford, the queen stayed all proceedings against Lady Mary Petre, Sir John's wife.[119]

A picture emerges of a patriarch protecting his family and ensuring that his children should be brought up in the faith by following the example of his father in obeying the law and taking part in public affairs in a manner that was always above reproach. It was not so easy for the next generation. William Petre (1575–1637), John's son and heir, and dedicatee of Byrd's Tenth Pavan and Galliard, began in the steps of his father and grandfather by representing Essex in the 1597–98 Parliament and by often appearing at court. He made an extremely good match with Katherine, daughter of the Earl of Worcester. But his participation in public life suffered a good deal owing to the increased persecution of the period from 1625 onward, and this may have hardened his resolve: he is reported to have founded the College of the Holy Apostles for Jesuit priests in the eastern counties in 1633 with an endowment of at least £4,000 on top of his annual contribution of £250 to the society.[120] His chaplain in these later years was Henry More, Jesuit provincial. It is important to see a certain continuity here. None of the Petres would have countenanced treachery or sedition. But they evidently never subscribed to the anti-Jesuit stance taken by some of the aristocracy. Later on, some of the family themselves became Jesuits. The central fact about their religious life is that it continued in the old faith, the patriarchs exhibiting a different attitude toward the outside world as seemed expedient for the maintenance of the family religion.

It is no wonder that Byrd fitted so well into a family in which he was treated as a trusted and distinguished friend rather than as a musical servant. The earliest notice of their association comes in a letter, dated 17 October 1581, that the composer wrote to Robert Petre, John's uncle and a high-ranking Treasury official, on behalf of a fellow recusant named Dorothy Tempest.[121] The first of Byrd's many recorded visits to Ingatestone occurs in October 1586; he was back at Christmas that year and stayed on until 16 January. Another visit occurred in July, and there are considerable details in the accounts about the Christmas season of 1589, when he was brought to Ingatestone on 26 December and stayed until 8 January. After Byrd came to live at Stondon Massey around 1593, the entries in the accounts are less prolific: they would not tell us, for instance, about the help Sir John or Sir William may have given him in his legal imbroglios, though from the various documents having to do with disputes over Stondon Place and its surrounding lands we know that Sir John tried to act as mediator from time to time. Byrd is the occasional recipient of a loan; in 1607 he recommends a tutor for William's children (an Andrew Foorde); he is paid in 1608 "for his riflinge for songe bookes"; an inventory of Thorndon Hall dating from the same year reveals that he has a room there, presumably somewhere he could stay the night on the occasion when he dined with Lord Petre and his guests on the Saturday before Christmas in 1609.

It could also have been somewhere he might have rested after a tiring rehearsal with members of the household designated to sing his music for the Mass. He may even have burned the midnight oil composing there, if a literal reading of his dedicatory epistle is to be allowed: "these musical products of my night labors have proceeded as copiously from your house (most dear to me and mine, by Hercules) as a harvest born from fertile soil, and they have produced fruits more pleasant and more abundant from that mild clime." A certain warmth lingers about the wording of this document, one of the more intimate and least fulsome of its kind, that bespeaks genuine respect and affection. John Petre was a great magnate, to be sure, but he and his family provided and guaranteed for Byrd and his offspring an ideal environment for the purposeful pursuit of religion and music.

PERFORMING BYRD'S *GRADUALIA*

No dogmatic assertions can be made about the nature of the performance of this music. We cannot even be certain that complete liturgical units were usually performed as such. As we have seen, one of the manuscript sets of part books from the library of the North Norfolk Roman Catholic gentleman Edward Paston contains a complete set of the Pentecost Propers in the order of the print (Tenbury 349–53, fols. 41r–43v), but it is the only such instance in the large extant remains of Paston's collection. Another set, Tenbury 369–73, gathers together most of the five-part music from book 1 yet manages almost perversely to avoid completing a single set of Propers.

Good introductions to the original performance context of *Gradualia* are John Bossy's evocative descriptions of Mass in the households of the recusant nobility:

> It may help us to grasp the extent of the . . . domestication of the Mass if we remember that it was for a long time unusual for it to be offered in anything that was architecturally speaking a Chapel. The idea that gentry families in any significant number had Mass said more or less continuously in their chapels from before the Reformation to modern times has been found attractive by some and irritating by others, but is in any case not true.[122]

On the whole the gentry avoided the use of their chapels if they had them, preferring to assemble in "fair, large chambers" where their activities would not be so obvious.

> In the bigger houses the liturgical cycle merged indistinguishably with the cycle of hospitality. At Easter or Christmas there would be a large company and sung Masses; the musicians who served for the Mass would also serve for the entertainment, and it was presumably on these occasions that Byrd's Masses were first performed.[123]

Another context must of course have been that of Jesuit enclaves such as the place some distance from London where Charles de Ligny, the man arrested in 1605 with *Gradualia* in his possession, was taken earlier in the year. There he found

> [Father Henry] Garnet in company with several Jesuits and gentlemen, who were playing music: among them Mr. Byrd, who played the organs and many other instruments. To that house came, chiefly on the solemn days observed by the Papists, many of the nobility, and many ladies by coach or otherwise.[124]

We are not dealing in either case with large Gothic interiors and serried ranks of choristers and lay clerks. The internal evidence of the music argues as much—the delicate filigree of such moments as the cadence to the phrase "et spiritui sancto" in the doxology of *Salve sancta parens*, to look no further than no. 6 in book 1, bars 57–59—tends to be obliterated in such performances.

We must also question the idea of liturgical music as a male preserve in this context. Bossy and other scholars emphasize the importance of women in the fabric of recusant Catholicism, and there is no reason to suppose that the women, who were in control of the important cycle of feasting and fasting, allowed themselves to be excluded from its music. Instrumental participation also cannot be ruled out, as de Ligny's testimony suggests. The lute arrangements of passages from *Gradualia* in one of Paston's books may have been for private delectation rather than use at Mass, but Catholic households that owned this music would surely have used whatever resources they had in order to give as good an account of the music as possible.[125] A further encouragement to instrumental accompaniment occurs in the annotation of the Rheims Bible to the expression "in Psalmes" that occurs in verse 2 of Psalm 94 (which happens to be part of the text of *Gradualia*'s final number, "Venite exultemus Domino"): "not only in singing his praise with voice, but also with musical instruments."

Alan Brown has written persuasively about the *Cantiones sacrae* of 1589 and 1591 as vocal chamber music, performed domestically in the same context as madrigals and the other secular repertory of Elizabethan times and with probably no more than one to a part.[126] The same is surely true of these works. "Versus" in this context is a liturgical term, not the performance direction it became in Anglican music of the period, and the rubric "Chorus sequitur" in the Christmas Mass in book 2 may simply refer figuratively to the return to full-voiced texture from a reduced-voice episode. That said, it must be admitted that in the Ascension and Pentecost Masses the sort of cadential eighth-note flurry so characteristic of most other parts of the entire collection, and so suggestive of one-on-a-part writing, is notably absent. One cadence in the Ascension introit incorporates a modest flourish, but in the rest of the five-part music eighth notes rarely appear more than two at a time.

The six-part music tells a different story. In spite of the richer texture, the individual voices tend to indulge in much greater activity, most notably of course at the clanking of the chains in the colorful *Solve jubente Deo* (no. 40) and at the rattling of the keys of heaven in *Hodie Simon Petrus* (no. 42), but also in the more usual context of the cadential gesture, as in *Tu es Pastor ovium* (no. 43). If the Ascension and Pentecost Masses were composed close to the date of the print, as has been suggested, then it is tempting to entertain the idea that the musically trained Catholic worship in and around the Petre household had expanded sufficiently for Byrd to compose intentionally in this instance for a small chorus of voices. The verse sections (*Omnes gentes* in the Ascension introit *Viri Galilei*, and *Exurgat Deus* in the Pentecost introit *Spiritus Domini*) mark a return to more complicated rhythmic texture, and the contrast, suggesting the introduction of soloists, also urges the point. The six-part music, because it marks a return to Byrd's more usual manner in *Gradualia*, should presumably be sung one to a part.

Gradualia pieces demand less stamina than the expansive earlier works, perhaps, but no less expertise and even greater sense of nuance. It is not hard to imagine Byrd writing them for the knowing, if amateur musicians of Ingatestone, and they will probably be heard to best advantage with one to a part, in a nonechoing acoustical space, at a tempo that strikes a balance between the often busy rhythmic texture and the overall contemplative atmosphere. The testimony of the Tenbury copy of the organ part of Tomkins's *Musica Deo Sacra* seems far distant from the context sketched out here, but its equation of the semibreve with two beats of the human heart or the swing of a pendulum two feet long (i.e., half note = ca. 72–76) is probably not far wrong as a norm. If a choral performance is ultimately preferred, then it would accord well with tradition to reduce voices during the three-part sections; the duos of the Easter sequence *Victimae Paschali laudes* (no. 22 in book 2) only make sense when sung by soloists.

The Marian masses all employ the same set of clefs and the same mode. Byrd keeps to this framework despite some chafing at the bit over tessitura; in *Diffusa est gratia* (no. 22 in book 1) the Contratenor usurps the range of the Medius, which in turn soars into the upper reaches of the Superius tessitura. This is all done at the reckless expense of ledger lines without changing clefs. Those who believe firmly in the relevance of a "clef-code" to pitch will probably interpret this information as support for the downward transposition they associate with this high-clef combination (i.e., the result of transposing down a fourth on account of the clefs and up a minor third on the basis of the pitch of English organs of the period in relation to modern standard).[127]

Absolute pitch, however, would not necessarily have been an issue unless the music was accompanied by an organ or other fixed-pitch instrument. In *Gradualia* as a whole there are in the music for four, five and six voices two sets of overall compasses, according to whether "low" or "high" clefs are employed, and they are pitched roughly a third to a fourth apart. If one assumes that Byrd was writing for a single group of singers, then one may be tempted to choose a *via media* that would reconcile the two sets, transposing pieces up or down as necessary. But as Alan Brown points out,[128] Thomas Morley's famous remarks, which are not so ambiguous as has sometimes been claimed, deserve as much consideration as the evidence of the Paston lute books, where transpositions approximate to those suggested by H. K. Andrews occur. There were obviously different schools of thought on the matter, then as now. Byrd's choice of the high clefs for the Marian masses may indeed have been (in Morley's words) "for more life"; and a performance with modern standard pitch equated with written pitch, and the vocal scoring of soprano (treble), mezzo (mean), alto (countertenor), tenor and bass, will probably be found satisfactory. In *Gradualia*, as in much of Byrd's music, the problem of pitch pales rather by comparison with the practical difficulty of finding voices able to articulate each extreme of the wide compass of the middle parts with equal clarity and grace.

Thus the four-part pieces in the low clefs (nos. 8–15 in book 1 and nos. 10–18 in book 2) can probably be sung by a S A T B group at pitch (providing a countertenor is available to sing the low Ds), or up a minor third. The Easter set (nos. 1–9 in book 2) has an anomalous set of clefs, neither high nor low, C1, C1, C3, C4, F3; the high bass range may be symbolic of the occasion and the set can for all intents and purposes be treated as belonging to the low-clef category. *Plorans plorabit* (⁵no. 28 in book 1) also sounds best at pitch, for S Ct Ct T B, but may benefit from transposing up a minor third in some circumstances.

The high-clef pieces may typically be sung down a tone by a S S A T B group. Add an extra T or B for SS. Peter and Paul. *Jesu nostra redemptio* (no. 19 in book 2), in very high clefs C1, C1, C3, C4, can be treated flexibly, being sung at pitch by M M A T or transposed down a fourth for male voices. As was apparent from the discussion of the Christmas music of book 2, a five-voice group is needed to sing this four-voice music on account of the change of voice nomenclature and clef in the inner parts. The countertenor who sings the second part in *Puer natus est nobis* and *O magnum misterium/Beata Virgo* (nos. 1 and 8–9) presumably sings the third part down in the other pieces, a separate tenor being required only for these outside pieces.

Finally, *Adoramus te Christe* (4no. 26 in book 1) requires a solo soprano or mezzo with treble, tenor and two bass viols and should be sung at pitch.

The other matter that will affect performance is the pronunciation of the words. This topic was first raised in connection with Latin words in English music of the period in my edition of Byrd's Five-Part Mass, published in 1973.[129] Much has changed since then, and there is no need to emphasize yet again the inappropriateness for Byrd's music of the modern Italian Latin pronunciation introduced into England by the Oxford Movement, hallowed in the prefatory pages to the English edition of the *Liber Usualis*, and applied to the point of caricature in the first complete recording of one of the Byrd collections.[130]

I encourage performers to adopt the English rather than the Italian consonants for this music. *C* and *sc* before *ae, e* and *i*, and *t* before unstressed *i* in hiatus, should be pronounced as *s* in "sing" (e.g., *as-sen-den-tem, prin-si-pi-o, lu-sis, vo-se, si-o, ex-pec-ta-si-o-ne, re-su-reck-si-o-nem, fa-sis*). *S* sounds as in "music" between vowels (*mizericordia*) and in final position after unstressed *e* (*omnez*). Consonantal *i*, and *g* before *e* and *i*, are both pronounced as *j* in "just" (*jubilatione, fugiant, gentes*); *g* is otherwise hard (*exurgat, gaudium, gloria, riga*) but may apparently be palatalized before *n*, as in *mangnus, ingnem* or *congnovisti* (the print's splitting of such words between the *g* and *n—mag-nus, ag-nus*—possibly was meant to discourage this practice). The *i* in *alleluia* must surely have been pronounced as *y*. Performers wishing to explore the contemporary English pronunciation of Latin can consult Harold Copeman's fully documented study, which gives a welcome stimulus to the whole question.[131] He raises the interesting possibility of a special pronunciation among the English Jesuits (119), which could be further explored.

The attempt to recapture an original pronunciation in all respects is a worthy aim that may be revealing of important aspects of the sonority of the music. It should be remembered, however, that such an attempt inevitably gives priority to an "archaeological" view of the music, and subverts an expectation shared by the composer and his audience that the words would be pronounced in a fashion natural to their ears. (It was a Byrd recording with exaggerated ultramontane Latin that first prompted me to raise the issue of an appropriate pronunciation for this music.) Approximating the sound of Latin to contemporary English, which is the main effect of preferring the "English" consonants over the "Italian" ones familiar from Anglo-American church Latin, achieves that aim, helps to make Latin words identifiable from their English cognates for a audience less widely educated in that language and serves to distinguish Byrd's music from other national styles of the period; it will in other words suffice for ordinary purposes. Whichever course is chosen, it is clearly of the greatest importance to pay heed to the significance the composer attributed to them by starting with the words and doing everything in our power to give them meaning through the music.

NOTES

1. A votive mass is a mass for a particular intention (from *votum*, meaning oath, wish, desire); it is not part of the office of the day or connected to a feast celebrated according to the rubrics. It can be offered to a person or a group of persons or, in this case, to a saint. Such masses appear early in the Roman Church, but their proliferation was curbed by the Council of Trent. The votive Mass of the Blessed Virgin is often called Lady Mass; it was traditionally offered on Saturdays.

2. James L. Jackman, "Liturgical Aspects of Byrd's *Gradualia*," *Musical Quarterly* (1963): 17–37; Joseph Kerman, *The Masses and Motets of William Byrd* (London, 1981), ch. 5. References to Jackman and Kerman are to these two works (unless others are specified), and consist of page numbers alone.

3. Graduals, because they were expensive to print and required the resources of large printing houses, are relatively few; nor has their survival rate been high. I have consulted the following:

P. Liechtenstein (Venice, 1580), Florence, Biblioteca Nazionale Mus.Ant.242

Plantin (Antwerp 1599), Oxford, Bodleian B.1.10.Th.Seld

Giunta (Venice, 1602), Boston, New England Conservatory of Music

Giunta (Venice 1613), London, British Library L.18.f.6

Societas Typographicae Librorum Officii (Paris, 1640), Cambridge, University Library Pet U.f.2

The 1602 and 1613 Giunta editions are exactly alike in pagination, transfer scheme and contents. Features in these are shared by the 1606 Giunta edition in the Vatican Library (Race. Gen. Liturgica Str. 33), but not by the Sanctorale of the two-volume Giunta Gradual of 1572 (Bologna, Biblioteca Communale di Archigenasio 16 cc. II 2–3). The prototype of these Giunta editions is likely to have been one of three Graduals published by the firm in the 1580s. The only other complete Gradual of the period I have been able to trace is a Gardano edition of 1591, edited by Ludovico Balbi, Andrea Gabrieli and Orazio Vecchi (copy in the University of Minnesota Library, Z783.23 fC285); containing one outlandish transfer all its own—the Assumption introit is found under the Feast of St. Agatha—it is closer to the Liechtenstein Gradual than to the Giunta editions in its rubrics and transfers. And I have been unable to find liturgical books Byrd may actually have used—the Petre family, for instance, owns no early Gradual.

I am grateful to Patrick Macey, Craig Monson and Lydia Hammessy for examining the 1606 Giunta, 1572 Giunta and Gardano editions respectively, and to David Crawford, who kindly allowed me use the census of Renaissance liturgical imprints that he and James Borders are compiling.

4. See Theodor Klauser, *A Short History of the Western Liturgy*, trans. John Halliburton, 2nd ed. (Oxford, 1979), 124–26. The feast only crept in to the last edition of the Sarum Great Breviary; see *Breviarum ad usam ecclesiarum Sarum*, ed. F. Proctor and C. Wordsworth II (Cambridge, 1879), 329. There is no indication that any special Marian feasts were observed in England in those difficult times when observing any church feast must have been fraught with danger; the *Missale Parvum ad usum Sacerdotibus in Anglia, Scotia, & Iberia iterantibus* ([St. Omer], 1626) has a few extra masses licensed by the bishop of Antwerp but none of them is Marian.

5. Quoted from transcripts at Jesuit House, Farm Street, London, by Godfrey Anstruther, *Vaux of Harrowden* (Newport, Monmouth, 1953), 275.

6. Klauser, 89–90. The Purification (also known as the Presentation of Christ in the Temple and Candlemass) and the Assumption were originally feasts of Christ, not Mary. The propers for the Assumption differ in modern service books: a new mass (Signum Magnum) was composed to commemorate the defi-

nition of the dogma in 1950 which made a clean sweep of the traditional texts (Archdale A. King, *Liturgy of the Roman Church* [London, 1957], 201). In the Clementine calendar the Assumption is a Double of the First Class and the Purification, Assumption and Nativity Doubles of the Second Class: see *The Generall Rubrics of the Brevarie, put into English* (St. Omer, 1617), repr. in *English Recusant Literature 1558–1640*, ed. D. M. Rogers, vol. 351 (Ilkley, Yorkshire, 1975).

7. The Visitation, announced by the pope in 1390, was added to the Sarum calendar long after; it fell on the same day as the commemoration of the indigenous St. Swithin, whose feast, so ominous from a meteorological point of view, was moved to 15 July. Our Lady of the Snow is the feast of the dedication of S. Maria Maggiore in Rome, turned into a Marian feast by Sixtus III (432–30) as a memorial to the Council of Ephesus. The Nativity and Assumption both had their octaves (a special observance on the eighth day of the feast) confirmed by Clement VIII's calendar reform of 1604.

8. The Plantin Gradual of 1599 prints only the alleluia under the Nativity, grouping the other chants in the votive mass section later in the book. The Paris Gradual prints the alleluia under the Conception.

9. There is an extra "sacra" in *Benedicta et venerabilis* (no. 7) found in none of Missals and Graduals I have examined. On the other hand the words "Christus Deus noster" that Kerman (222) reports as missing from *Felix es* (no. 9) were introduced in Clement VIII's revision of the Missal in 1604, being absent from the Pian text of 1570.

10. A good example is the three consecutive trios that result when the gradual *Speciosus forma* is followed by the tract *Gaude Maria Virgo* in the votive mass from Christmas to the Purification, on the rare event of Septuagesima occurring before the Purification.

11. For the strong evidence for this, see Kerman 81, 244–45, 251.

12. The Sarum Graduals of 1528 and 1532, by contrast, print the offertory under the feast. The Sarum rite for the Purification specifies a different alleluia verse, *Adorabo ad templum*, and includes a sequence, *Hac clara die*. The Common of Virgins is part of the Common of Saints, where chants prescribed for the feasts of various classes of holy people—martyrs, bishops, doctors—are found.

13. I am indebted to Jane Frogley for this suggestion. By the same token, however, the Visitation, which the Book of Common Prayer includes, would have been a more likely choice than the Nativity, which is not an Anglican feast.

14. Quotations are from the facsimile edition in the series *English Recusant Literature 1558–1640*, vols. 265–67 (see note 6). The books are entitled—in volume order from Old Testament to New—*The Holie Bible Faithfully Translated into English out of the Authenticall Latin* (Douai, 1609), *The Second Tome of the Holie*

Bible, etc. (Douai, 1610), and *The New Testament of Iesus Christ Translated Faithfully into English out of the Authenticall Latin* (Rheims, 1582). Page references are given here under OT for *The Holie Bible* (1609) and *The Second Tome* (1610), and NT for *The New Testament* (1582).

15. The New Testament was printed in 1582, as noted above, but the Old Testament translation, most of it finished when the principal translator, Gregory Martin, died in 1584, was not printed until 1609–10. Yet the psalm texts in Byrd's *Psalmes, Songs and Sonnets* (1611) are so close to it that it seems reasonable to suppose that Byrd had access to an unrevised pre-publication version. See Joseph Kerman, *The Elizabethan Madrigal: A Comparative Study,* American Musicological Society Studies and Documents 4 (New York, 1962), 110.

16. It is likely that the notes were written by Richard Bristow, fellow of Exeter College, Oxford, and prefect of studies at the English College; see A. C. Partridge, *English Biblical Translation* (London, 1973), 95.

17. In 1588 alone, 22 priests and 16 lay people were put to death, between 1590 and 1603, 53 priests and 35 lay people; see Alan Dures, *English Catholicism, 1588–1642: Continuity and Change* (London, 1983), 32. Altogether 125 of the 463 English seminary priests suffered death—a 27 percent casualty rate; see Patrick McGrath, "Elizabethan Catholicism, a Reconsideration," *Journal of Ecclesiastical History* 35 (1984): 425.

18. The key-clef combination is the same as that of *O quam gloriosum,* a motet from the 1589 *Cantiones* which links two All Saints texts, the Magnificat antiphon and the chapter at Nones, by means of a few added words.

19. For once Byrd was not prompted by his Bible, which does not annotate this passage. Unlike Pius V, who excommunicated Queen Elizabeth, Clement VIII cultivated good relations with James, whose accession was celebrated by a solemn Mass at the English College in Rome in 1603 and even accepted by the Jesuits. Furthermore, the Rheims annotations avoid challenging royal authority and do not press home the political implications of the 1570 bull of excommunication, *Regnans in excelsis;* see Peter Holmes, *Resistance and Compromise; the Political Thought of the Elizabethan Catholics* (Cambridge, 1982), 39–41.

20. J. D. Chrichton, "The Manual of 1614," *Recusant History* 17 (1984): 162.

21. Translation from John Morris, S. J., *The Troubles of Our Catholic Forefathers related by themselves* (London, 1872–75), 2:142, where nearly all the material relating to Byrd and the Jesuits will be found (141–46). For another translation, see William Weston, *An Autobiography from the Jesuit Underground,* trans. Philip Caraman (New York, 1955), 622.

22. *Unpublished Documents Relating to the English Martyrs (1584–1603),* ed. John Hungerford Cullen, Catholic Record Society Publications 5 (London,

1908), 1:308. July contained no major feasts between the Visitation (1 July) and St. James Apostle (25 July).

23. Bodleian MS Eng.th.b.2, p. 136.

24. Royal Historical Manuscripts Commission, *Calendar of Salisbury MSS,* Reports and Calendars Series 17 (London, 1938), 611.

25. Robert Parsons, *Memorial for the Reformation of England* (ed. Edward Gee, as *The Jesuit's Memorial,* 1690), 259.

26. Klauser, 37–38.

27. Anstruther, *Vaux,* 137–38.

28. By both Anstruther, *Vaux;* and Philip Caraman, *Henry Garnet, 1555–1606, and the Gunpowder Plot* (London, 1964), 320n. See also D. Shanahan, "The Gunpowder Plot and an Essex Country House," *Essex Recusant* 17 (1975): 89.

29. Kerman, who points this out, also effectively suggests "that by echoing this false relation later in the piece—at 'O dulcis, o pie,' and most directly at 'miserere mei'—Byrd meant to keep the Eucharist more clearly before our eyes than the text manages to do" (Kerman 81, 288).

30. "What survived . . . was the idea that Mass-time was mainly a specially auspicious time for exercises of interior devotion": John Bossy, *The English Catholic Community, 1570–1850* (London, 1975), 130–31.

31. Christopher Haigh, "The Continuity of Catholicism in the English Reformation," *Past and Present* 93 (1981): 65, drawing on material in Morris, *The Troubles of Our Catholic Forefathers,* 3:390–94, 467–68; *An Elizabethan Recusant House: Comprising the Life of the Lady Magdalen, Viscountess Montague (1538–1608),* by Richard Smith, trans. Cuthbert Fursdon (1627), ed. A. C. Southern (London, 1954); *Chronicle of the English Augustinian Canonesses,* ed. A. Hamilton (Edinburgh, 1904), 1:80–82; W. Palmes, *Life of Mrs Dorothy Lawson,* ed. G. B. Richardson (Newcastle, 1851), 33–40. See also chapter 4.

32. *An Elizabethan Recusant House,* 43, 49.

33. The song "With lilies white," an elegy for her death in 1608, was almost certainly written not directly for her family but at the request of Byrd's friend and patron Edward Paston, whose eldest son married Lady Montague's granddaughter, Mary Brown; see *An Elizabethan Recusant House,* 15, 149–51 and 178. See also chapter 4

34. *An Elizabethan Recusant House,* 47.

35. "It is supposed by some that the name *Primer* was derived from *Prime,* the first of the Hours. But most authorities believe that from the start the name was applied to what was naturally regarded in many households as their first book (*liber primarius*)," Charles C. Butterworth, *The English Primers (1529–1545)* (Philadelphia, 1953), 3. The Jesus Psalter comprised not psalms, but a series of

"devout and godly petitions" numbering 150 (like the Psalms) and divided in certain ways that recall the Rosary; see A. C. Southern, *Elizabethan Recusant Prose 1559–1582* (London, [1950]), 219–23. The Manual, similar to the Primer in that it contained private prayers and hymns, but not so imitative of the Breviary, gradually outstripped it in popularity during the seventeenth and eighteenth centuries.

36. These were included in the contemporary Breviary, where they were called the "little" offices to distinguish them from those said on feasts of the Virgin Mary.

37. J. D. Crichton, "The Manual of 1614," *Recusant History* 17 (1984): 161.

38. Edgar Hoskins, *Horae beatae Mariae Virginis, or Sarum and York Primers with Kindred Books and Primers of the Reformed Roman Use* (London, 1901; repr. in W. W. Gregg, *A Companion to Arber* [Oxford, 1967]), 107–56 and 159–92. The revised *Short-title Catalogue* lists around 200 editions, compared to about 40 editions of the hymnal and about 100 editions of the Breviary. The shelfmark of the British Library copy is C.65.k.9.

39. J. M. Blom, *The Post-Tridentine English Primer,* Catholic Record Society Publications 3 (London, 1982), 1–2.

40. Anstruther, *Vaux,* 87–88.

41. Anstruther, *Vaux,* 151; the list contains twenty-two works, some printed, some manuscript.

42. Kerman mystifies Byrd's versions of these hymns by claiming that they do "not follow the Pian Breviary, but rather hold to the traditional versions current both in England and abroad before 1571" (329). Byrd does follow the Pian Breviary (or rather Primer, as I would think) to the letter, the divergences in three of the hymns (all but *Ave maris stella*) in the modern books being the result of the 1629 revision of Urban VIII, who "being himself a Humanist and no mean Poet, . . . desired that the Breviary hymns . . . should be corrected according to grammatical rules and put into true meter," as Fernand Cabrol puts it in the article on the breviary in *The Catholic Encyclopedia,* 2:775. The revised texts first appeared in a typical edition entitled *Hymni Breviarii Romani* (Rome, 1629); the British Library copy is C.28.f.1. On the Urban revision see also Blom, 11–12.

43. Byrd Edition 3:47–52; see Kerman 81, 323–25.

44. The Clementine revision changed some rubrics, expanded and reformed the calendar significantly and made some small changes to the biblical texts of the liturgy by substituting the Vulgate text of 1591 for the old Itala version previously used: see King, *Liturgy,* 44.

45. Byrd Edition 8:156–67.

46. See Crichton, 169.

47. See Neighbour 78, 87 and 92.

48. The opening alleluia of *Alleluia. Vespere autem Sabbathi* is a rewriting of the small motet *Deo gratias*.

49. For the plainsong and a note on the sources, see Byrd Edition 6b:142 and 175.

50. The second "crucifige," in chorus 10, is the same as the setting of "et laetemur" in *Haec dies*, bars 13–14.

51. The three voice parts, which are in separate books, are reproduced in facsimile in Byrd Edition 6b:145–68.

52. His arms are stamped on the cover of an edition of 1604. The quotation is from David Harris Willson, *King James VI & I* (London, 1956), 212.

53. "Rome and the Elizabethan Catholics: A Question of Geography," *The Historical Journal* 7 (1964): 135–49.

54. For references to the visits of Thomas Byrd (8 days) and Colford (9 days) to the English College at Rome, see Henry Foley, S.J., *Records of the English Province of the Society of Jesus* (London, 1877–82), 6:566 and 571. Colford appears to have passed through Antwerp on his way, as reported in a letter of Verstegan to Robert Persons, dated 27 May 1593. In 1600 Verstegan paid on Colford's behalf the account for purchases he had made at the Plantin house. See *The Letters and Despatches of Richard Verstegan (ca. 1550–1640)*, ed. Anthony G. Petti, Catholic Record Society Publications 52 (London, 1959), 155–57.

55. The Rheims Passion with its supporting annotations is printed in Byrd Edition 6b:vii–xii.

56. Frederick J. McGuinness, *"Roma sancta* and the Saint: Eucharist, Charity, and the Logic of Catholic Reform," *Historical Reflections* 15 (1988): 103.

57. The Church of the Gesù became famous for such spectacles, as noted by Mark S. Weil in "The Forty Hours and the Roman Baroque Illusion," *Journal of the Warburg and Courtault Institutes* 37 (1974): 218–48, which also includes a useful history of the devotion, based on Angelo de Sancti, *L'Orazione delle Quant'Ore e i temi di calamita e di guerra* (Rome, 1919).

58. Weston, 246–47. See Craig Monson, *Voices and Viols 1600–1650: The Sources and the Music* (Ann Arbor, 1982), 96.

59. F. G. Emmison, *Tudor Secretary; Sir William Petre at Court and Home* (London, 1961), 213.

60. Emmison, *Tudor Secretary*, 293. For more on this episode, see pp. 208–9.

61. Fellowes 48, 44–45.

62. See Joseph Kerman, "William Byrd, 1543–1623," *Musical Times* 114 (1973): 687–90, with an analytical edition of the piece as the July Musical Supplement.

63. The liturgical text jumps to this phrase at the end of Acts 2:11 and omits

the reference to speaking in tongues, but it is clear from the music that Byrd sought to include the entire picture in his interpretation.

64. Ludwig Einsenhofer and Joseph Lechner, *Liturgy of the Roman Rite*, trans. A. J. and E. F. Peeler, ed. H. E. Winstone (New York, 1961), 216 (see note 1).

65. The association of *Venite exultemus* with the morning office is a strong one: Psalm 94 in the Rheims version is accompanied by an initial marginal note that reads "This inuitation is most fitly ordayned for the Church for the proeme or beginning of Mattins" (OT, 175).

66. *Butler's Lives of the Saints*, rev. Herbert Thurston and Robert Attwater (London, 1956), 2:667–68, 3:236–37. See also Einsenhofer and Lechner, 235, and King, *Liturgy*, 205 (see note 1).

Butler points out that 1 August was also known as Lammas-day, i.e., "Loaf-Mass," an early harvest festival or thanksgiving for the first fruits. The Rheims annotation to Acts 12:6 show that Byrd would have known this: "These chaines are famous for miracles, and were brought from Ierusalem to Rome by Eudoxia the Empresse, wife to Theodosius the yonger, where they were matched & placed with an other chaine that the same apostle was tied with by Nero, & a Church founded thereupon, named *Petri ad vincula*, where they are religiously kept and reuerenced to this day, and there is a feast in the whole Church for the same, the first of August, which we call *Lammas Day*" (NT, 326).

67. "Petre is pronounced Peter; Pet-tree and Pea-tree are solecisms." A. C. Edwards, *John Petre: Essay on the Life and Background of John, 1st Lord Petre, 1549–1613* (London, 1972), p. 9.

68. Kerman 81, 315–18. John Harley notes an additional cause for celebration that summer, William's being knighted at Theobalds on 3 May 1603 after going to York to meet James I (*William Byrd, Gentleman of the Chapel Royal* [Brookfield, VT, 1997], 335). Almost the entire gentry got something out of the new king, who was prodigal with such honors.

69. See pp. 133–39.

70. H. C. Collins, "Byrd's Latin Church Music for Practical Use in the Roman Liturgy," *Music & Letters* 4 (1923): 259.

71. The annotations, in small type, cover two pages: NT, 46–47.

72. "For thy fathers, sonnes are born to thee. Thou shalt make them princes ouer al the earth, This is the Catholic Church. Her children are made princes ouer al the earth, her sones are constituted for fathers. Let them acknowledge this that are cut of[f]: let them come to the vnitie, be they brought into the temple of the king" (OT, 91).

73. (NT, 47). Peter Holmes makes the point that this would have been the

obvious place to refer to *Regens in excelsis*, the papal bull of excommunication against the queen, and finds the annotations "extremely tame" (41); see note 20.

74. See David Mateer, "William Byrd's Middlesex Recusancy," *Music & Letters* 78 (1997): 1–14 for documentary evidence that Byrd received "favor for his recusancie" in the previous reign from the Privy Council through the attorney general, as he claimed in his post-1604 letter to Salisbury (Historical Manuscripts Commission, *Hatfield*, Reports and Calendars Series 24, 219).

For Byrd's examination in the aftermath of the Throckmorton plot, see John Bossy, *Giordano Bruno and the Embassy Affair* (New Haven, 1991), 121. The document referred to there is a letter dated 22 February 1584 from Dr. William Parry, the "presumably spurious [Catholic] conspirator," executed for treason on 2 March 1585, to Charles Paget, another conspirator living in Paris. It contains the sentence "Mʳ Byrd is at libertye and hath bene very honorably intreated [i. e., dealt with] by my Lords of the Councell." Both Charles and his brother Thomas, Lord Paget, were composition students of Byrd: see Christopher Harrison, "William Byrd and the Pagets of Beaudesert: A Musical Connection," *Staffordshire Studies* 3 (1990–91): 51–61.

75. Antony Weldon, *The Court and Character of King James* (London, 1650), 22, as quoted by G. P. V. Akrigg, *Jacobean Pageant* (London, 1962), 36. Willson, 349.

76. Linda Levy Peck, *Patronage and Policy at the Court of James I* (London, 1982), and "Problems in Jacobean Administration: Was Henry Howard, Earl of Northampton, a Reformer?" *The Historical Journal* 19 (1978): 831–58.

77. E. F. Rimbault, *The Old Cheque-Book of the Chapel Royal* (London, 1872), 60–62.

78. See Caraman, 349.

79. Aided by the antiquary Sir Richard Cotton, Northampton wrote the defense of the government's case, *A True and Perfect Relation of the whole proceedings against the late most barbarous Traitors, Garnet, a Jesuit, and his Confederats*, and Linda Peck notes that the tone of his speeches on religious matters in the Star Chamber changed radically after that (*Patronage*, 81, 111).

80. E. Arber, *A Transcript of the Registers of the Company of Stationers in London, 1555–1640* (London, 1876), 267.

81. Historical Manuscripts Commission, *Salisbury*, 612; the original is in French.

82. Shelfmark P 2/1-5. It is in a contemporary binding that also includes other prints: *Gradualia* is found between Byrd's 1589 *Cantiones* and Richard Dering's *Cantiones sacrae* (1617) and *Cantica sacra* (1618).

83. "The Printed Part-Books of Byrd's Vocal Music," *The Library*, 5th s., 19

(1964): 10. His mistake in reflected in the revised *Short-title Catalogue*, nos. 4143–45 and 4244.

84. It is in turn the source of a manuscript copied by John Danby for the Madrigal Society (British Library Madrigal Society C.28 [MS 239]).

85. Neither of these manuscripts can have been copied from the York exemplar because of certain details in the text: their different reading of the underlay in the medius at the end of *Oculi omnium*, for example.

86. This was pointed out to me by Davitt Moroney, who made the transcription of the Marian masses for the *Byrd Edition*, helped me to work out the presentation and contributed in other ways too numerous to mention. As regards *Adorna thalamum*, Moroney noted the anomaly of its inclusion in the Easter music section of the index. In the Superius, Tenor and Bassus it pushes the index on to the inside form (³C1v–³C2r). Even though the other books could accommodate the index on a single leaf, East evidently preferred to use a half sheet. This is confirmed by the binding of the York copy, in which this double leaf has been folded back around all the other sheets except the lone title page in all the part books. The order of leaves at the beginning of this copy is therefore Superius, Tenor and Bassus A1, ³C2, B1, etc.; Medius, A1, ²E2, B1 etc.; and Contratenor (reversing the position of the index entirely) A1, F1, B1, etc.

87. Further on costs, see pp. 202–3.

88. This is presumably the copy of STC 4244 erroneously located by the *Short-title Catalogue* at the royal library at Windsor Castle. Like the York copy, it is also bound together with Continental prints: Peter Philips, *Cantiones Sacrae* (Antwerp, 1612), *Florilegium Sacrarum Cantionum* (Antwerp, 1609), and *Giardino novo*, I and II (Copenhagen, 1605, 1606) (RISM 1605⁷, 1606⁵). The binding is more modern, and the copy is badly cropped—nearly all the running heads are missing in the Superius.

89. Without the index gathering and with the three fascicles bound in reverse order; the Medius also lacks A² (i.e., dedication and epistle).

90. The Cambridge Superius has an index page, signed "F.1," bound in after the five-part music; it must derive from a Contratenor book, and is in addition to the usual index (mis-signed "E.ij") at the end. The Bassus lacks the dedication as well as the title page, and has the three fascicles bound in reverse order. It is bound last in a sequence consisting of Morley's *Canzonets a 3* (1602), *Madrigals a 4* (1594) and *Triumphs of Oriana* (1601), and Byrd's *Psalmes, Sonets & Songs* (1588; 4th ed., ca. 1599).

91. The Christ Church set and the Lincoln set are parts of parallel omnibus Byrd collections: see Alan Brown's remarks in the preface to Byrd Edition's vol. 2. The Lincoln books include all of Byrd's major printed collections except

the 1575 *Cantiones* and the Three-Part Mass, bound together, possibly in the 1640s, for Michael Honywood, dean of Lincoln from 1660–81. The Christ Church set includes all of Byrd's major printed collections except the 1575 *Cantiones* and John Mundy's *Songs and Psalms* (1594), bound together for Henry Aldrich, dean of Christ Church from 1689–71. On C 2v of the Tenor is written "Miles Mayhen his booke"—probably the original owner, whom I have been unable to trace.

92. See Teruhiko Nasu, "The Publication of Byrd's *Gradualia* Reconsidered," *Brio* 32(1995): 119. A Richard Redmer is listed in 1628 among "such Booke sellers, as deale in old Libraryes Part Bookes or any other"; see Philip Gaskell, *A New Introduction to Bibliography* (Oxford, 1972), 241.

93. See note 104 below.

94. "The Printed Part Books," 9 (see note 83).

95. A similar case is mentioned by Fredson Bowers, *Principles of Bibliographical Description* (Princeton, 1949), 47.

96. The Tenbury manuscripts now belong to the Bodleian Library, Oxford.

97. It is more revealing to list what is missing from Tenbury 369–73 than what it contains:

Purification: verses of the gradual, alleluia, and tract *(Quia viderunt . . . omnium popularum)* and communion

Nativity: verses of the alleluia and gradual *(Quis ascendit . . . alleluia)*

Advent votive Mass: verses of the gradual and alleluia (except for the alleluia)

Post-Christmas votive Mass: introit (except for the alleluia), gradual and offertory

Paschal votive Mass: alleluia (no. 20)

Annunciation: gradual *(Diffusa est gratia)* and tract *(Audi filia . . . templum Regi)*

Assumption: alleluia verse and offertory

No complete mass can be made up out of the selections. The excerpts run continuously and in the order of the print from fol. 41 to fol. 50; after that occur *Adoramus te Christe* and the All Saints Mass, without its offertory. *Plorans plorabit* occurs earlier at fol. 37v. An eighteenth-century manuscript score, British Library Add. 5058, apparently copied from Tenbury 369–73 or a related source, contains the Assumption introit (fol. 5) alone.

98. Fellowes 48, 240; M. C. Boyd, *Elizabethan Music and Musical Criticism*, 2nd ed. (Philadelphia, 1962), 84.

99. See Joseph Gillow, *Biographical Dictionary of English Catholics* (London, 1887), 356–57; and Godfrey Anstruther, *The Seminary Priests* (Great Awakening, Surrey, 1975), 2:120–21.

100. See Gregg, calendar items 20, 44, 78, 99, 107, 125, 151.

101. See Historical Manuscripts Commission, *Hatfield*, 219; the entry is undated but must be "before May 24, 1612" (as the editor indicates), i.e., before Salisbury's death; it must also date from after 4 May 1605, when Sir Robert Cecil was created Earl of Salisbury.

102. Gaskell, 178.

103. Margaret Dowling, "The Printing of John Dowland's *The Seconde Booke of Songs or Ayres*," *The Library*, 4th s., 12, no. 4 (1932): 365–80. The quotations from East and Eastland in the following text appear on page 374.

104. Humphrey Lownes can be identified by his type ornament as well as his initials; see R. B. McKerrow and E. S. Ferguson, *Title-page Borders used in England and Scotland, 1485–1640*, Illustrated Monographs of the Royal Bibliographical Society 21 (London, 1932), nos. 179, 181, 183 and 186. In the absence of a Tenor book with the original title page, absolute certainty that every sheet of the 1610 issue came from the 1607 edition is lacking, but the context of the entire *Gradualia* strongly suggests that not a single note was reprinted. I am indebted to Davitt Moroney for the explanation of the discrepancies between the cancellans title pages of the 1610 issue.

105. See Byrd Edition 2:vi.

106. MSS 17–19 contain nos. 1 (verse), 2, 3, 4, 5, 6, 8, 9, 10 (verse), 19 and 20 (verse). MSS 1–6 contain all the Ascension and Pentecost music, in a slightly garbled order, two numbers from Easter (nos. 21 and 24), and all the six-part music except for *Solve jubente Deo*, *Hodie Simon Petrus* and *Tu es Pastor ovium*.

107. For the manuscripts of Hamond and Merro, see Monson, 77–115, 149–53. A list of *contrafacta*, including "All ye people, clap your hands," can be found in Byrd Edition 12:xiii–xiv.

108. In his article "John Petre, William Byrd, and Oxford Bodleian MS Mus.Sch. E. 423," *Royal Musical Association Research Chronicle* 29 (1996): 21–46, David Mateer suggests that a large loan made to Byrd by William Petre, Lord Petre's son and heir, at some undisclosed date, and discharged in 1608 (William gave £8, a "parcell" of it, to his wife, Katherine, on 15 February), may have enabled the publication. O. W. Neighbour reminds me that if the masses had been published without dedication perhaps Petre would have been embarrassed by such acknowledgment at an earlier date; if so, the dedication of book 1 to a key government minister, Northampton, can be seen as a necessary step to clear the path of any difficulties arising from such a gesture.

109. Bossy, *English Catholic Community*, 101.

110. Lawrence Stone, *The Crisis of the Aristocracy, 1558–1641* (Oxford, 1965), 731.

111. Emmison, *Tudor Secretary,* 8, 88, 185.

112. Emmison, *Tudor Secretary,* 214, which also lists Byrd's earlier visits to the family homes in Essex from 1586 on. Mateer (see note 108) usefully transcribes all the relevant passages about Petre's musical education and interest, as well as Byrd's connection to him.

113. Emmison, *Tudor Secretary,* 288, from a letter to Sir Francis Englefield.

114. Count Magalotti, *Travels of Cosimo III, Grand Duke of Tuscany,* quoted by Jennifer C. Ward in *The History of Old Thorndon Hall* (Chelmsford, 1972), 7. The quotation would equally apply to Ingatestone Hall (somewhat altered since Byrd's time), which has the feeling of a much extended farmhouse; the Petres' wealth appears not to have led them into undue ostentation.

115. Edwards, 22, summarizing Joel's Samaha's app. F to F. G. Emmison's *Elizabethan Life: Disorder* (Chelmsford, 1970), 321–26.

116. Edwards, 9.

117. For this detail, as well as matters addressed in the paragraph on Sir John's heir, see Nancy Briggs, "William, and Lord Petre (1575–1637)," *Essex Recusant* 10 (1968): 51–64. This is an exception to many articles in this journal which merely summarize secondary sources.

118. Foley, 2:558–59, from British Library Landsdowne MS 33, fols. 145–49, also in "The Religious Beliefs of the Petre Family under Elizabeth I," *Essex Recusant* 3 (1961): 58–65, in a literal transcription kindly corrected for me by David Mateer.

119. For a good account of the Payne case, see Emmison, *Elizabethan Life,* 50–52. A full account of the trial was printed at the time by William Allen, Payne's superior at Douai, in *A Briefe Historie of the Glorious Martyrdom of XII. Reverend Priests* (Rheims, 1582).

120. Foley, 2:585, wrongly attributes the gift to Robert; William signed himself "Cephalini" in letters to Richard Blount, the first provincial.

121. The letter (which Byrd addressed to "ye worshipful and my verye good friend Mr Petre on[e] of ye officers of her Maties escheuquer at Westminster") is printed in Fellowes 48, 39–40, where the recipient is mistakenly identified as Sir William Petre, who died in 1572.

122. Bossy, *English Catholic Community,* 126.

123. John Bossy, "The Character of Elizabethan Catholicism," *Past and Present* 21 (1962): 40.

124. Historical Manuscripts Commission, *Salisbury,* 612; the original is in French.

125. The more puritanical reformers at Trent, like Cardinal Borromeo, excluded all instruments except the organ from the liturgy, of course. See Lewis

Lockwood, *The Counter-Reformation and the Masses of Vincenzo Ruffo* (Venice, 1970), 110.

126. Byrd Edition, 2:viii.

127. This approach was outlined by H. K. Andrews in "Transposition in Byrd's Vocal Polyphony," *Music & Letters* 42 (1962): 25–37.

128. See Alan Brown's remarks in the preface (1988) to Byrd Edition, 2:viii–ix.

129. Byrd Edition 4: xii–xiii.

130. *Cantiones sacrae* (1575), Cantores in Ecclesia, dir. Michael Howard, Oiseau Lyre SOL 311, rec. 1969.

131. *Singing in Latin, or, Pronunciation Explor'd* (Oxford, 1990).

APPENDIX

PUBLICATIONS BY PHILIP BRETT
ON ELIZABETHAN AND
JACOBEAN MUSIC

EDITIONS

The English Madrigal School, edited by E. H. Fellowes, revised by Thurston Dart
[et al.] as *The English Madrigalists*. London: Stainer & Bell, 1961–65. Volumes
revised by Brett:

vol. 14, *Psalmes, Sonets & Songs*, by William Byrd (1588) = vol. 12 of *Collected
Works of William Byrd*, edited by E. H. Fellowes, revised by Thurston
Dart [et al.]. London: Stainer & Bell, 1963.

vol. 15, *Songs of Sundrie Natures*, by William Byrd (1589) = vol. 13 of *Collected
Works of William Byrd*, 1962.

vol. 30, *Second Set of Madrigals*, by Michael East (1606).

vol. 31a, *Third Set of Books*, by Michael East (1610).

vol. 31b, *Fourth Set of Books*, by Michael East (1618).

vol. 35b, *Songs and Psalms*, by John Mundy (1594).

vol. 36, *Madrigals to Five Voices*, by Michael Cavendish et al. (1598, 1601).

Do not Repine, fair Sun, by Orlando Gibbons. London: Stainer & Bell, 1961.

The Western Wind: Mass for Unaccompanied Choir, by John Taverner. London:
Stainer & Bell, 1962.

Mater Christi: Motet or Anthem for Unaccompanied Choir, by John Taverner. London, Stainer & Bell, 1964.

Spem in alium nunquam habui, by Thomas Tallis. In vol. 6 of *Tudor Church Music*,
rev. version. London: Oxford University Press, 1966.

Consort Songs. Musica Britannica 22. London: Royal Musical Association, 1967.

The Byrd Edition. London: Stainer & Bell, 1970–2004. Philip Brett, general editor.

Volumes edited by Brett:

vol. 4, *The Masses (1592–1595)*, 1981.
vol. 5, *Gradualia I (1605):The Marian Masses*, 1989.
vol. 6a, *Gradualia I (1605): All Saints and Corpus Christi*, 1991.
vol. 6b, *Gradualia I (1605): Other Feasts and Devotions*, 1993.
vol. 7a, *Gradualia II (1607): Christmas to Easter*, 1997.
vol. 7b, *Gradualia II (1607): Ascension, Pentecost, and the Feast of Saints Peter & Paul*, 1997.
vol. 15, *Consort Songs for Voice and Viols*, 1970.
vol. 16, *Madrigals, Songs and Canons*, 1976.

Other volumes:

vol. 1, *Cantiones Sacrae (1575)*, ed. Craig Monson, 1977.
vol. 2, *Cantiones Sacrae (1589)*, ed. Alan Brown, 1988.
vol. 3, *Cantiones Sacrae (1591)*, ed. Alan Brown, 1981.
vol. 8, *Latin Motets I (from Manuscript Sources)*, ed. Warwick Edwards, 1984.
vol. 9, *Latin Motets II (from Manuscript Sources)*, ed. Warwick Edwards, 2000.
vol. 10a, *The English Services I*, ed. Craig Monson, 1982.
vol. 10b, *The English Services II, (The Great Service)*, ed. Craig Monson, 1980.
vol. 11, *The English Anthems*, ed. Craig Monson, 1983.
vol. 12, *Psalmes, Sonets and Songs (1588)*, ed. Jeremy Smith, 2004.
vol. 13, *Songs of Sundrie Natures (1589)*, ed. David Mateer, 2004.
vol. 14, *Psalmes, Songs and Sonnets (1611)*, ed. John Morehen, 1987.
vol. 17, *Consort Music*, ed. Kenneth Elliott, 1971.

The Lamentations of Jeremiah, by Thomas Tallis. London: Oxford University Press, 1969; new version, transposed for SAATB, with English translation, 1995.

The City Cries; the Country Cries, by Richard Dering. Reprinted from Musica Britannica 22 [1967], with new preface. London: Royal Musical Association, 1984.

ARTICLES

"Songs by William Byrd in Manuscripts at Harvard." *Harvard Library Bulletin* 14 (1960): 343–65. Coauthored with Thurston Dart.

"The English Consort Song, 1570–1625." *Proceedings of the Royal Musical Association* 88 (1961–62): 73–88.

"Edward Paston (1550–1630): A Norfolk Gentleman and His Musical Collection." *Transactions of the Cambridge Bibliographical Society* 4 (1964): 51–69.

"*Musicae Modernae Laus:* Geoffrey Whitney's Tributes to the Lute and Its Players." *Lute Society Journal* 7 (1965): 40–44.

"Did Byrd Write 'Non nobis Domine'?" *Musical Times* 113 (1972): 855–57.

"Word-Setting in the Songs of Byrd." *Proceedings of the Royal Musical Association* 98 (1971–72): 47–64.

"The Two Musical Personalities of Thomas Weelkes." *Music & Letters* 53 (1972): 369–76.

"Editing Byrd." *Musical Times* 121 (1980): 492–95, 557–59.

The New Grove Dictionary of Music and Musicians, edited by Stanley Sadie. London: Macmillan, 1980; and the 2nd ed. (2001), revised, s.vv. "Consort Song," "Morley, Thomas," "Paston, Edward."

"Homage to Taverner in Byrd's Masses." *Early Music* 9 (1981): 169–76.

"English Music for the Scottish Progress of 1617." In *Source Materials and the Interpretation of Music: A Memorial Volume to Thurston Dart,* edited by Ian Bent, 209–26. London: Stainer & Bell, 1981.

"Facing the Music." *Early Music* 10 (1982): 347–50.

"Pitch and Transposition in the Paston Manuscripts." In *Sundry Sorts of Music Books: Essays on the British Library Collections Presented to O. W. Neighbour on his 70th Birthday,* edited by Chris Banks, Arthur Searle, and Malcolm Turner, 89–118. London: British Library, 1993.

"Traditionalist and Innovator: Aspects of William Byrd." *Southern California Early Music News* 18, no. 3 (November 1993): 1–15.

REVIEWS

The Technique of Byrd's Vocal Polyphony, by H. K. Andrews (London: Oxford University Press, 1966), *Musical Times* 180 (1967): 134–35.

Collected Anthems, by Thomas Weelkes, edited by David Brown, Walter Collins, and Peter Le Huray, Musica Britannica 23 (London: Royal Musical Association, 1966), *Journal of the American Musicological Society* 20 (1967): 134–38.

Four Hundred Songs and Dances from the Stuart Masque, edited by Andrew Sabol (Providence: Brown University Press, 1978), *Shakespeare Quarterly* 31 (1980): 109–11.

Patrons and Musicians in the English Renaissance, by David C. Price (Cambridge: Cambridge University Press, 1981), *Early Music* 9 (1981): 353–56.

Masses, by Christopher Tye, edited by Paul Doe, Early English Church Music 24 (London: British Academy, 1980), *Early Music* 9 (1981): 545–49.

LINER NOTES

John Taverner, *Tudor Church Music*, Choir of King's College, Cambridge, dir. David Willcocks. Argo 2RG 5316, rec. 1965.

Thomas Tallis, *Tallis for King's*, Choir of King's College, Cambridge, dir. David Willcocks. Argo 2K 30–31, rec. 1966.

Thomas Tallis, *Lamentations of Jeremiah* [et al.], King's Singers. EMI, rec. 1978.

William Byrd, *Mass for Four Voices*, The Sixteen. Virgin Classics, 719933, rec. 1990.

Wiliam Byrd, *The Marian Masses*, William Byrd Choir, dir. Bruno Turner. Hyperion A66451, rec. 1990.

INDEX

Italic page numbers refer to examples and figures.

Brown, Alan, 213, 215
Brown, David, 66–68; on Weelkes, 69, 70–71, 75
Browne, Sir Anthony, 49
Buckingham, Earl of (George Villiers), 83
Bull, John, 9; in Paston manuscripts, 42
Bull, Stephen, 37
Burney, Charles, 102
Butler, Alban, 224n66
Butler, Charles, 76n8
Byrd, Julian, 126; recusancy charges against, 181
Byrd, Thomas, 170, 223n54
Byrd, William: on *afflatus*, 142; Anglican liturgical compositions, 2, 100, 121; authorial persona of, 123, 124, 125; and caesura, use of, 109; Catholic liturgical compositions of, ix, 15, 20, 79 (see also *Gradualia; Masses*); celebrations honoring, xi; Continental style of, 1, 124, 125, 126; counterpoint of, 20, 74, 160, 190; and Counter-Reformation, 143; on creative impulse, 141–42; decorum of, 115, 116, 127, 143, 161; dedicatees of, 141, 193, 194–95, 201, 206–7; and elegy, use of, 108, 112; and Elizabeth I, 2, 121–22, 123–24, 143; and Elizabethan age, role in, 121; and Ferrabosco, 15, 124; formalism of, 75; and Henry Garnet, 152, 153; genres of, 1–2; and Gibbons, influence on, 92, 95; and Guidetti, knowledge of, 170; and Gunpowder Plot, 174–75; historical sense of, 20, 122; at Ingatestone, 178, 210; instrumental music of, 4, 5, 126; interiority of, 125; and Jesuits, 122–23, 125, 126, 134, 152–53, 168, 171; keyboard music of, 5; late music of, 4–5, 20, 117; Latin songs of, 124; lawsuits of, 195; and London, arrival in, 51; lyrical style of, 20; medievalism of, 126; models for, 9; and Morley, 67; motets of, 9, 52, 100, 187; and

Northampton, 194; as outsider, 2, 20, 122, 193; and Paston, 51, 62; in Paston manuscripts, 32, 40, 49, 50, 52, 56, 110–12; patrons of, 122, 193–211; performances by, 212; and Petre family, 178, 188, 210–11; polyphony of, 2, 125, 127; and predecessors, 103; and printing, 116, 122, 123, 203–4; and public life, retirement from, 2, 8, 9, 126, 127; recusancy of, 2, 122, 145, 195, 225n75; Redford's influence on, 18; Roman Catholicism of, 2, 8–9, 122–23, 127, 145, 168–69, 195, 225n75; as royal musician, 2; secular music of, 3, 100; and Sidney, settings of, 3; and Sidney circle, 51, 119n17; songs for solo voice and viols, 52; and Spenser, 121–23; at Stondon Massey, 2, 8, 126, 206, 210; and Tallis, 15, 78, 107–8; at Thorndon Hall, 210–11; and Throckmorton plot, 193, 225n74; traditionalism of, 3–4; and Weelkes, 67, 70–71. *See also* Consort songs; Six-part music; Vocal music; *and titles of compositions*

Cabrol, Fernand, 222n42
Caesura, Byrd's use of, 109
Calendar, liturgical: Clement VIII's reform of, 219n7; saints' days in, 133
Cambridge University Library: Syn 6.60.6, 198, 226n90; Syn 6.61.15, 198; Syn 6.61.16, 204
Cambridge University Musical Society, 27
Campion, Edmund, 208
Campion, Thomas, 68, 79
Candlemas, processional antiphons for, 169
Cantiones sacrae (Byrd, 1575), 9; counterpoint in, 190; dedication of, 123–24; six-part music of, 187
Cantiones sacrae (Byrd, 1589), 113, 145, 220n18; authorial strategy of, 124; as vocal chamber music, 213

Purification, 130, 132, 134, 139, 140, 141, 162; repetition in, 138; transfer schemes of, 132–38, 140, 166, 173; Visitation, 134
Mateer, David, 228nn108,112
Matthew, Sir Toby, 201
Maximilian (duke of Milan), 63
McGrady, Richard J., 119n10
Medicine, Galenic, 125
Medievalism: Byrd's, 126; at Elizabeth's court, 20, 117
Melismas, in Byrd's word setting, 111, 116
Melville, Andrew, 82
Memento salutis auctor (Gradualia), 160
Meres, Francis, 87
Merro, John, 86–87, 206
Mildmay, Sir Thomas, 208
Missals: *ad usum Sacerdotibus in Anglia*, 218n4; Clement VIII's revisions to, 219n7
Missals, Tridentine, 138; Forty Hours Devotion in, 176
Mixolydian mode, Tallis's use of, 24
Monson, Craig, 9, 87, 124
Montague, Lady Magdalen, 49, 111, 221n33; devotions of, 157–58
Monte, Philippe de: "Dolce mio duol," 59n29
Montemayor, George of: *Diana*, 35, 51
Monteverdi, Claudio, 1; *Missa In illo tempore*, 28
Montrose, Louis A., 123
More, Henry, 209
Morehen, John, 76n5
Morley, Thomas, 44, 167, 215; and Byrd, 67; ditties, rules for, 103–4; *First Booke of Ayres*, 202; Italianate idiom of, 72; on madrigals, 116; madrigals of, 4, 79; on motets, 161; at Norwich, 57n10; Oxford B.Mus. of, 63, 76n5; printing patents of, 203; repetition, use of, 67; at Thorpe Hall, 36; *Triumphes of Oriana*, 63;
Moroney, Davitt, x, 226n86, 228n104

Motets, Byrd's, 100; models for, 9; in Paston manuscripts, 52; techniques of, 187
Motets, medieval, 89
Mush, John, 157
Music, close listening to, 26
Music, early: medieval, 89, 108; performances of, 27, 29
Music, early English: counterpoint in, 11–12; French influence on, 78–79; Italianate, 69; medieval, 89, 108; in Nomine tradition, 4; Puritan suspicion of, 2–3; secular, 3, 74, 79–80, 100; Stuart, 78
Music, Elizabethan: archives of, 31; Brett's study of, viii; Byrd's, 121; manuscripts of, 31; songs, 117
Music, French: influence on English music, 78–79
Music, Italian: English counterparts to, 69
Music, Jacobean: Anglican, 69, 71, 72; court, 90
Music, Tudor: court, 109; establishments of, 78; line in, 18–19; masses, 18; songs, 107
Musica Britannica, Brett's contributions to, viii
Musical Times (journal), 22
Musicology: analytical technique of, 26; critical theories in, 28–29; historical focus of, 25; stylistic analysis in, 28; after World War II, viii
Myriell, Thomas, 79

Nasu, Teruhiko, 202, 227n92
Nativity of Christ the Savior, Byrd's music for, 172
Nativity of the Blessed Virgin Mary, Byrd's music for, 130, 133, 134, 135, 139; in Clementine calendar, 219n6
Neighbour, Oliver, 9, 228n108; *The Consort and Keyboard Music of William Byrd*, xiii, 18

Compositor:	Binghamton Valley Composition
Indexer:	Roberta Engleman
Music engraver:	Rolf Wulfsberg
Text:	10/15 Janson
Display:	Janson
Printer/Binder:	Maple-Vail Manufacturing Group